IMAGES
of America

WICKENBURG

On the Cover: "The Big Hat" was a souvenir shop operated by the Wickenburg Chamber of Commerce in downtown Wickenburg from the 1930s until the 1960s. (Courtesy Desert Caballeros Western Museum.)

IMAGES
of America

WICKENBURG

Lynn Downey and
Desert Caballeros Western Museum

ARCADIA
PUBLISHING

ISBN 978-0-7385-8504-8

Published by Arcadia Publishing
Charleston, South Carolina

Printed in the United States of America

Library of Congress Control Number: 2011939323

For all general information, please contact Arcadia Publishing:
Telephone 843-853-2070
Fax 843-853-0044
E-mail sales@arcadiapublishing.com
For customer service and orders:
Toll-Free 1-888-313-2665

Visit us on the Internet at www.arcadiapublishing.com

This book is dedicated to the people of Wickenburg, who embody the generous spirit of the West.

Contents

ACKNOWLEDGMENTS

When I first visited Wickenburg in 2003, I had no idea that the friendships I formed would lead to writing this book. As a Californian, it is a singular honor.

Many thanks to Cindy Thrasher, of the Wickenburg Historical Preservation Society, and Julie Brooks, of the Wickenburg Chamber of Commerce, who recommended me to the publisher. They were also generous with their local knowledge.

I am grateful to Dr. James Burns, Mary Ann Igna, Michelle Duncan-Gilbert, and the staff and volunteers of the Desert Caballeros Western Museum. They supported my work and indulged me as I flitted through the museum archives. I now feel like one of the exhibits, which is just what I wanted. Mary Ann did double duty as fact-checker and typo-catcher.

I could not have written this book without Joe Stevens. Over the course of three visits to the museum, a rainy ride down the Constellation Road, and in countless emails, I pumped Joe for information about mines, natural history, architecture, dude ranches, Native Americans, and Henry Wickenburg. He always had an answer. He also fact-checked the manuscript with an enviable eye for historical detail.

Paul Hughes, tireless local everyman, took original photographs around town and helped me tell the story of modern Wickenburg. I learned more history on our desert dune buggy rides, and I will always cherish the barbed wire scar I received on one memorable trip.

The committed individuals and important work of the Vulture Mine Preservation and Restoration Association fueled my research into the history of this storied mine.

Steve and Andrea Taylor, of the Flying E Ranch, helped me understand the dude ranch experience over the course of five memorable days.

Betty Hammer-Joy set me straight on the life of her extraordinary grandmother, Angela Hammer.

Pieter Burggraaf cleared up the history of "Hassayampa."

Visual Presentation of San Francisco did the digital magic.

Thanks also to editors Jared Jackson and Stacia Bannerman.

All images belong to the Desert Caballeros Western Museum unless otherwise specified. Additional photographs were provided by Paul Hughes, Melissa Oehler, Jeanne Hangauer and Taina Kissinger, Jeremy Rowe, Del E. Webb Center for the Performing Arts, Flying E Ranch, Arizona Historical Society, and Levi Strauss & Co. Archives.

INTRODUCTION

It is somehow fitting that the city of Wickenburg is situated so close to Arizona's capital, Phoenix, for like that mythical bird, Wickenburg has risen from the ashes more than once since its wobbly beginnings 150 years ago. Today, it is a thriving, family-oriented town, popular with tourists and road trippers, but Wickenburg's peaceful present belies its colorful past.

The area was first home to the Hohokam and then the Yavapai people, who farmed and hunted near the Hassayampa River. The Spanish gave them a wide berth during their explorations in the 16th century, but when rumors of gold brought miners into the area in the early 1860s, clashes were inevitable. In 1863, the American military established a fort north of what would become Wickenburg, and violent conflicts filled the region for nearly a decade. Despite the dangers not only of warfare, but also the perils inherent to the desert—heat, predators, prickly plants—men still wandered into the area looking for elusive metals. Abraham Peeples, Pauline Weaver, and Joseph Walker all found gold, registered claims, and formed mining districts by 1863, the year that Arizona was declared a territory.

Another visitor was German immigrant Henry Wickenburg. The details of his arrival and founding of the Vulture Mine, one of the richest mines in the Southwest, are still open to debate. But unlike other miners, and despite years of setbacks, Wickenburg made his mining claim—and eventually his farm—his home. Partners and prospectors swarmed there as well, and Wickenburg Ranch officially became the town of Wickenburg with the establishment of the post office in 1865. Incorporation came later, in 1909.

The Hassayampa River made both mining and Wickenburg's future possible. It flows for nearly 100 miles, and throughout most of this course it actually runs underground, thanks to unusually deep bedrock. It resurfaces when the rock rises to the level of the riverbed and creates a riparian oasis much favored by both Native Americans and early settlers, who found its rich soil perfect for farming.

A succession of companies bought and sold the Vulture Mine, and its fortunes waxed and waned. Stagecoaches were robbed of their bullion, gold carriers were murdered, and miners worked six days a week for the Vulture's owners, sifting the ore-rich tailings for themselves on Sundays. However, the mine's output and fame helped spur investment in Jack Swilling's canal project, which in turn enabled the growth of Phoenix and the settlement of central Arizona.

Even an infamous stagecoach massacre in 1871 had no effect on the migration of fortune hunters to the Vulture and other mines that had been discovered in the mountain ranges that ring the Wickenburg area. Their names, and the names of the districts that sprang up around them, were just as colorful: Octave, Monte Cristo, Constellation, Gold Bar, and Congress are just a few examples. They enriched some and impoverished others, but their presence gave additional impetus for people to wander into the area to see what it could do for them.

As the 19th century drew to a close, Wickenburg began to thrive as a place to live, rather than just a place to pass through. Ranching and agriculture grew, and the Santa Fe, Prescott &

Phoenix Railroad set up a depot in town, taking over from the stage companies. Newspapers, churches, schools, cemeteries, dry goods stores, and restaurants soon appeared. The boom and bust nature of mining meant that the city's population fluctuated with the fortunes of its miners, but numerous people had started to make a modest living and made Wickenburg their home. They felt that the town had a future, even in the face of disasters like the Walnut Grove dam break of 1890, which took dozens of lives and wiped out local agriculture.

The town might have become a simple pinpoint on an Arizona map if not for the popularity of the guest (or "dude") ranch, a favorite destination for easterners who wanted a taste of the old West. Highways 60 and 89 were completed in 1922, making Wickenburg even more accessible to visitors. A number of local ranchers and entrepreneurs took advantage of the new roads and the ease of train travel from Phoenix and began to market Wickenburg as a dude ranch destination.

The Sonoran Desert landscape and its vistas of red rock and saguaro cactus fulfilled visitors' fantasies of the old West (and what it looked like on movie screens). Places like the Remuda Ranch, Kay El Bar, and later, Flying E and Rancho de los Caballeros, were among the most popular guest ranches in the area, offering Western-themed activities ranging from the rustic to the elegant.

World War II saw the closure of the Vulture Mine, as well as others, and the mining industry left Wickenburg for good. Personal mining never went away, however; even today, a pile of rocks on an out-of-the-way trail marks the boundary of a claim.

Locals were fascinated with Wickenburg's history, and the Desert Caballeros Western Museum opened in 1969 with great support from community leaders, longtime families, and retirees who had relocated for the sun and other amenities. Dude ranches, gold panning, rodeos, and other Western pursuits fueled Wickenburg's popularity as a destination well into the 1960s. In the 1970s, interest in the West began to wane and many of the ranches closed. But the year-round residents who had discovered the area's beauty, climate, and closeness to a major city helped breathe new life into Wickenburg.

Today, some of the former guest ranches are now recovery or rehabilitation centers, the Del E. Webb Center for the Performing Arts brings major cultural events to town, and the Desert Caballeros Western Museum hosts exhibitions of major Western artists. As part of a public art project that delights visitors and locals alike, life-sized bronzes of classic Western characters and native wildlife are sprinkled throughout the city.

Wickenburg's history blends a bit of the old West with a touch of luxury living, a contradiction that makes it continually fascinating to residents, visitors, and historians. This book is meant to be a taste of Wickenburg's rich heritage through a look at its people, mines, ranches, and cultural institutions. The author hopes that the book will lead readers to further explorations of this story at the museum, the Wickenburg-Boetto House, the Hassayampa River Preserve, a guest ranch, or any of a dozen other historic sites in the area. There, visitors can witness what the writer of a promotional brochure said of this region in 1898—Wickenburg "is throbbing with the intense life of the splendid West."

One

First People, First Settlers

Between the 16th and 18th centuries, when Spanish explorers and gold-seekers wandered into what is now central Arizona, they found few precious metals, but did encounter the Yavapai. The native people ranged from the present-day location of Globe, Arizona, to the Colorado River as well as in the valley of the Hassayampa. The Yavapai moved seasonally to various encampments or rancherias to hunt game and gather local plants. They also tended crops of beans, pumpkins, and tobacco in the fertile river soil. The Yavapai are actually four different peoples, and those who lived in the region of the Hassayampa were called the Tolkepaya.

For centuries, the Yavapai were undisturbed in the Southwestern desert, and even the Spanish visitors did not interrupt the patterns of their lives. The discovery of gold in California in 1848 brought thousands across the country and through Arizona, but these Argonauts bypassed Yavapai territory, staying south. All of this changed, however, in the early 1860s.

In 1862, the Pauline Weaver party found gold north of Fort Yuma and established the town of La Paz. Another group, headed by Abraham Peeples, left La Paz in the spring of 1863 with Weaver as a guide. About 15 miles north of present-day Wickenburg, they found a massive gold deposit in a place they named Rich Hill.

Joseph Walker headed a mining exploration party in the mountains above the Hassayampa River region in early 1863. Setting up camp near present-day Prescott, he formed the Pioneer Mining District after making a strike. When Walker went to Pima Indian villages to buy supplies, he probably met Weaver and others from the Peeples party. After they shared information about their discoveries, word got out and the region was soon home to hundreds of other gold-seekers.

The miners' encroachment onto Yavapai lands led to inevitable bloodshed. As the Civil War raged, the military set up Fort Whipple in December 1863 and began a campaign to subdue the native peoples, which ended a decade later on the Rio Verde reservation.

Despite the dangers, the promise of marvelous metals continued to bring the hopeful to the Hassayampa Valley.

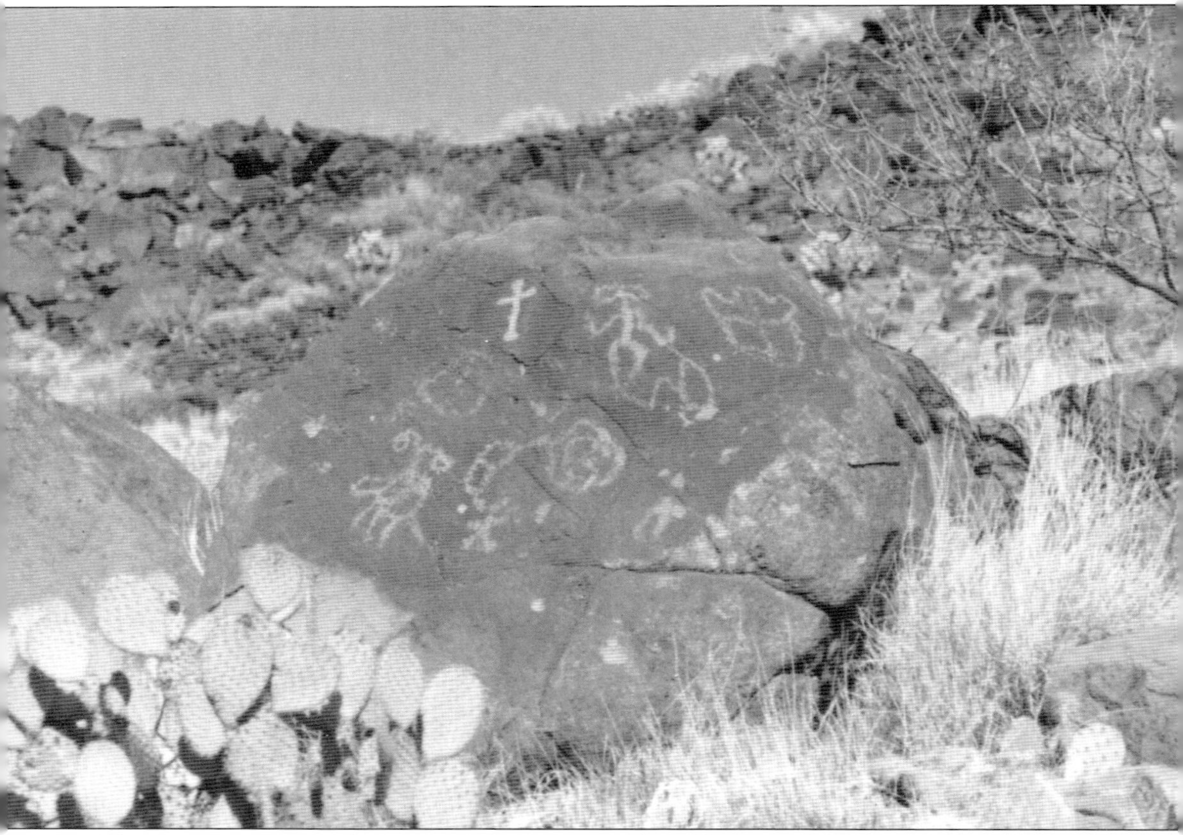

The first footprints in the Wickenburg area were placed by the ancient Hohokam Indians, who farmed throughout the area that would become the Salt River Valley. The Hohokam disappeared around 1450, leaving behind mysterious petroglyphs and a sophisticated canal system that would later be reinvented by an American entrepreneur and lead to the development of Phoenix.

Although they are dressed in modern clothing, the Yavapai men and woman pictured in these photographs from around 1900 kept their identity and traditions even as white settlers moved onto their traditional lands. The Yavapai were on good terms and traded with most of the other tribes in the Colorado River area, but had conflicts with the Apaches. The two tribes did not share many cultural similarities, but early explorers misidentified the Yavapai as Apache for many years. For example, the person who took these photographs wrote "Apache" on the back of them. The Yavapai helped early miners and explorers by serving as scouts and also performing labor in mining camps, but the friendly relations would not last.

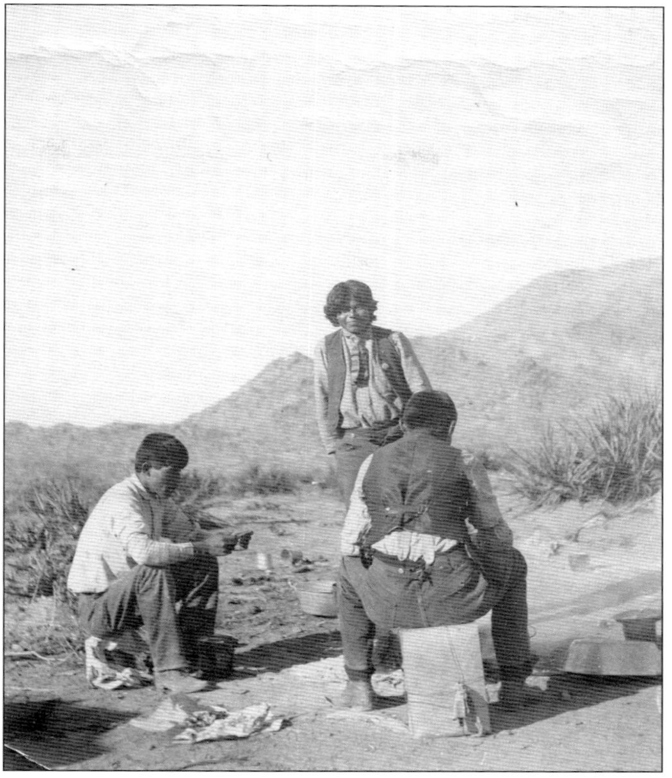

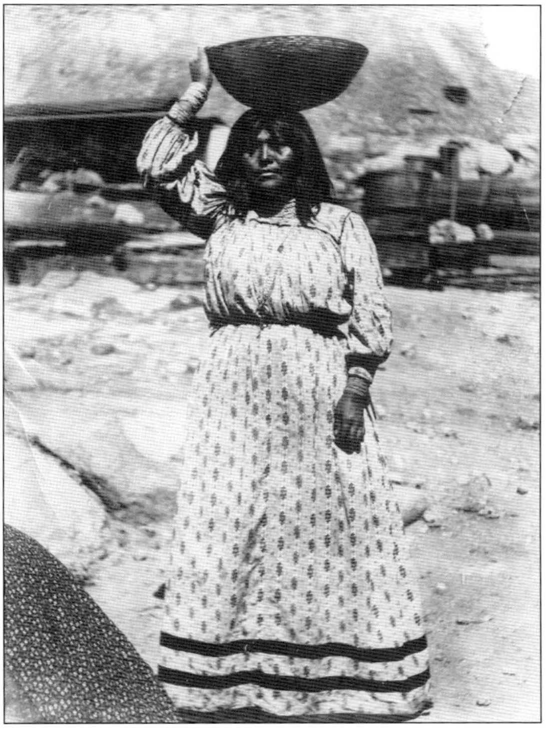

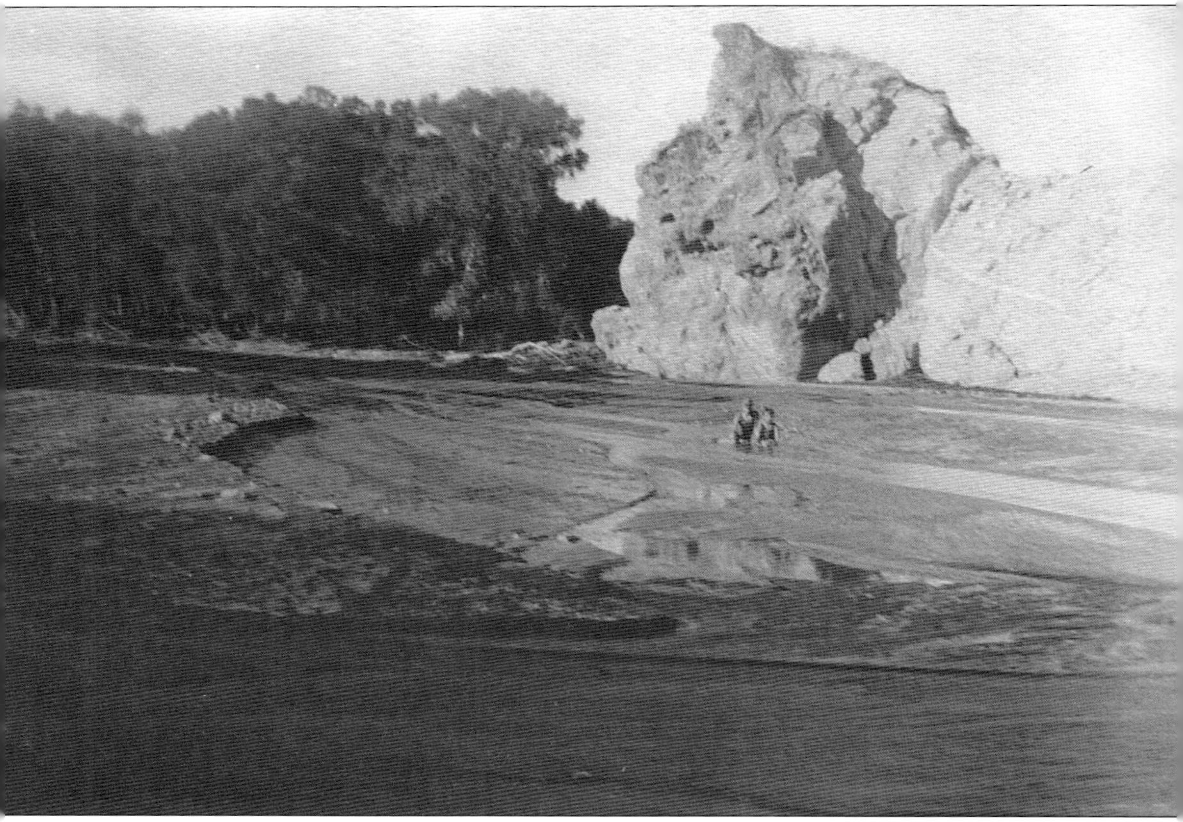

The Hassayampa River was the lifeblood of the Yavapai, who planted seasonal crops at Wickenburg's future townsite. For decades, its nickname was "The Upside-Down River" because of its habit of disappearing underground; the phrase was first used in a 1947 publicity brochure designed to add a zippy legend to a local landmark. The name does have Native American origins—the Mohave and Yavapai, who shared the Yuman language, referred to the portion of the river nearest Wickenburg as Haviamp. A Yavapai boy adopted by a cavalry officer called it Ha-sa-ya-mo, meaning "following the water as far as it goes." But Hassayampa is an American invention. The recording secretary for the first mining district established in the area thought Haviamp needed a Spanish pronunciation and came up with Hassayampa. A c. 1885 map of Maricopa County spells the name "Hassayamba" and calls the waterway a creek. When Arizona guidebooks were published in the early 20th century, they perpetuated the story. The origin of the word may be fiction, but the Hassayampa remains a powerful presence in Wickenburg.

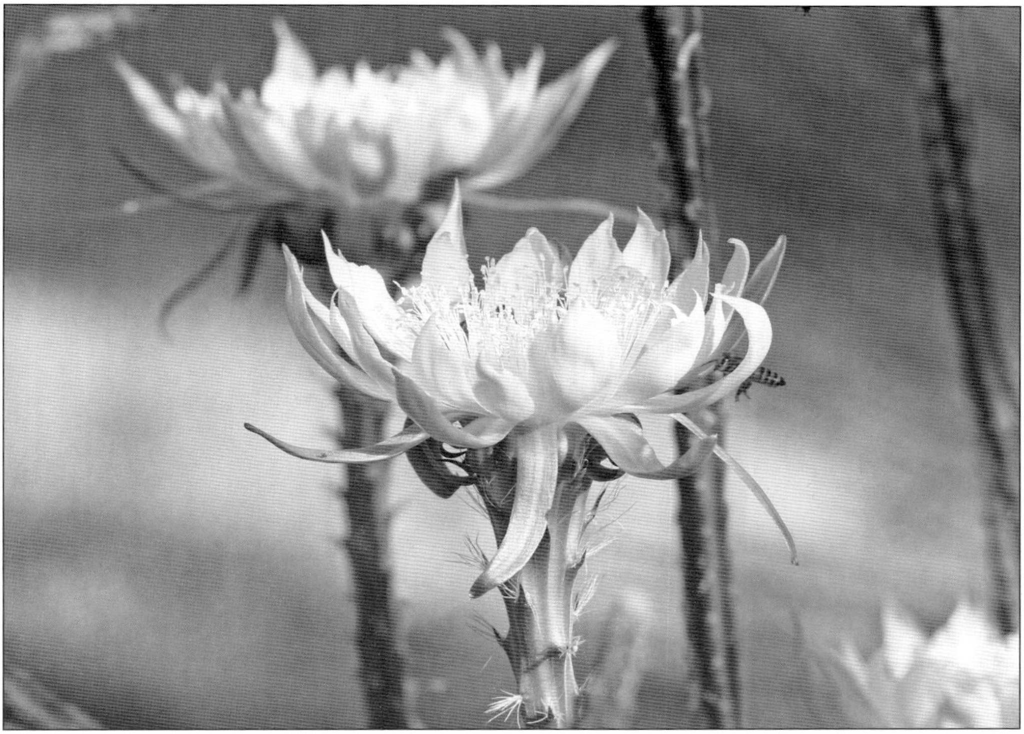

The beautiful landscape of Wickenburg, located in the Sonoran Desert, is astonishing to visitors whose idea of a "desert" is something barren, stark, and lifeless. If travelers are lucky enough to see this flower—the fragrant night-blooming cereus—they never look upon the desert quite the same way. Also called "Arizona Queen of the Night," the flowers of this cactus are so prized that it is listed as endangered in some of the states where it grows. (Photograph by Melissa Oehler.)

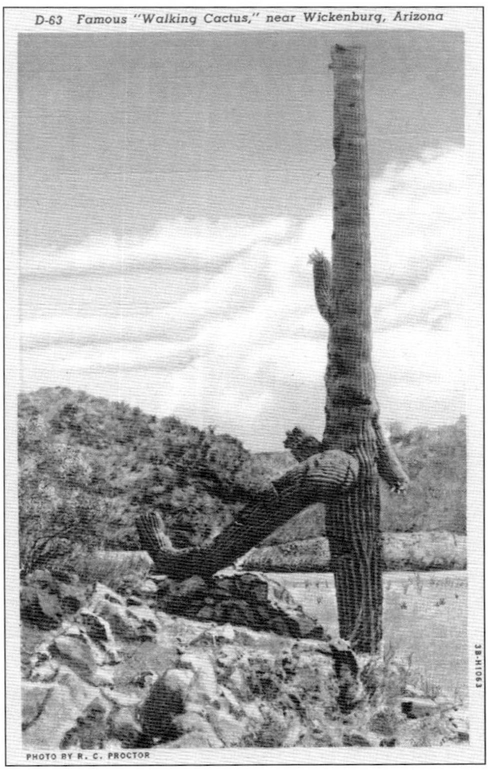

The mighty saguaro is practically the trademark of the desert, and these ancient cacti grow in profusion all around Wickenburg. It can take 75 years for a saguaro's "limbs" to begin their growth, and when they do appear, they can take very interesting shapes. In the 1920s, the arms of this peculiar plant caused a photographer to dub it the "Walking Cactus," and he printed up postcards for local travelers to send to curious relatives outside the West. (© Lollesgard Specialty Co. Collection of the author.)

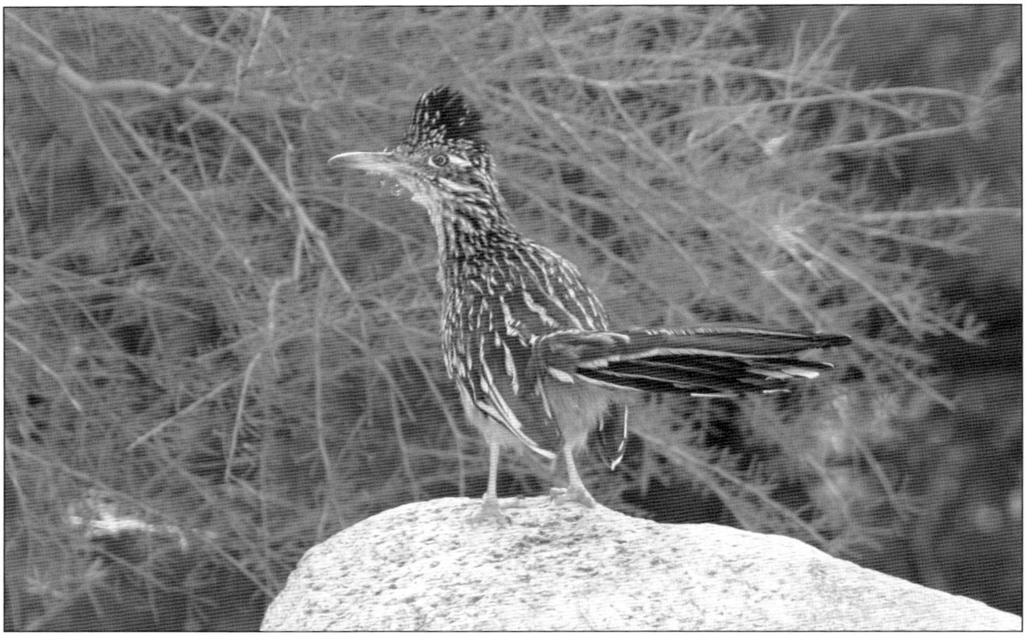

They may not look much like their cartoon counterparts, but roadrunners are some of the swiftest denizens of the desert, clocked at up to 20 miles per hour on a dead run. These birds are aggressive snake eaters, even ingesting the occasional rattlesnake, and are smart enough to rest during the heat of the day. (Photograph by Melissa Oehler.)

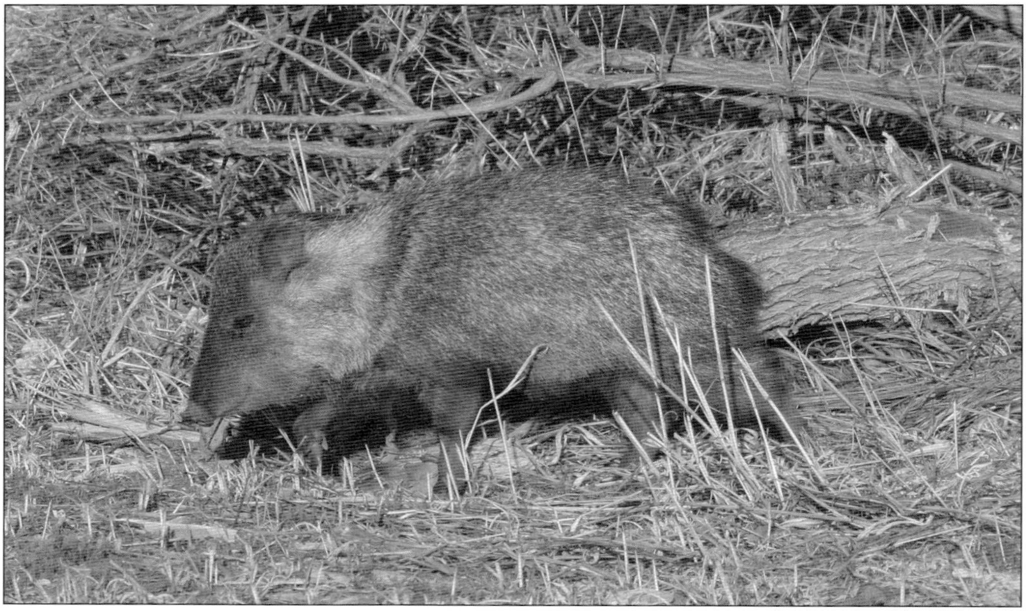

Although a javelina, also called a peccary, may appear to be a species of wild pig, these animals—from a mammal family called *Tayassuidae*—are more closely related to the rhinoceros. Javelinas thrive in the Sonoran Desert, where one of their principal foods is the abundant prickly pear cactus. They are not dangerous when encountered alone, but a band of javelinas can be formidable. (Photograph by Melissa Oehler.)

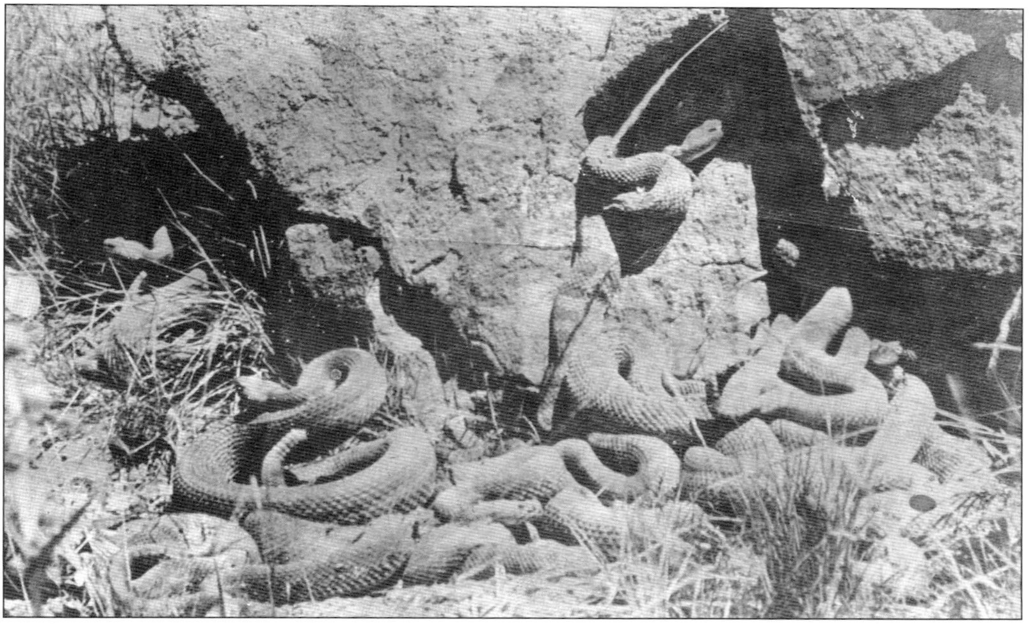

Rattlesnakes, whether alone or in nests, are perfect desert dwellers. Though they "sleep" during the winter, they proliferate in the warmer months, and residents are always alert to their presence. Visiting hikers and riders often see rattlesnakes, but the creatures are just as afraid of humans as humans are of them. A brave photographer captured this image of a rattlesnake nest around 1900.

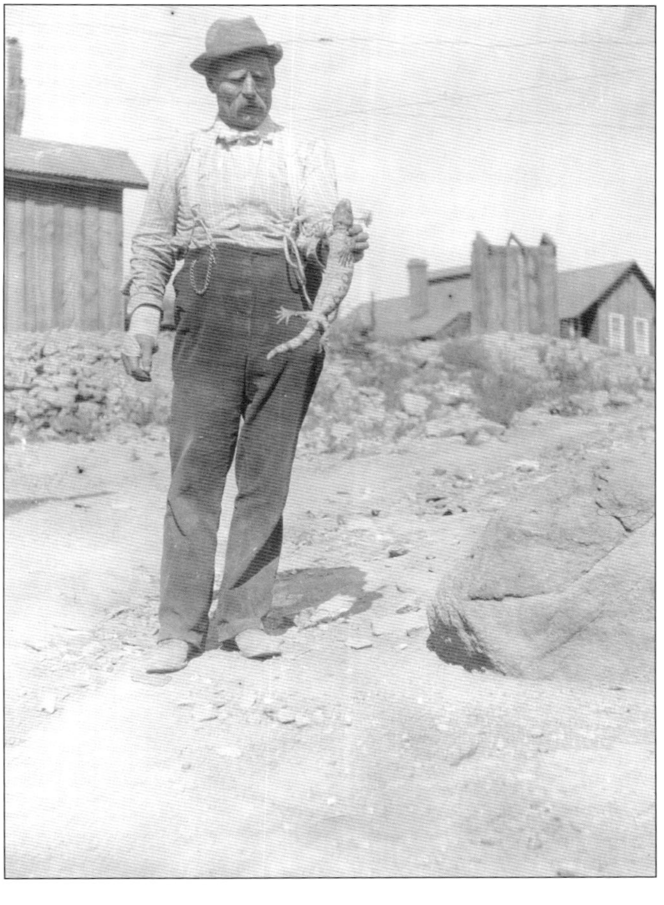

The venomous Gila monster is a rarely seen Sonoran Desert resident. These lizards spend most time in their subterranean burrows, venturing out during the warmer seasons. The Gila monster will avoid confrontation if it can, but it will bite if provoked and will hold on tenaciously to inject its venom. The man in this early-20th-century photograph managed to get the upper hand over this specimen.

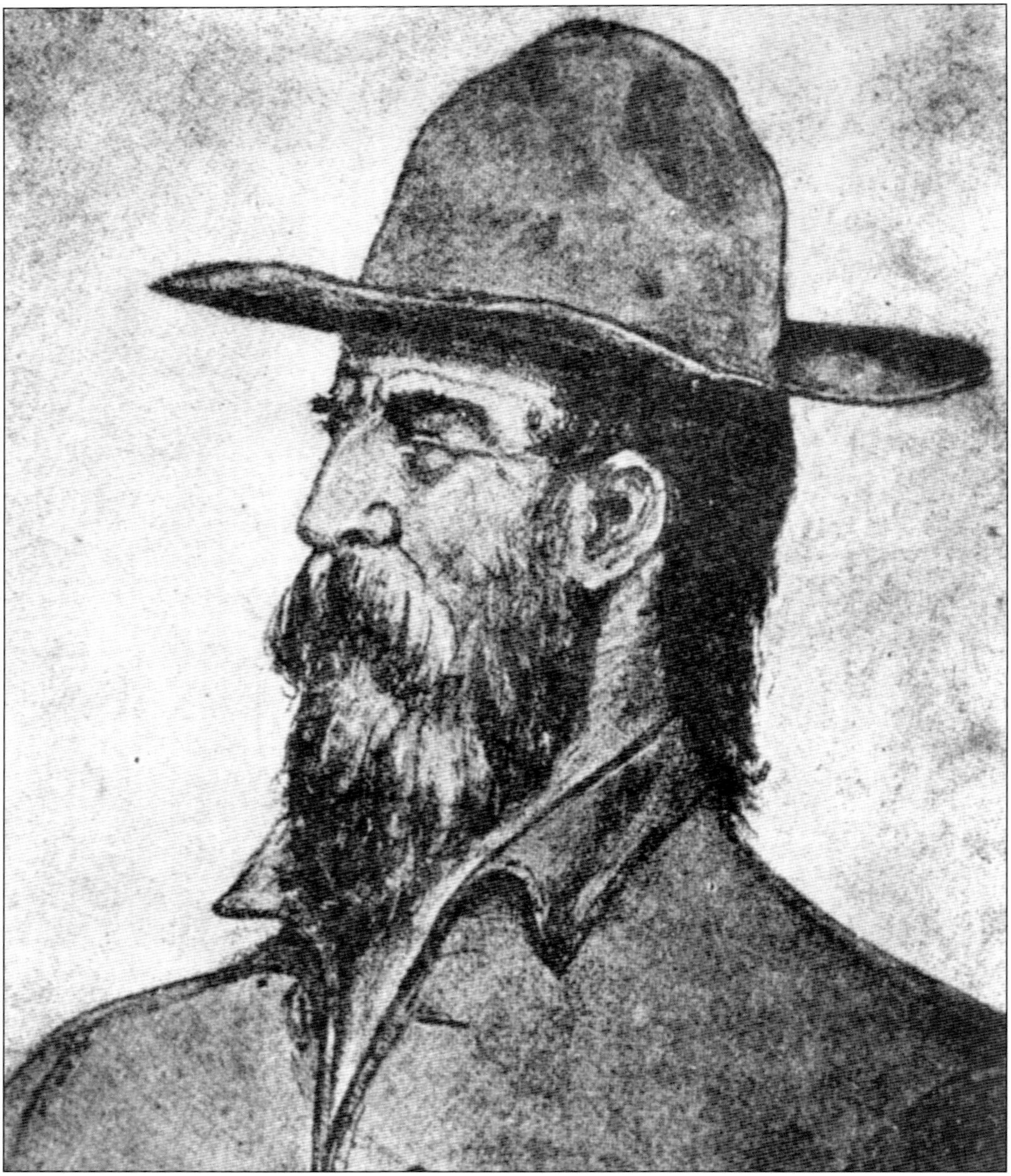

Born Powell Weaver in Tennessee, the man known as Pauline Weaver was a trapper, "mountain man," scout, and rancher throughout the Southwest before showing up in the Wickenburg area in 1863. Weaver accompanied Kit Carson when he traveled east from Southern California to deliver news of California's occupation by the Americans to Gen. Steven Watts Kearny in 1846. He then joined the Mormon Battalion, which supported the Army during the Mexican War. Later, after ranching in California, Weaver moved to the Yuma area in the late 1850s. In 1862, rumors of gold sent him prospecting along the Colorado River east of La Paz, a now-vanished town near present-day Ehrenberg. Soon named the Weaver Mining District No. 1, the area experienced a minor gold rush until the ore was played out a year later. The next spot that lured prospectors was the Hassayampa Valley and nearby Bradshaw Mountains, and Weaver's skills and knowledge of the area made him the perfect choice to guide the next group of explorers.

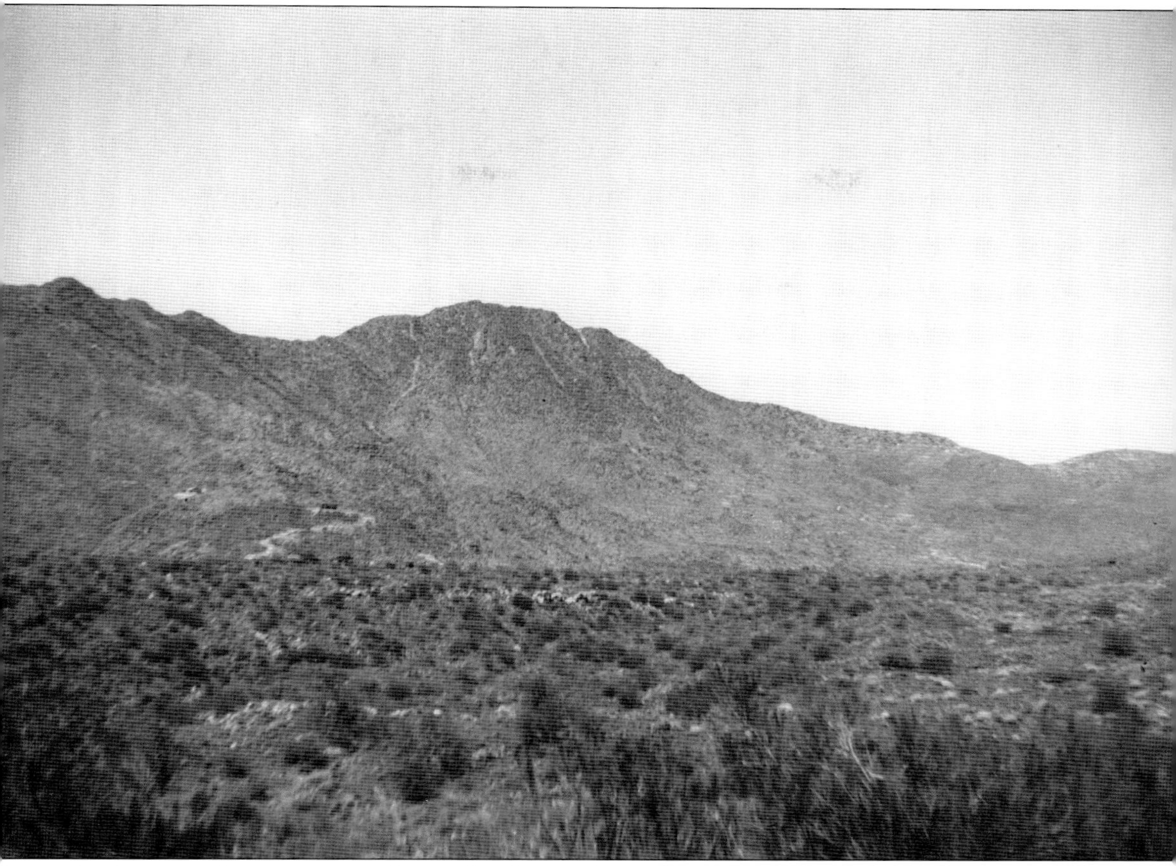

Abraham Peeples was born in North Carolina in 1822. Moving west, he fought in the Mexican War and was lured to California during the gold rush. By 1863, Peeples was in the Yuma area and led the group of men who left La Paz with Pauline Weaver that spring. Among the large party was Henry Wickenburg, whose fame would come later. The group traveled north along the Colorado River and then turned east. About 15 miles north of present-day Wickenburg, they found a gentle peak with gold deposits so abundant that the men were able to dig them out with knives; the place was dubbed Rich Hill. Needing supplies, they headed to the Pima Indian villages, where they met Joseph R. Walker and his own group of prospectors, which included a man named Jack Swilling, who later joined the Peeples party. Walker had already found gold and formed the Pioneer Mining District near present-day Prescott. When Mexican miners also made strikes in the same area, word got out and new mining districts were soon formed. This photograph of Rich Hill was taken in the 1950s.

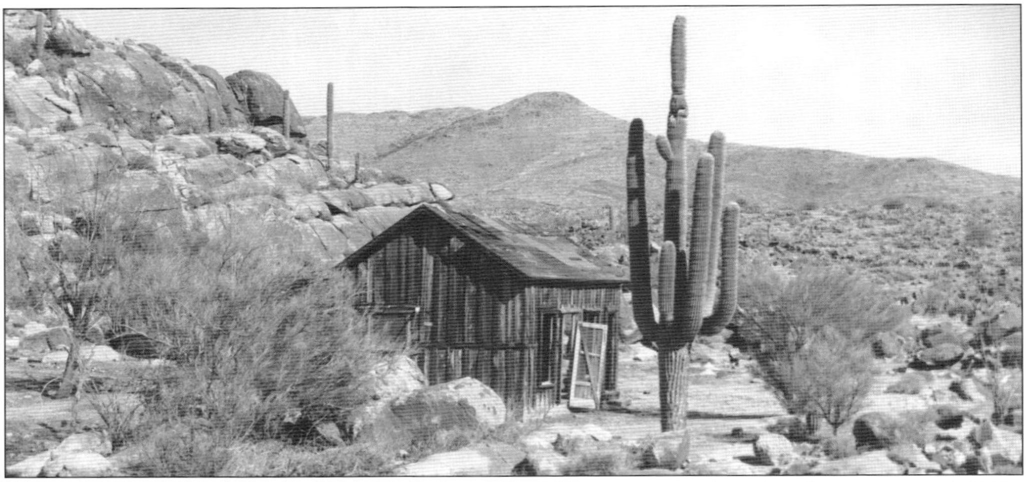

The Walker Mining District and the town of Walker were in place by the summer of 1863. Weaver Mining District No. 2 was organized in May 1864, and its small settlement was named for the famous guide, Pauline Weaver. Abraham Peeples settled into the valley that now bears his name and was a businessman and politician in the town of Wickenburg. He died in Phoenix in 1892 and is buried in the City Loosley Cemetery. Joseph R. Walker, born in 1798, ended up in California; he died in 1876 and is buried in the Alhambra Cemetery in Contra Costa County. (Photograph © Moulton B. Smith.)

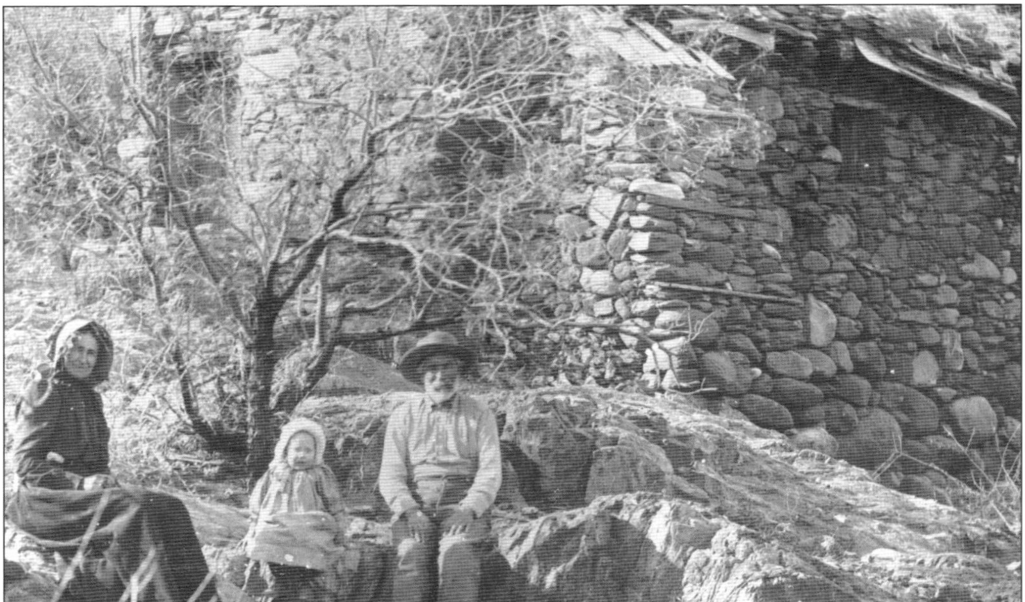

A group of early residents poses in front of a derelict house in the abandoned town of Weaver in the late 19th century. Pauline Weaver spent his remaining years as a scout and guide for the military. He died in 1867 and was buried at the Camp Verde Army post. The camp was closed in 1890, and his body was exhumed and reburied in San Francisco in 1892. In the 1920s, some Arizona citizens campaigned to have Weaver brought back to the state, and on October 27, 1929, Boy Scouts carried Weaver's casket to his new burial site on the grounds of the Sharlot Hall Museum in Prescott.

Two

Henry Wickenburg and the Vulture Mine

The most famous resident of the Hassayampa Valley—for whom a tiny settlement was first named—was German immigrant Henry Wickenburg. Born in 1819 in Essen-Holsterhausen, the records of his arrival and early years in the United States are a bit contradictory, so it is difficult to pin down how he came to Arizona. Described by journalists as a "staunch old pioneer," the story of his life that has come down through history seems to have started with his arrival in Arizona around 1862, when he was doing some placer mining in the La Paz region.

In the fall of 1863, Wickenburg found himself in the middle Hassayampa River valley with two partners, and in October, they found a quartz outcropping rich with gold. Whether Wickenburg himself came up with the name "Vulture Mine," and how that came to be, is another enduring historical mystery of the famous mine. Did he see a turkey vulture on a nearby rock, as some claim? Did the shape of the nearby mountain—later named Vulture Peak—suggest the shape of a vulture's head?

Whatever the reason for the name, it is known that Wickenburg and the two men posted a claim notice, and Wickenburg's partners then left the area. In May 1864, Wickenburg returned with a few other miners and found the area deserted and unworked. He immediately organized the Wickenburg mining district and registered the claim in Prescott, the county seat.

Two years later, Wickenburg sold his interest in the Vulture Mine and opened up other claims nearby. He endured litigation (which he won) with his first partners over ownership of the original claim. Over the next decades, the Vulture went through many owners, reflecting the rising and falling tide of hope that accompanied all western mining ventures.

Wickenburg's future and inclination lay in farming, and while still scratching out a living through his mining ventures, he also took advantage of the Hassayampa's rich bottomland, setting down crops and rooting himself forever in the town that bears his name.

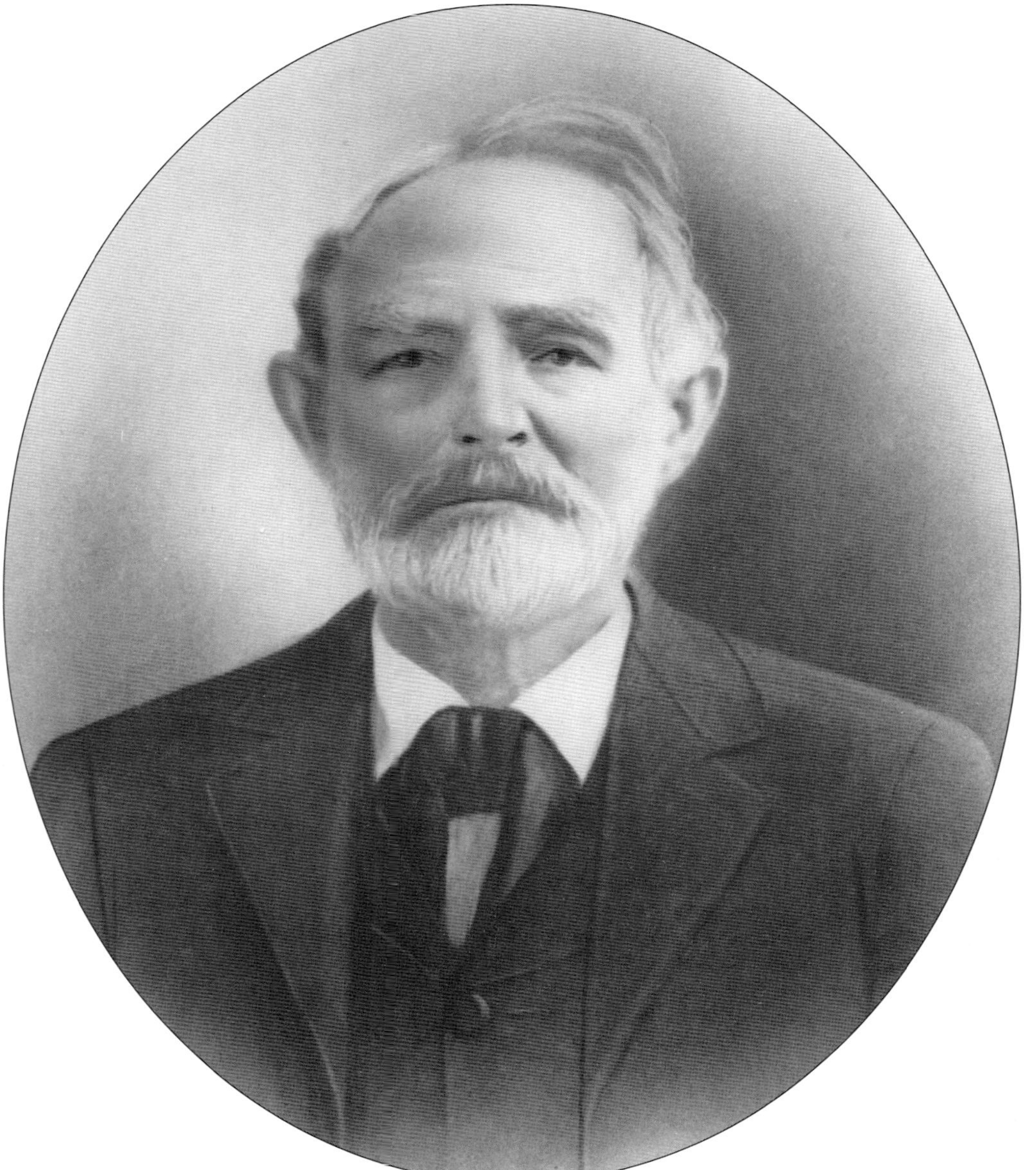

A newspaper article about the life of Henry Wickenburg, which ran in the April 20, 1932, edition of the *Arizona Republic*, began as follows: "It certainly took brave men to go prospecting alone in the hills and mountains of Arizona in 1863. And Henry Wickenburg, discoverer of the famous Vulture Mine, was among those who braved the frontier perils." He certainly was brave, and although he was a wanderer in his early life, he found his home in the town that was eventually named after him. Born in Germany in 1819, Wickenburg made his way to New York around 1847 and traveled to San Francisco in 1853, where he was first naturalized (he was apparently naturalized again in Arizona in 1882). The year 1862 saw him in La Paz, where he joined the Peeples party, which eventually found Rich Hill. Some research suggests he had mining experience in Germany, but records of Wickenburg's early years are spotty. Most of what is known about him begins with his life in the new territory of Arizona

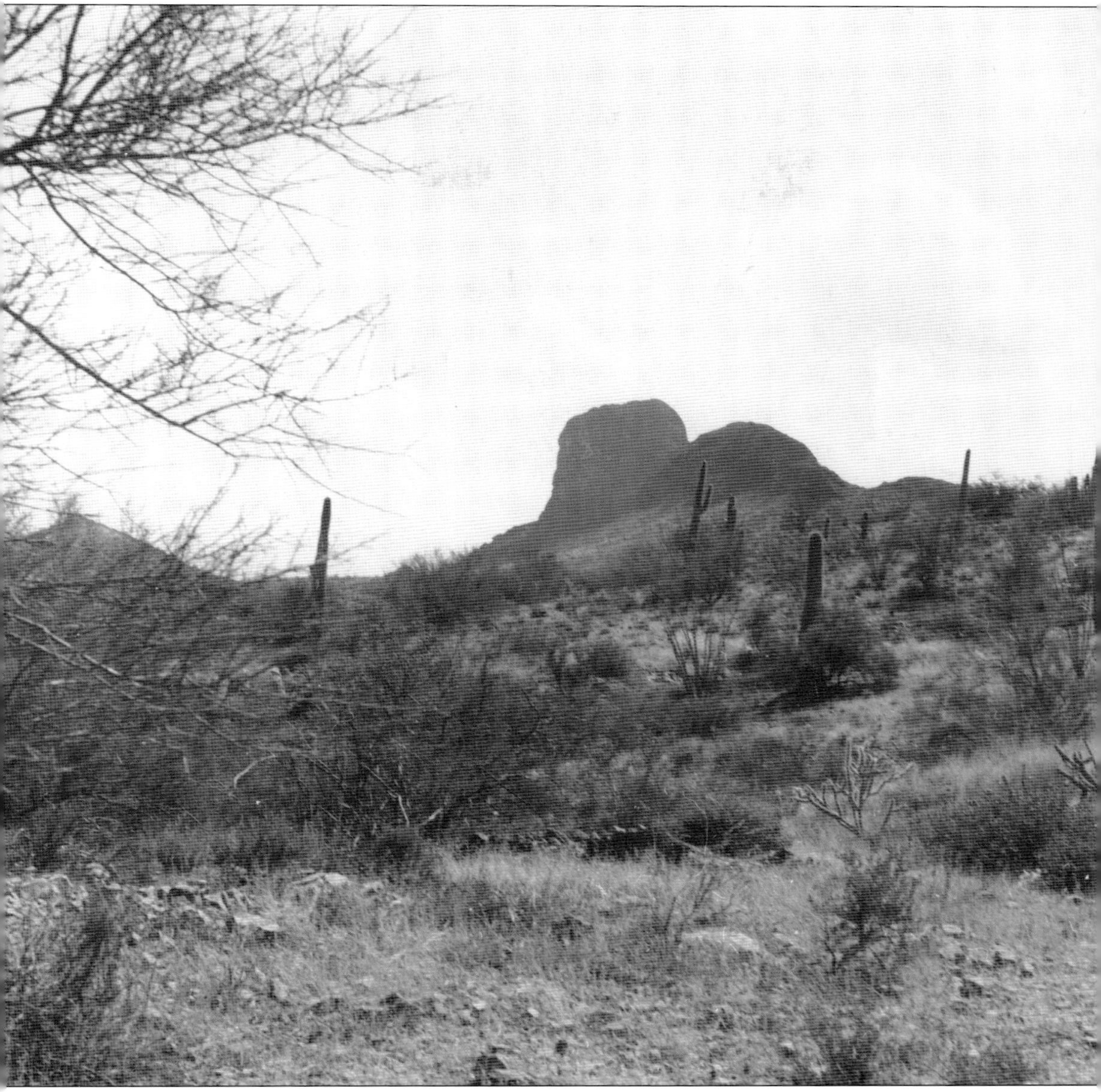

By the fall of 1863, Henry Wickenburg had two mining partners—Van Bibber and Rusk. They were working a dry claim in an area near a distinctive mountain peak on the Hassayampa Plain, south of present-day Wickenburg, where they discovered a quartz outcropping that Wickenburg thought looked promising. His partners disagreed, but Wickenburg went back later, found gold-bearing samples, and showed them to the two men. They did not develop the site and Rusk and Van Bibber took off, though Wickenburg stayed nearby and returned to the area the following spring. He organized the Wickenburg Mining District with four new partners and registered the claim in Prescott. The origin of "Vulture" is a bit convoluted. Wickenburg himself told conflicting stories about the name, ranging from the fanciful to the prosaic. Eastern newspapers, which preferred juicy tales from the Wild West, have been blamed for some of the stories. The real story will likely never be known, but the mine and the unusual peak that shares its name will always be legend in the history of western mining.

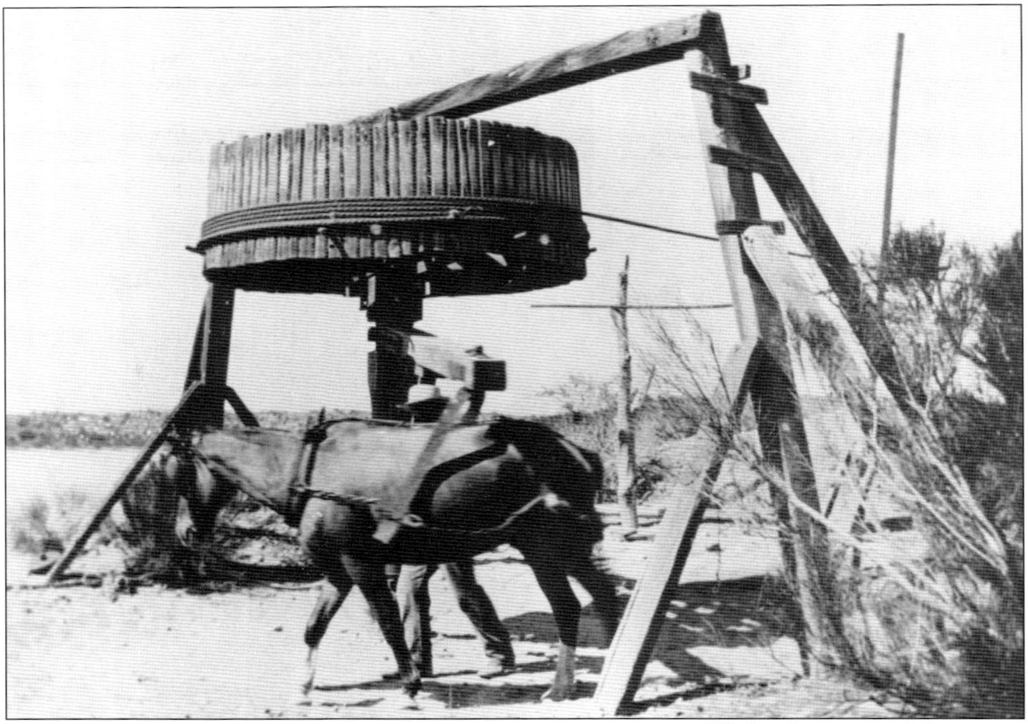

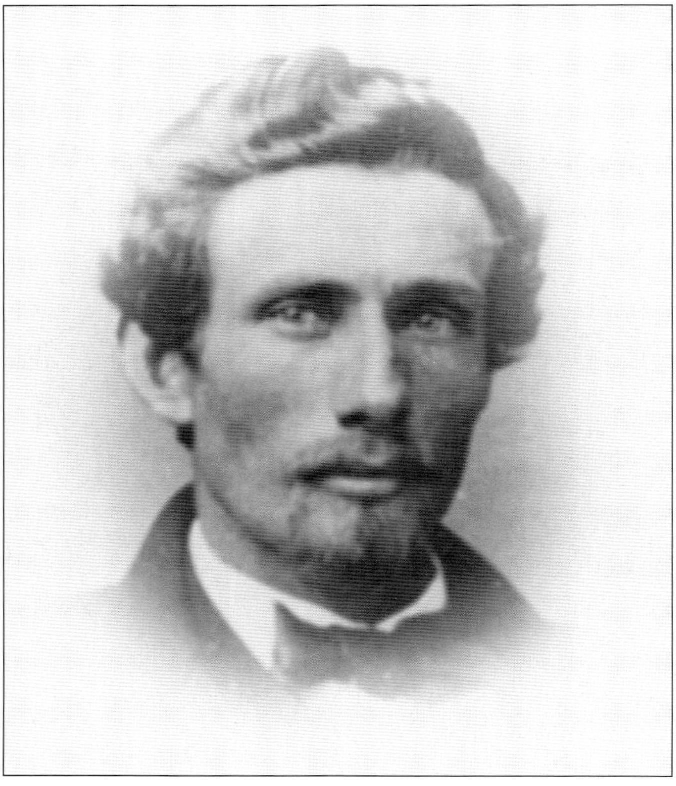

Wickenburg mined the Vulture's gold via the arrastra method first used by Spanish and Mexican miners. The quartz rock containing the gold was hauled 12 miles away, to the Hassayampa River. The ore was dumped onto a flat area with a circle of stones around the outside. A timber was set in the middle with a crossbar to which large boulders were attached on the inside of the circle. Mules or horses walked around the circle, dragging the large stones over the ore and crushing it so the gold could be retrieved. Charles Genung (1839–1916), pictured here, was a mining man who worked a number of claims in the Rich Hill area. Genung met Henry Wickenburg in the summer of 1864 and helped him build his first arrastra.

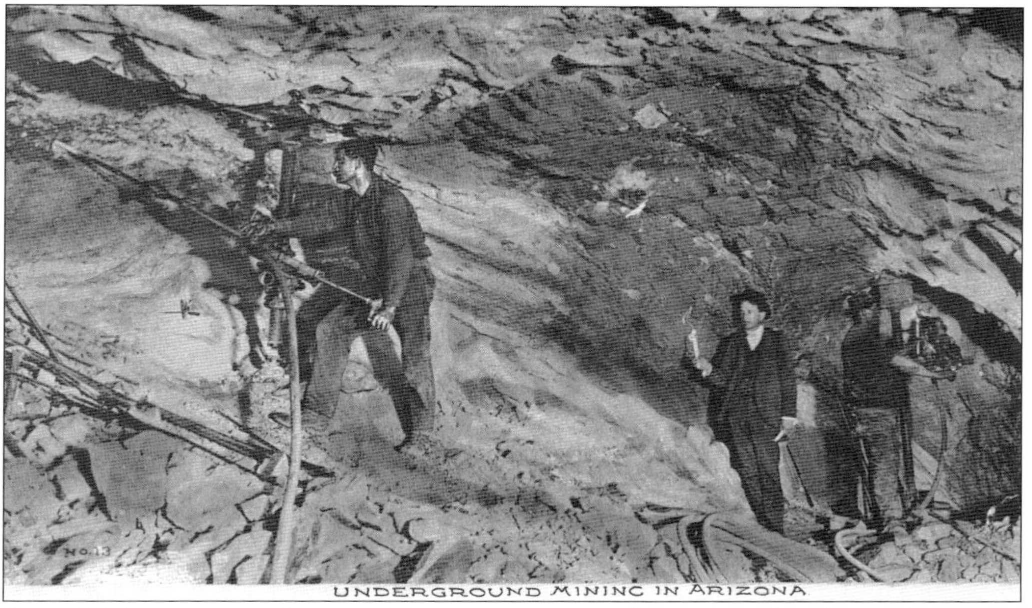

Henry Wickenburg soon discovered that mining is a tough way to make a living. Once news of the strike at the Vulture Mine got out, arrastras were built up and down the banks of the Hassayampa. Instead of working his claim, Wickenburg charged people $15 per wagon to haul out the ore themselves. Within a decade, miners had the option of using the newly invented pneumatic drill, as seen in this c. 1900 postcard. (Collection of the author.)

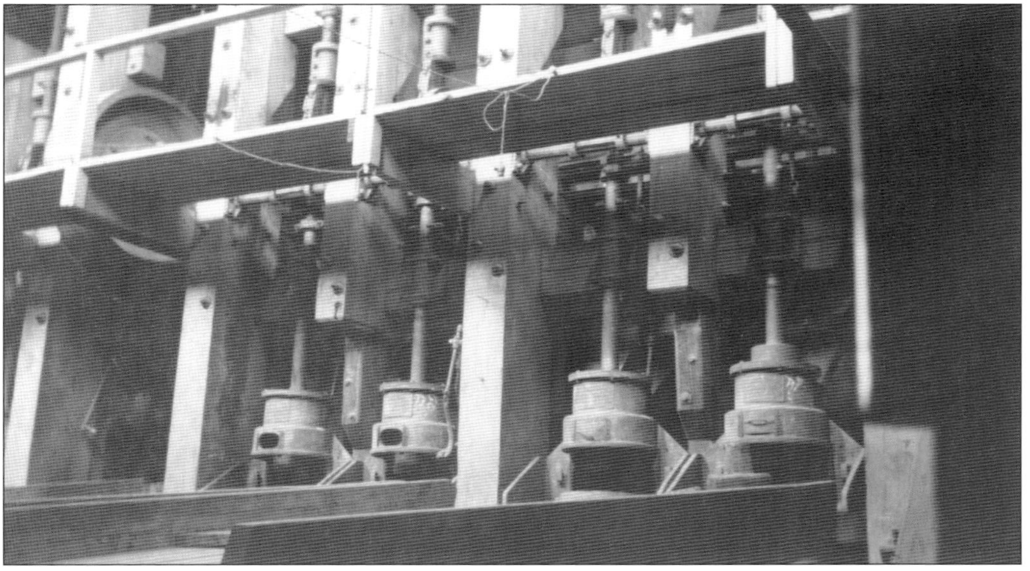

By 1865, a stamp mill had been erected in a dry wash, called Martinez, north of the mine site. The automated machinery did the labor of an individual miner and crushed more ore in a day than one man could dream of. There was a price to pay, though; the constant pounding of the heavy metal stamps could be heard and felt for miles, and the mills often ran for 24 hours a day. However, as some mining historians have written, to some this was the sound of prosperity. (© Bate photograph, Prescott.)

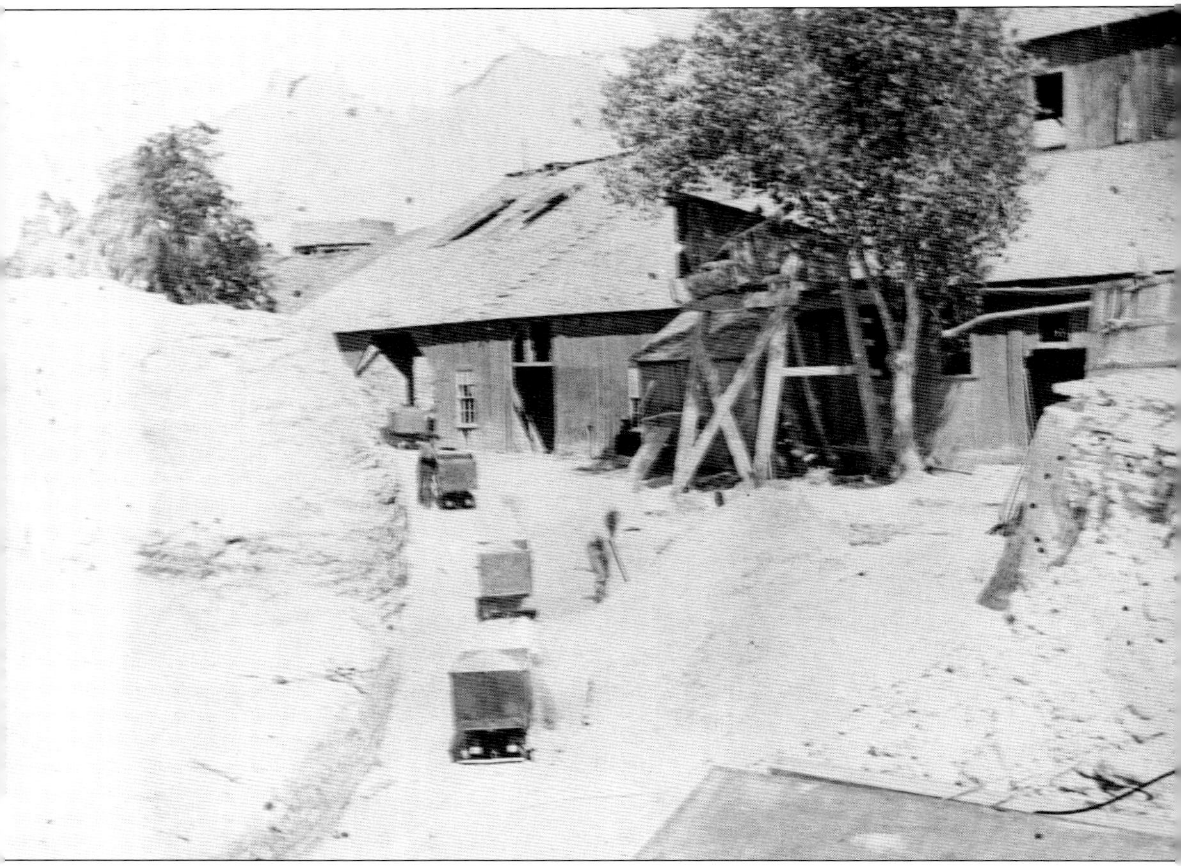

In 1865, the Wickenburg Post Office was established 12 miles from Vulture Mine, the name having been shortened from "Wickenburg Ranch." The following year, Henry Wickenburg sold the Vulture Mine to Benjamin Phelps for around $80,000, though he never received all of the money. Phelps and his partners then formed the Vulture Mining Company. Two years later, they erected a 20-stamp mill near Martinez Wash (having started with 10 stamps) and contracted with a firm in Fort Yuma to haul 20 tons of ore to the mill per day. By the end of the year, the annual production was reported to be $250,000 and rumors of big strikes and rich veins continued to make the newspapers.

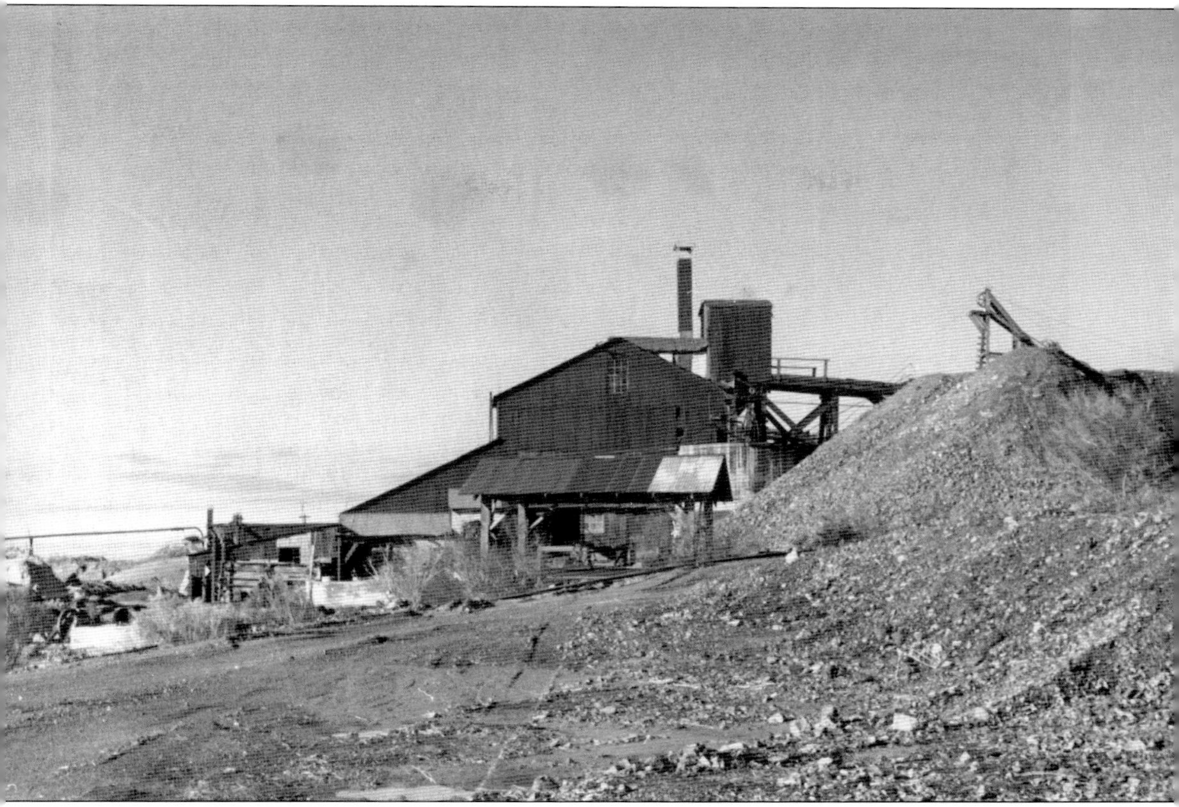

Over the years, the name "Vulture" was applied to a variety of locations throughout the Wickenburg area, though only two were actually associated with the mine. The first was probably Vulture Town, the small settlement that sprung up around the 10-stamp mill erected by the Vulture Mining Company about a mile north of present-day Wickenburg. Vulture City is recognized as the official name of the community at the mine's site, which became a fully functioning town by the 1870s. In 1870, for example, a judge named John A. Rush bought a storehouse and its contents in Vulture City. As reported in the February 26, 1870, issue of *The Miner*, the store "is next to the Vulture Quartz Mill, Vulture City, and patronized by the Vulture Mining Company and its numerous employees." Judge Rush was reportedly making plans to go to San Francisco to get more goods for his new store.

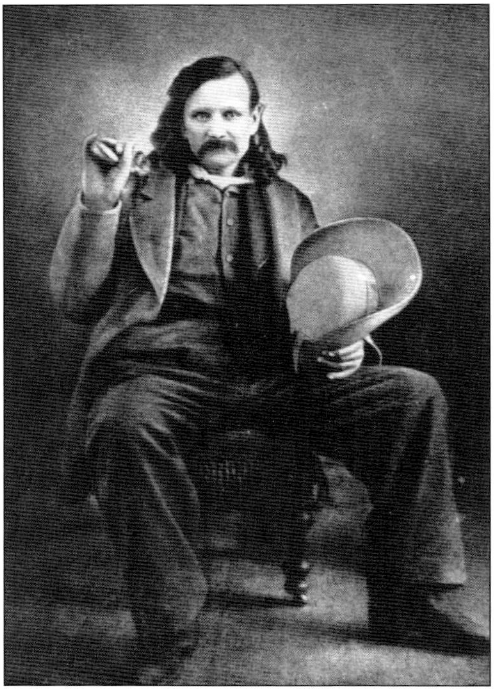

Jack Swilling (1830–1878) was born in South Carolina, lived in California, and arrived in Arizona around 1858. He belonged to the Gila Rangers, a militia company formed to repel Indian attacks. In January 1860, Swilling's men wandered into the Prescott Basin, near the Hassayampa, where they found traces of gold. After his return in 1863, he settled in the area and prospected on Rich Hill. Swilling and his family lived in Wickenburg, where they farmed the lower Hassayampa. In 1867, he noticed the ancient Hohokam canals near present-day Phoenix, and in September of that year, he formed the Swilling Irrigating Canal Company and began constructing modern irrigation canals. Henry Wickenburg was an early stockholder, and Swilling moved to Phoenix, where his own farm benefited from the water now flowing through the canals. Near the end of his life, Swilling was wrongly suspected of taking part in a deadly stagecoach robbery, and he died in jail in Yuma awaiting a hearing. The location of his grave is unknown. (Arizona Historical Society.)

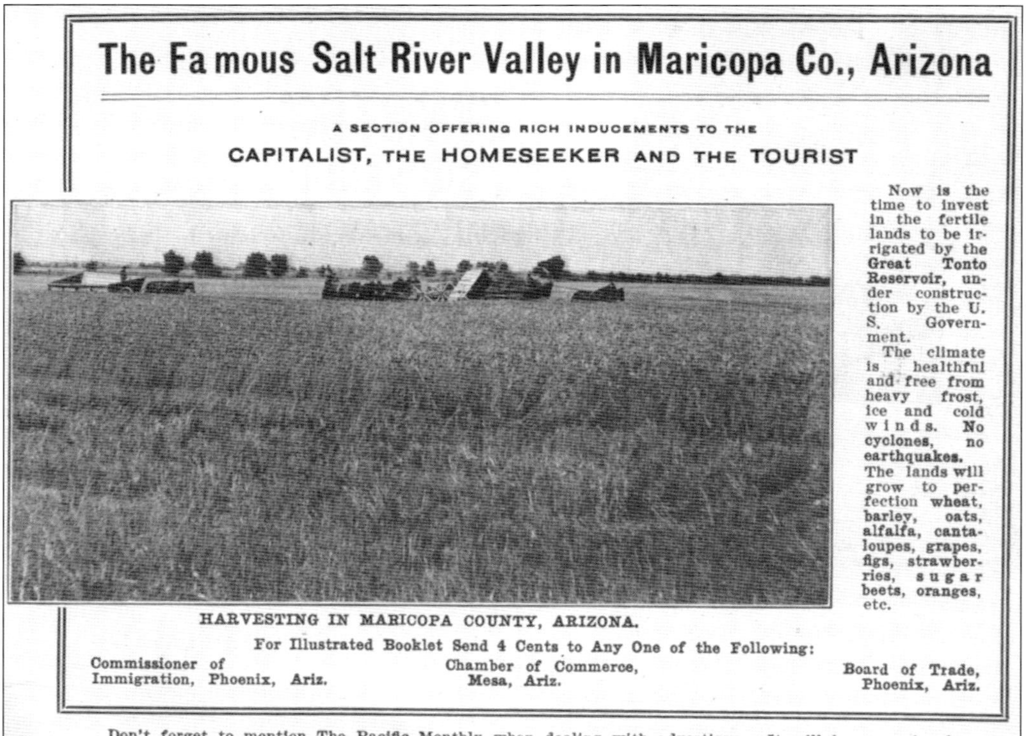

This 1906 advertisement for Phoenix's fertile Salt River Valley is a reminder of the pioneering efforts of Jack Swilling. (Collection of the author.)

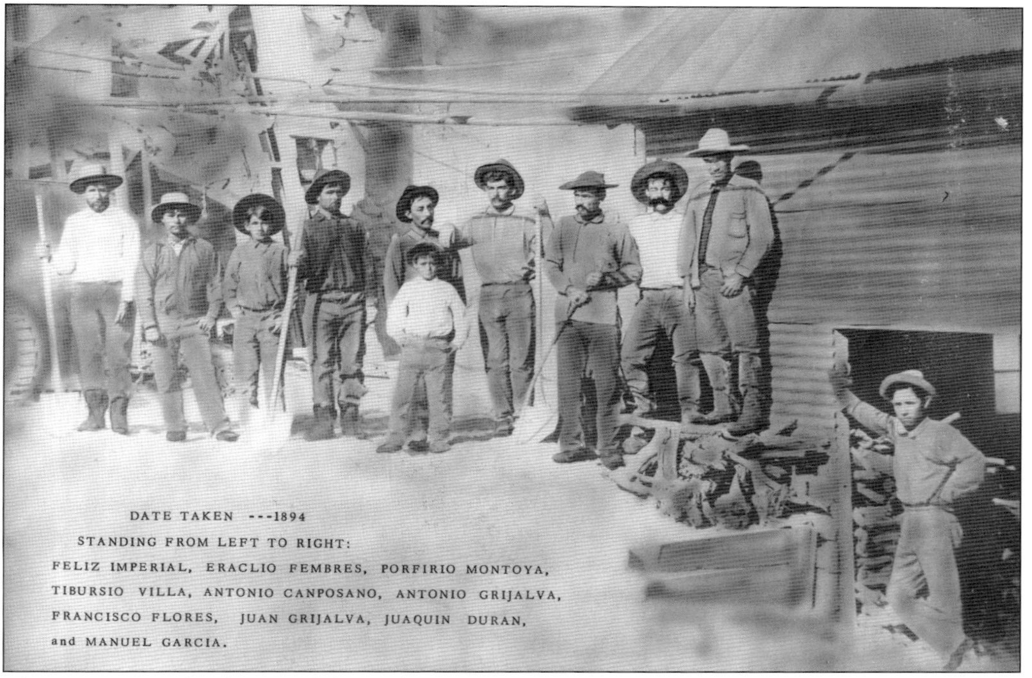

The town of Wickenburg and the Vulture Mine site always had Hispanic residents and workers. In the 1880 census, for example, half of Wickenburg's population had Spanish surnames. This 1894 image of the Vulture Mine was reprinted with the names of the workers pictured in the photograph and is frequently used in exhibits at the Desert Caballeros Western Museum.

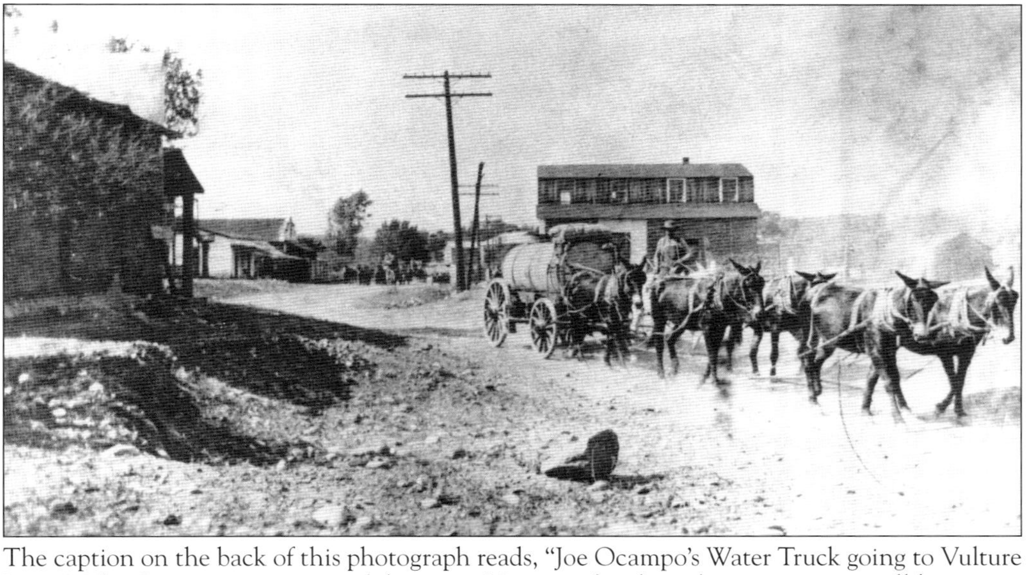

The caption on the back of this photograph reads, "Joe Ocampo's Water Truck going to Vulture Mine." The Ocampos were one of the many Hispanic families whose names are still known in Wickenburg, including Quesada, Macias, Garcia, Ortega, Valencia, and others. In the last few years, many family papers have been donated to Arizona State University, and books have been published about Hispanic contributions to Wickenburg and Arizona history, making research easier for new generations.

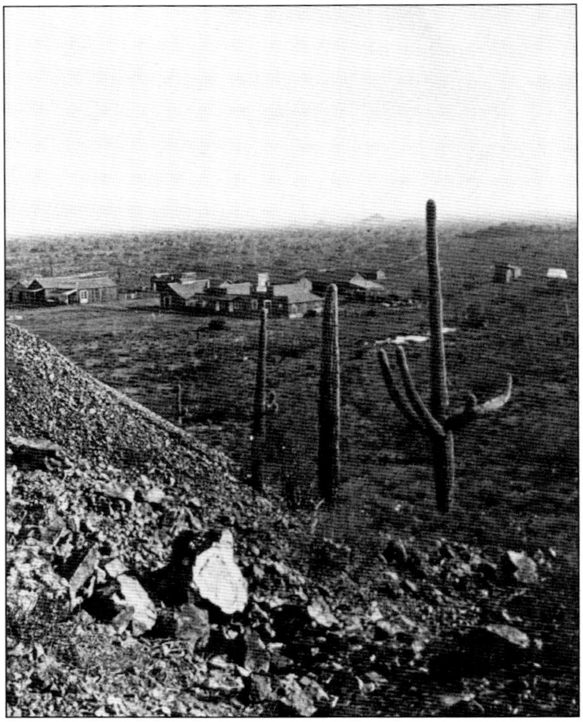

The fortunes of the Vulture Mine continued to make headlines. It was bought and sold more than once as the century progressed and for a time was owned by Horace Tabor, the flamboyant Silver King of Leadville, Colorado. A post office was established at Vulture City around 1880, though it was closed a few years later. But the biggest thing to happen at the Vulture was the construction of a water pipeline from nearby Seymour, 14 miles away. Completed in 1880, it was made of hand-riveted sheet iron and brought water to the mine so a stamp mill could be built on-site, thus saving the men the chore of hauling the ore to the Hassayampa for processing.

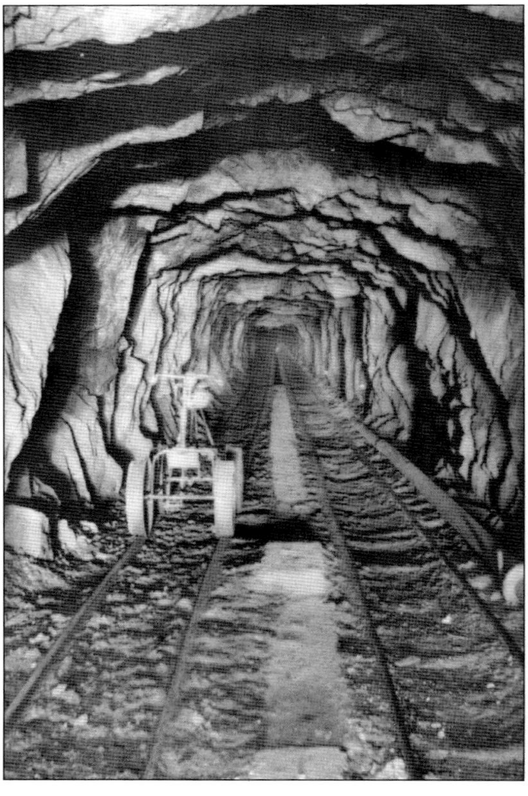

The Vulture Mine might have been modernized, but it was still a dangerous place to work. In 1887, a miner named Alejandro Valenzuello was killed in a cave-in and two companions barely escaped. However, disaster was sometimes averted. In 1888, a wagon of supplies bound for the Vulture got stuck in the mud a few miles from Wickenburg, and the teamster had to unload 1,750 pounds of "giant powder" (dynamite). Another teamster came along and tried to shoot a coyote sniffing at the boxes. As reported in the December 8, 1888, issue of the *Mohave County Miner*: "His shot struck the giant powder and people for ten miles around thought there was a fearful earthquake. The coyote has not been seen since."

Three

Mines and Mayhem

Wickenburg's beginnings reflected the financially risky nature of western mining. Henry Wickenburg not only discovered the Vulture Mine, but also bought and sold other claims, and men and their dreams made way to the Hassayampa.

As the century progressed, other mines were discovered in the area and given names like Octave, Monte Cristo, Congress, and Gold Bar. The wealth of these strikes and the mirage of easy riches attracted danger and crime as well as hard workers. Wickenburg's early history is full of the kind of mayhem regularly associated with the West, the most notorious of which is the Wickenburg Massacre of 1871.

The end of the century also spelled the end of the traditional way of life for the Yavapai. By 1873, warfare with the US military ended with the final expulsion of the Yavapai to reservations. Today, they again thrive in their ancestral lands, and there are three federally recognized Yavapai tribes: Fort McDowell Yavapai, Camp Verde Yavapai-Apache, and Yavapai-Prescott.

The fortunes of the Vulture Mine fluctuated in the decades after its discovery. It closed in 1873 and reopened in 1878, a cycle that was repeated throughout its history. The Vulture's wealth led to robberies and murders, all of which were described in regional newspapers with relish. Accidents were also common.

The town of Wickenburg showed signs of real settlement. Arizona was declared a territory in 1863, and a post office was established at Wickenburg in 1865. The townsite was platted (though not recorded) in 1868. The US Census of 1870 recorded 442 people (of which 74 were women) in Wickenburg and the surrounding region, and in 1875, the town became part of the newly formed Maricopa County. The first school was opened in 1879, the same year that Pres. Rutherford B. Hayes deeded 160 acres of land to Henry Wickenburg. By 1887, plans for a dam on the Hassayampa—a project with grave consequences for everyone in the valley—were on the drawing board.

But that was a few years away. In the late 1800s, despite the occasional mine-related robbery, Wickenburg's future looked bright.

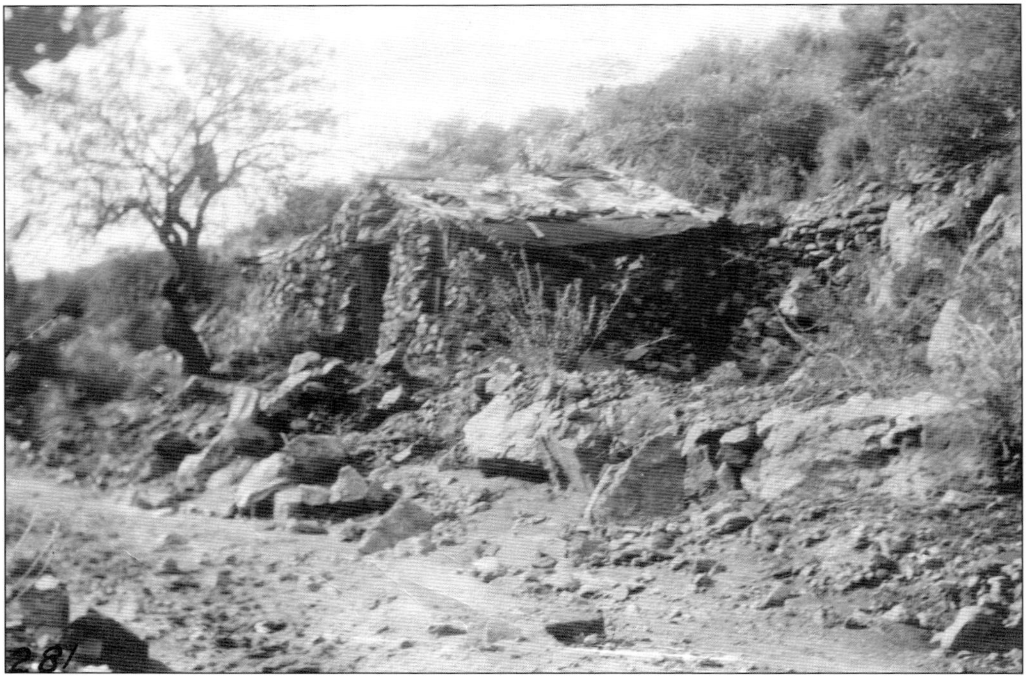

This 1920s photograph is captioned, "Relic of Mining Days." By this decade, mining was seen as something from Wickenburg's past. But miners still swarmed through town and the surrounding mountains as new strikes were found and new companies were formed. An article in the April 25, 1901, issue of the *Arizona Republican* said of Wickenburg, "One hears of little but mines."

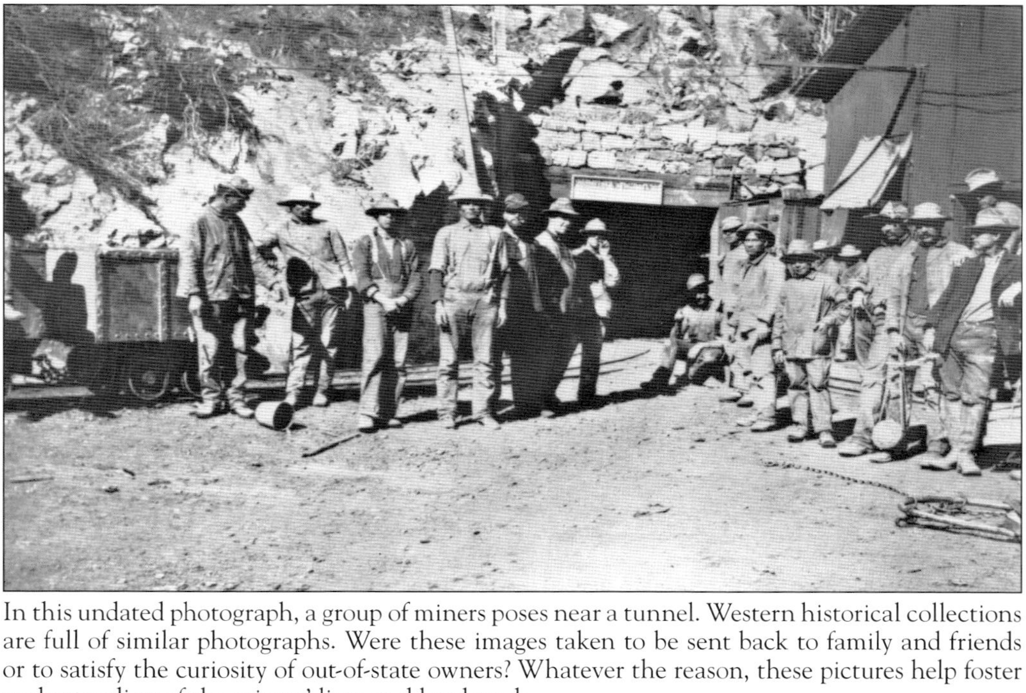

In this undated photograph, a group of miners poses near a tunnel. Western historical collections are full of similar photographs. Were these images taken to be sent back to family and friends or to satisfy the curiosity of out-of-state owners? Whatever the reason, these pictures help foster understanding of the miners' lives and hard work.

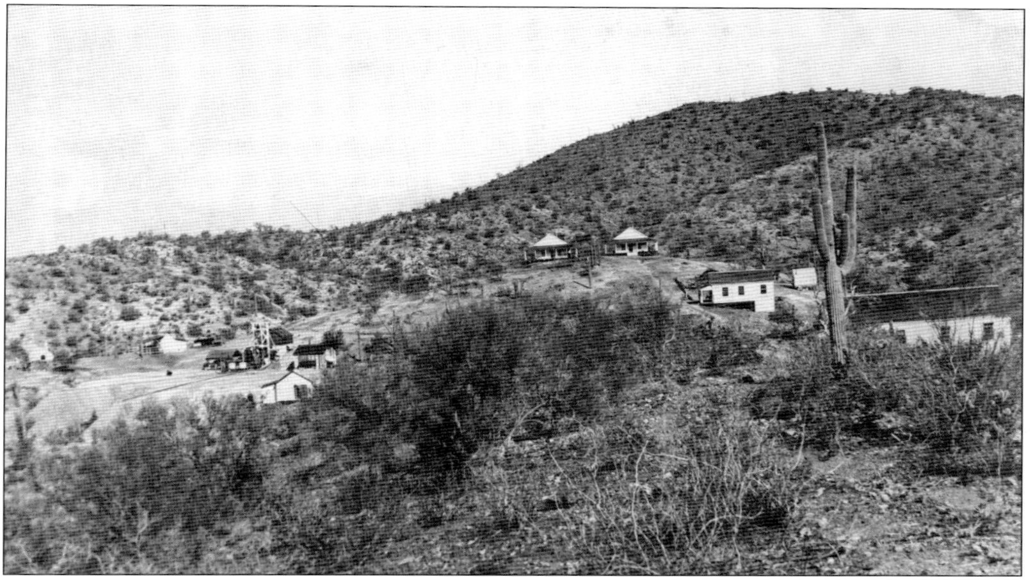

The Oro Grande Mine (pictured), with rich deposits of copper and silver, was discovered in the 1870s about five miles north of Wickenburg in the Black Rock District. A major gold strike was also made in the area. One of the mine's owners, a Mr. Hatfield, showed a "door-stop"–sized nugget, weighing three or four pounds, to a reporter from the *Arizona Republican*.

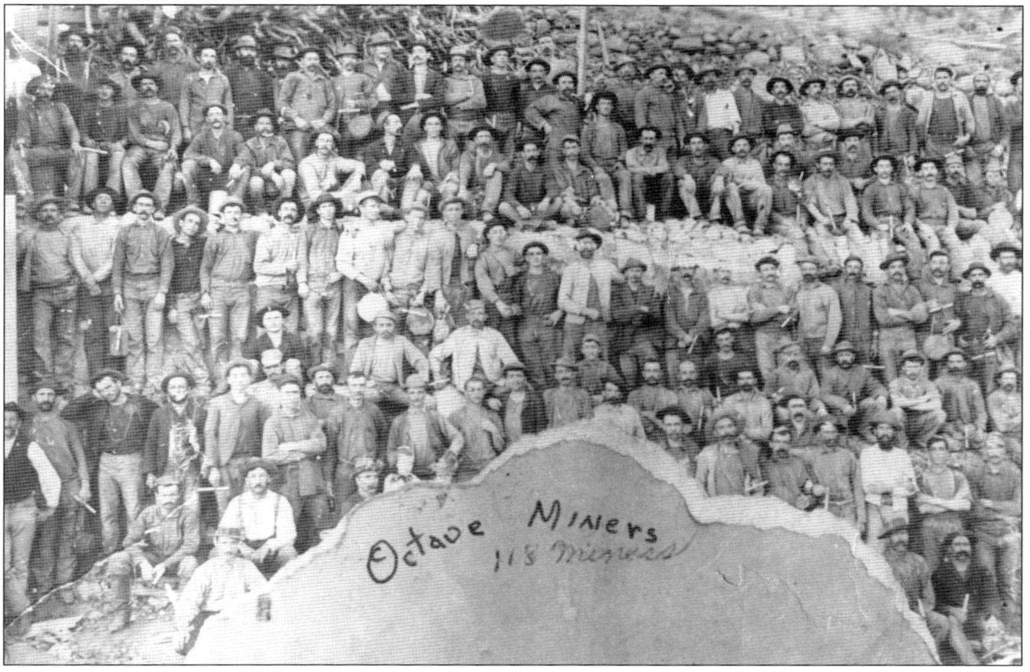

The Octave Mine was also in the region north of Wickenburg. According to Charles Genung, he and other prospectors discovered the Octave vein near Rich Hill in June 1864. Recovering the gold barely repaid the miners' efforts, though Genung worked the area for over 20 years. By 1895, the property was sold to a syndicate called the Octave Gold Mining Company; various companies worked the mine until it closed in 1942.

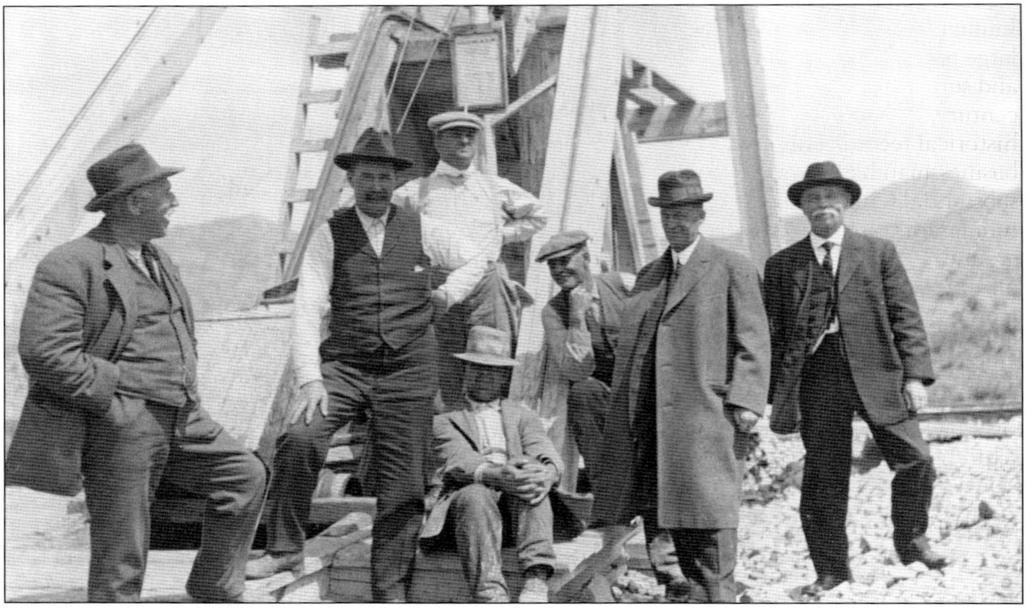

One of the men in this undated photograph is Ezra Thayer, Phoenix hardware merchant and owner of the Monte Cristo Mine, a silver strike from the late 19th century. Thayer acquired the site as payment for a debt, and when he was unable to find the rumored vein of ore, he hired renowned mining engineer Frank Crampton to locate it. Crampton discovered that the previous owners had hidden the rich seam of silver with lumber and rocks.

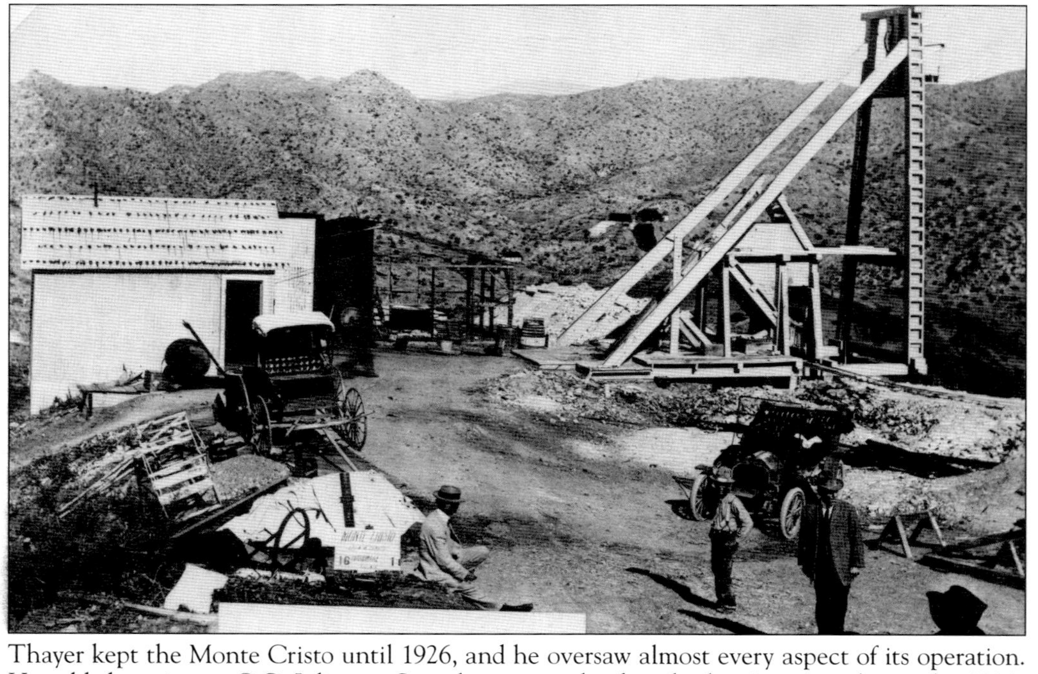

Thayer kept the Monte Cristo until 1926, and he oversaw almost every aspect of its operation. He sold the mine to C.C. Julian, a Canadian man who found oil in Los Angeles in the 1920s and was then embroiled in a stock swindle that rivaled the Teapot Dome scandal of the same era. The Monte Cristo site can still be visited today.

Immigrants from China did not make up a large portion of the population in Wickenburg and surrounding Arizona cities in the 19th century, but they were present and in the historical record. This prosperous Phoenix businessman had counterparts in the fairly substantial Chinese community in Prescott. Immigrants also worked the mines in and around Wickenburg, where the harshness of mining life sometimes had tragic results; a man named Wong Tie killed another Chinese miner at the Vulture in 1885. But it was not all bad news—in 1889, the *Mohave County Miner* reported that local rancher Frederick Brill had leased part of his property to two Chinese men, "Ling Sing . . . and a Phoenix celestial." (Cabinet card, F.A. Hartwell photographer, c. 1898. Courtesy Jeremy Rowe, vintagephoto.com.)

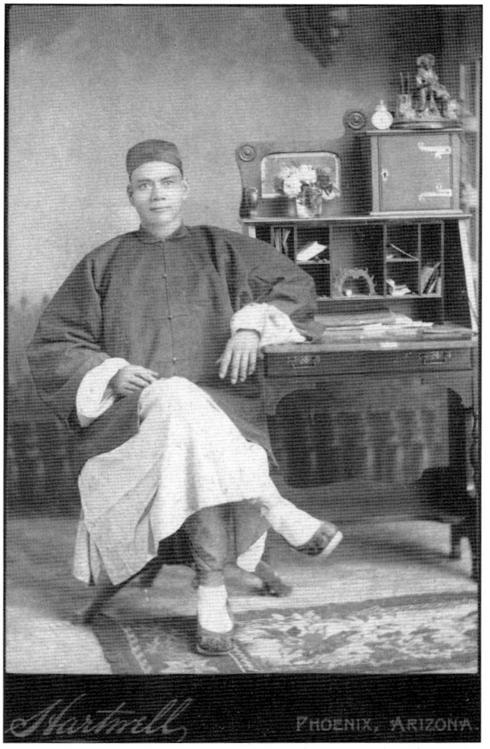

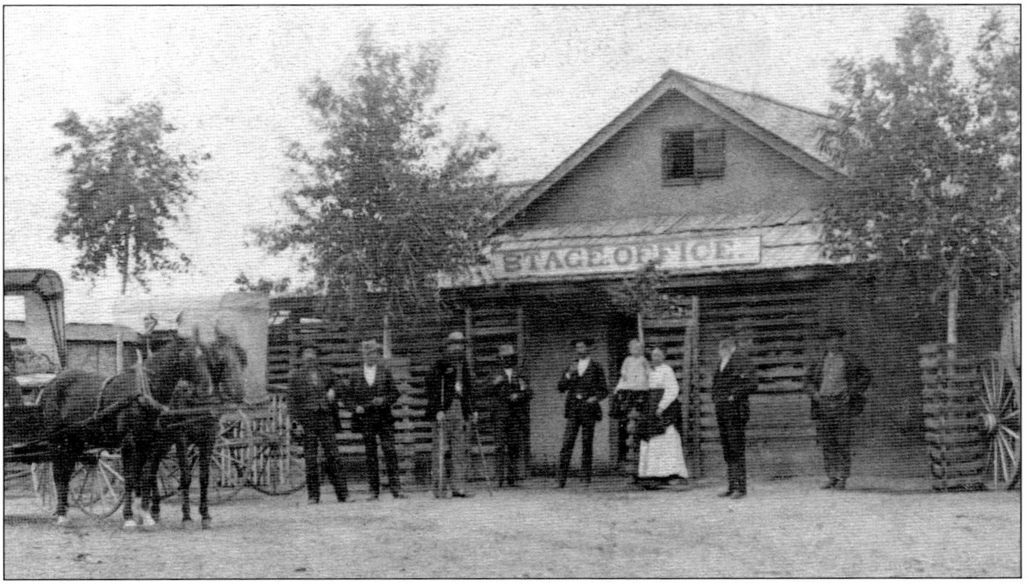

In the early years, stagecoach companies ran both mail and passengers from Prescott to Phoenix and other southwest cities. This shot of Grant's Station is probably the oldest image of a Wickenburg stage stop. Early firms included the Arizona Stage Co.; the Tucson, Arizona, City & San Diego Stage Co.; and the Santa Fe & Prescott Mail Line, whose buckboards left Prescott for Santa Fe every Wednesday and Saturday. (Stereograph by Dudley P. Flanders, spring 1874. Courtesy Jeremy Rowe, vintagephoto.com.)

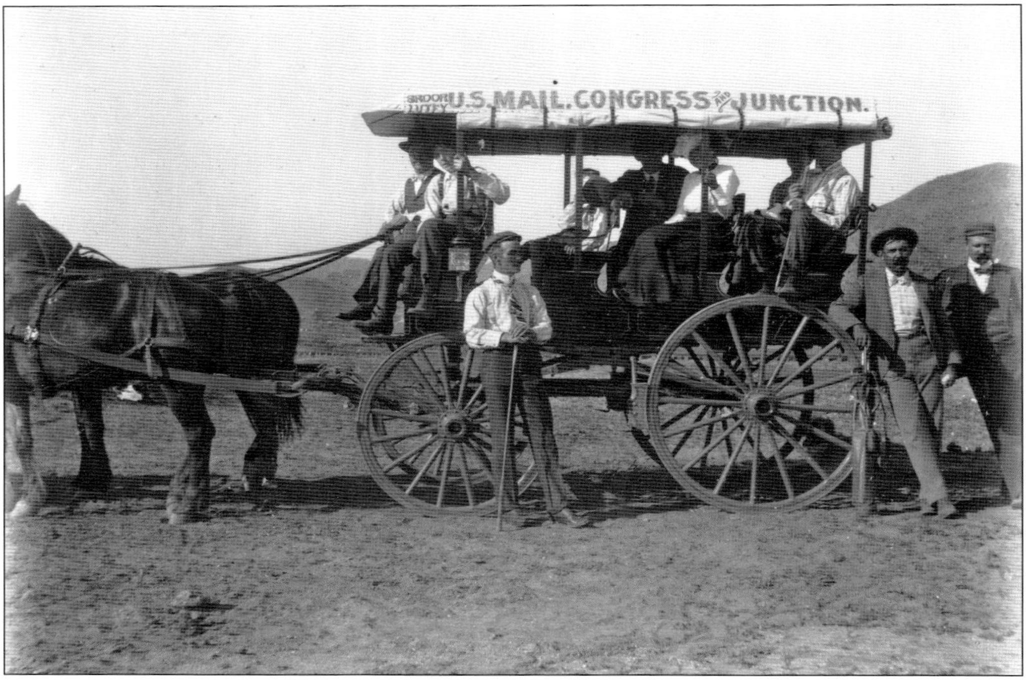

Gold was discovered in the Congress region of nearby Yavapai County in 1884, and Congress Junction was soon a bustling railroad and mail stop. During its heyday, from 1891 to 1910, the mine produced nearly $8 million in precious metals. The former mining site is now a "ghost," but the town of Congress is a comfortable small community.

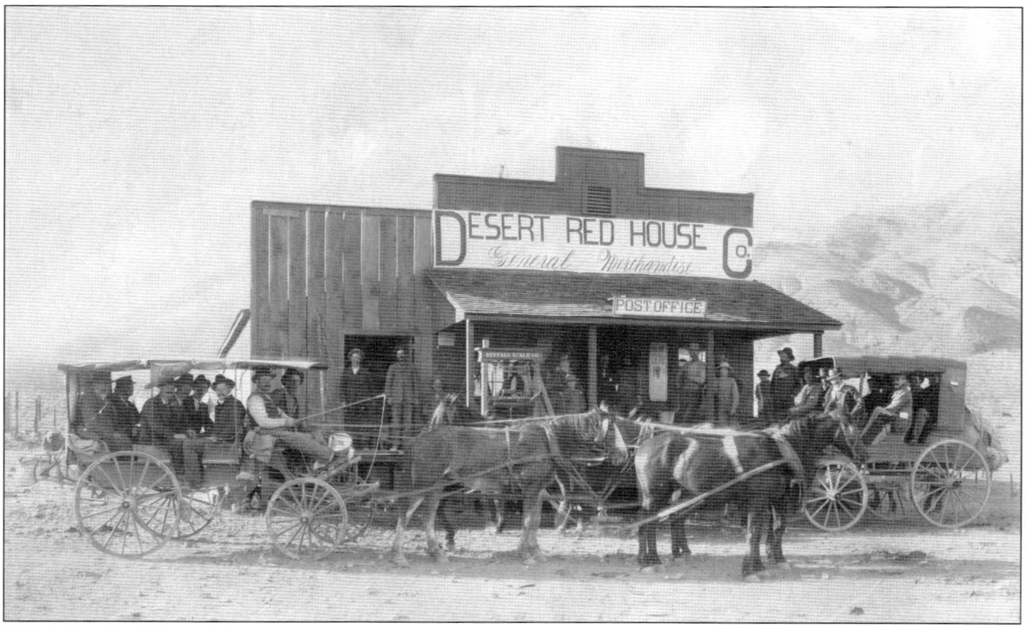

This photograph of Congress Junction from around 1900 encapsulates what all local miners needed—a mercantile store for clothing and supplies, a post office to send mail to loved ones, and reliable transportation.

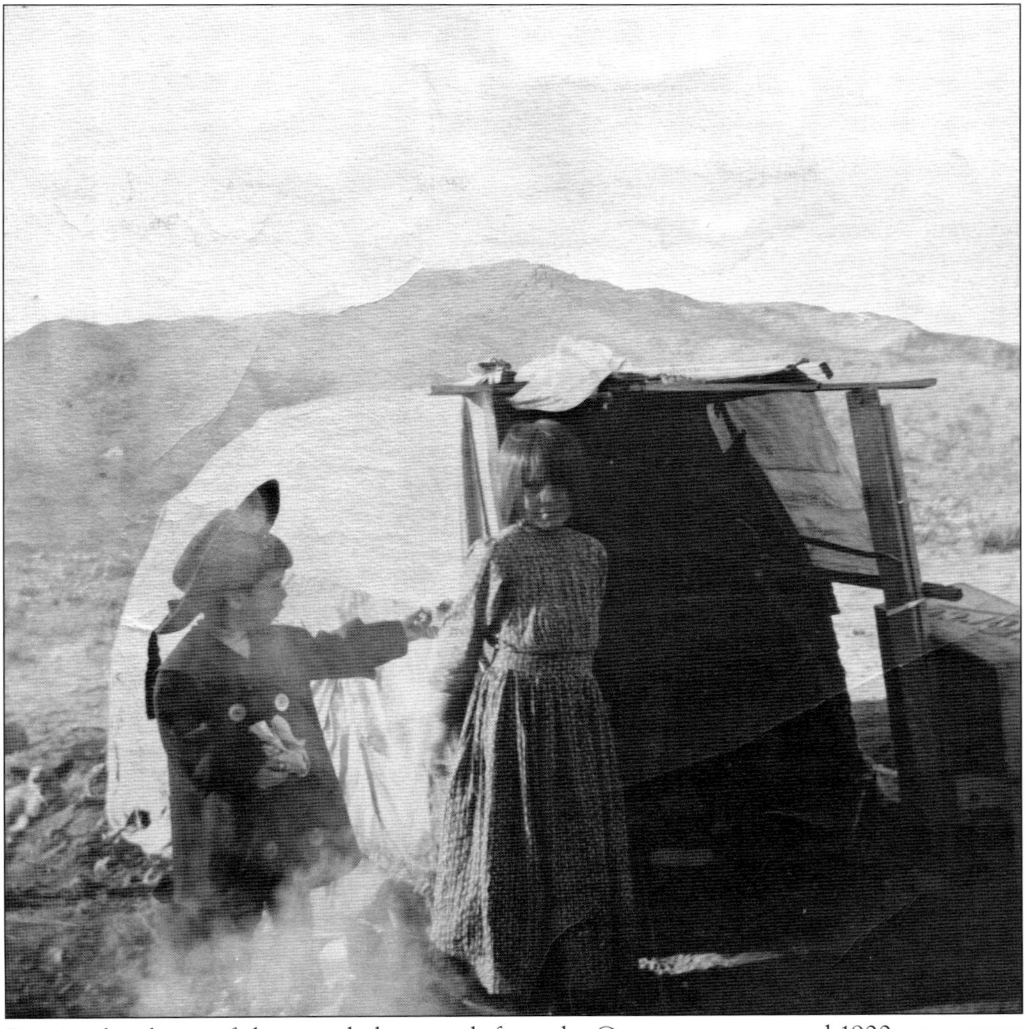

Despite the charm of this posed photograph from the Congress area around 1900, encounters between the Yavapai and the miners and settlers in the Wickenburg area led to inevitable conflict. Everyone competed for resources, and the attitude toward Native Americans was almost universally hostile. Over the course of a decade, armed conflict led to nearly 1,000 deaths of Yavapai, Anglos, and Mexicans. Military posts were built and abandoned all over the region, beginning with Fort Whipple near Prescott. From 1865 to 1866, some soldiers were briefly stationed in Wickenburg though it was never an official outpost. A temporary post was set up at Date Creek, about 25 miles north of Wickenburg on the stage road to California, and made permanent in 1867. In September 1872, the Army's new commander, Gen. George Crook, mounted a fierce campaign against the Yavapai, eventually crushing their resistance and forcing them onto a reservation at Date Creek. In 1873, the Date Creek reservation was closed and the Indians moved to the Rio Verde reservation.

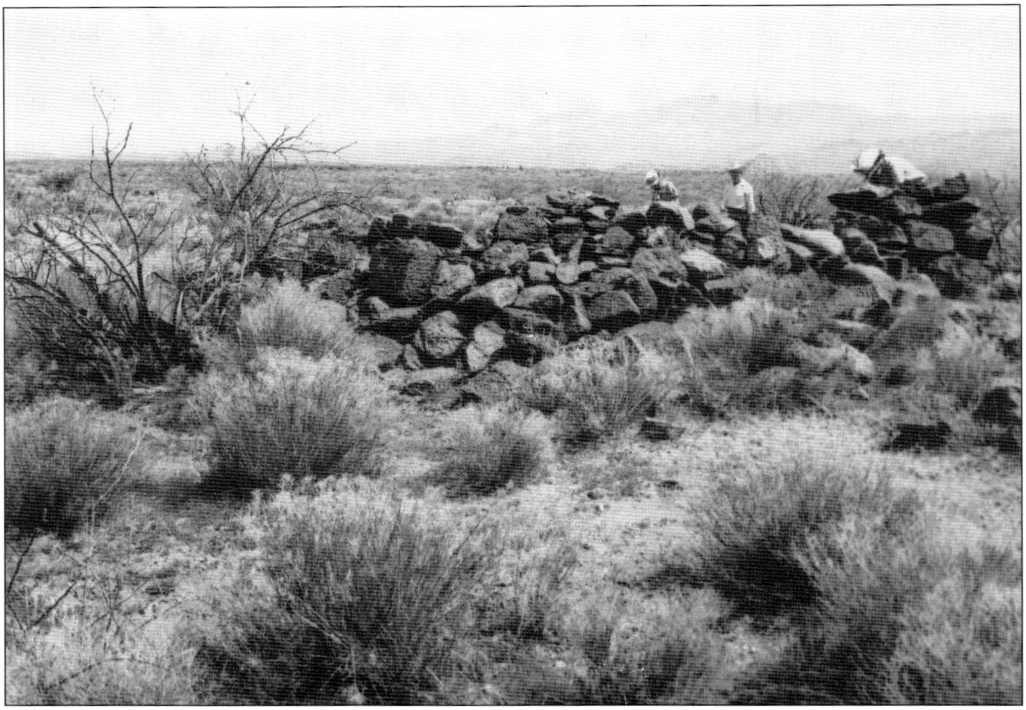

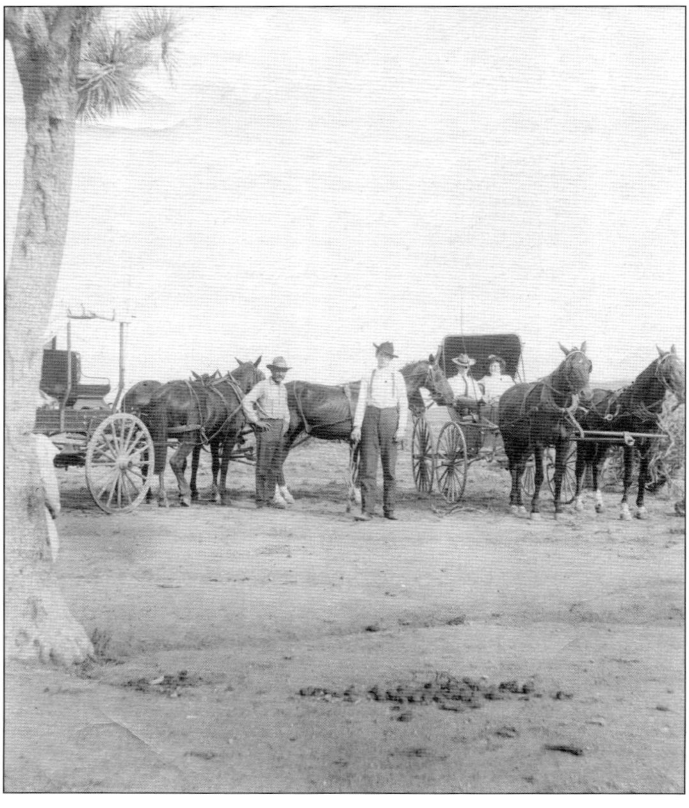

The Army's Date Creek fort quickly fell to ruin after its closure, and the site became a tourist attraction in the early 20th century.

Date Creek's original purpose as a fort did not deter revelers from using the site for picnics or other recreation. This creatively captioned photograph from the early 1900s states: "This picture is another Picknick at the old fort . . . When we go to Date Creek we usualy [sic] take a 4 horse team."

On the morning of November 5, 1871, the westbound Wickenburg-Ehrenberg stagecoach was ambushed about eight miles from present-day Wickenburg. Six of the eight people on board were killed, and the survivors claimed that the attackers were Apache Indians. More than 130 years later, the jury is still out on the question of who really robbed the stage and did the killing. Was it the Yavapai, who were regularly mistaken for Apaches? Was it a group of Mexican robbers dressed as Indians? Did the two survivors plan the attack and come back later for the loot? Or was it white settlers trying to make it look like an Indian attack in order to further Anglo encroachment in the area? Every book and article written about the massacre seems to have an answer, but the truth will probably never be known. A monument at the entrance to the Flying E guest ranch on Highway 60 marks the tragedy.

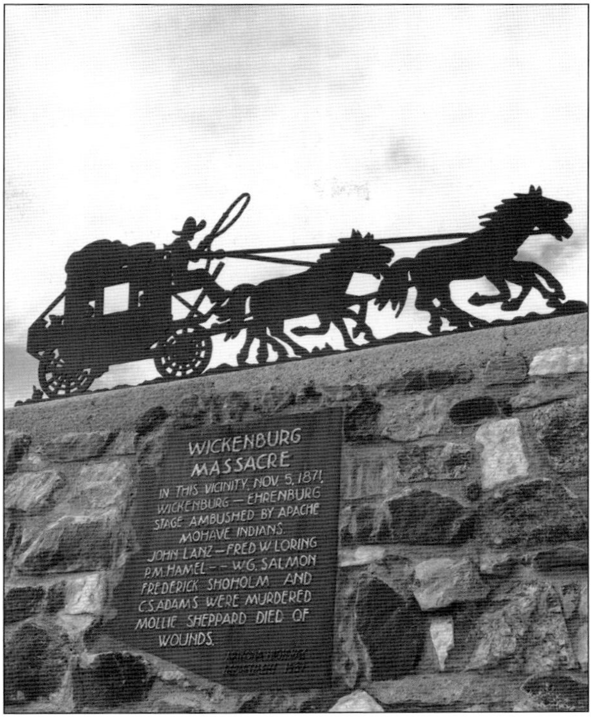

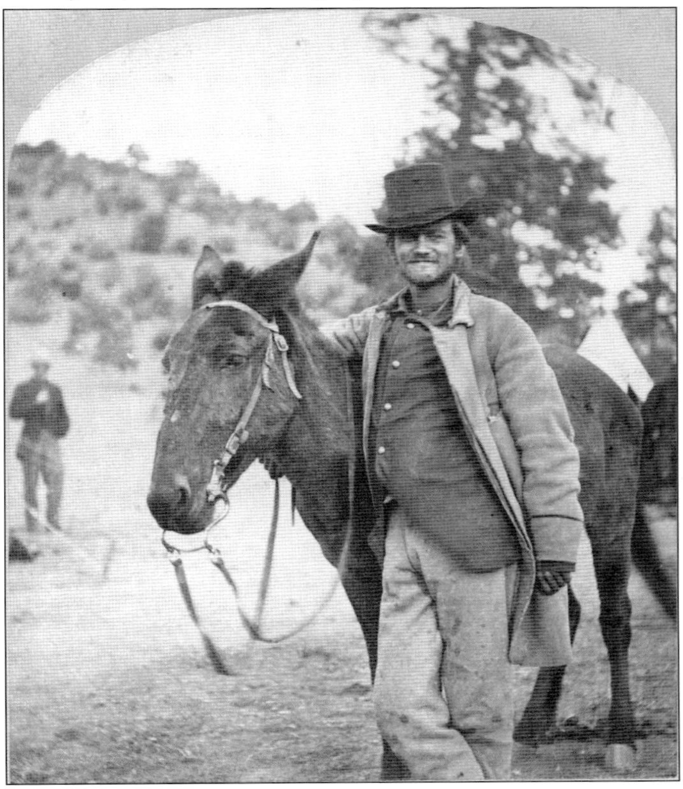

One of the victims of the Wickenburg Massacre was 22-year-old journalist and illustrator Fred Loring. A Boston native and a Harvard graduate, he joined a Grand Canyon expedition led by George Wheeler as a reporter for *Appleton's Journal*. Loring and two members of the survey team, William Salmon and P.W. Hamel, were on their way to California via the Wickenburg stage to report on the expedition when they were killed. (Stereograph by Timothy O'Sullivan for the Wheeler Expedition, November 1871. Courtesy Jeremy Rowe, vintagephoto.com.)

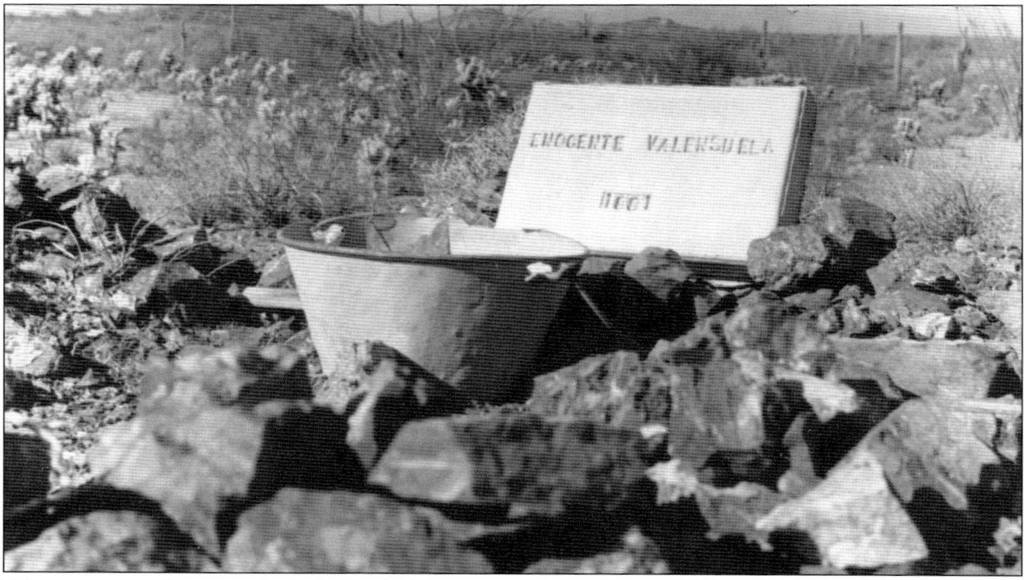

The promise of easy riches always led to crime and violence in mining regions. The workers, stage drivers, and citizens at Vulture Mine were particularly susceptible to mayhem, given its staggering volume of gold production. One of the worst incidents took place in March 1888. Vulture's superintendent, Cyrus Gribble, along with driver John Johnson and engineer Charles Doolittle, were murdered while escorting a wagon of bullion to Phoenix. Inocente Valenzuela was later found to be in possession of one of the gold bars and Gribble's watch and was killed in a gunfight with authorities. Valenzuela was also suspected of killing the Barney Martin family two years earlier. When two men accused of taking part in the Gribble murder were captured, the *Sacramento Daily Union* headline screamed the news: "Capture of a Brace of Outlaws and Cutthroats in Arizona." Valenzuela's grave is at the Verde Flat Cemetery near the Vulture Mine with his name misspelled on his gravestone.

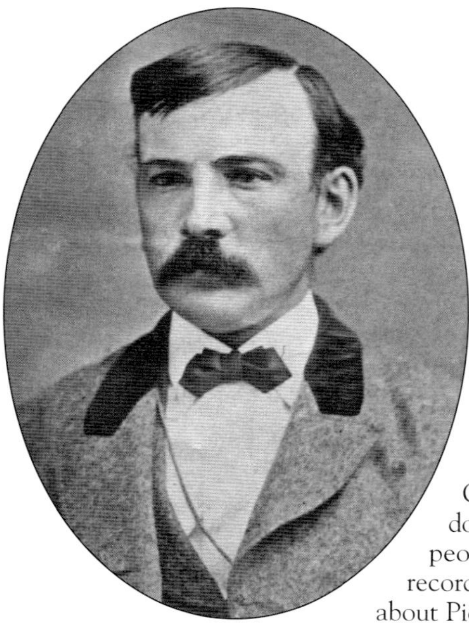

Dr. John Pierson was another colorful local character. This photograph is captioned "Vulture Mine physician and manager California & Arizona Stage Line, 1872," but that is only part of the story. Early settler Charles Genung said Pierson deliberately poisoned another local doctor and that he defrauded the Vulture's workers. Other people allegedly died at Pierson's hands, but historical records cannot keep up with the rumors and stories printed about Pierson over the last century.

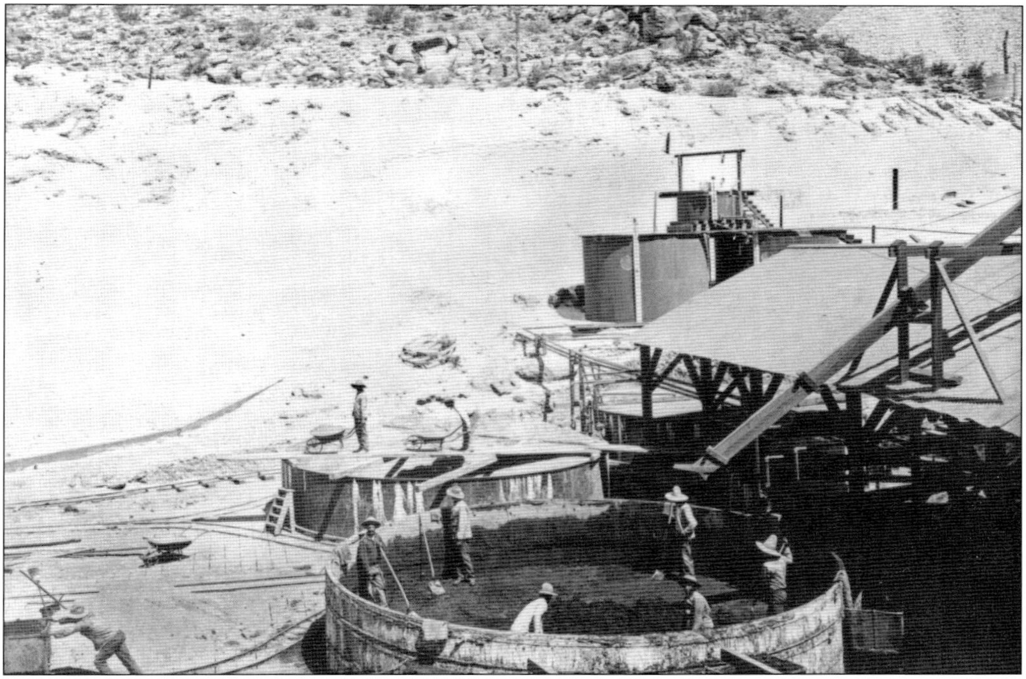

Beginning in the 1890s, cyanide was used to extract gold and silver from raw ore. A diluted solution was washed through rocks that had been ground down to sand. The cyanide attached itself to the metal and when zinc was added, the metal was easily recovered. The Congress Mine had a working cyanide tank in place around 1900.

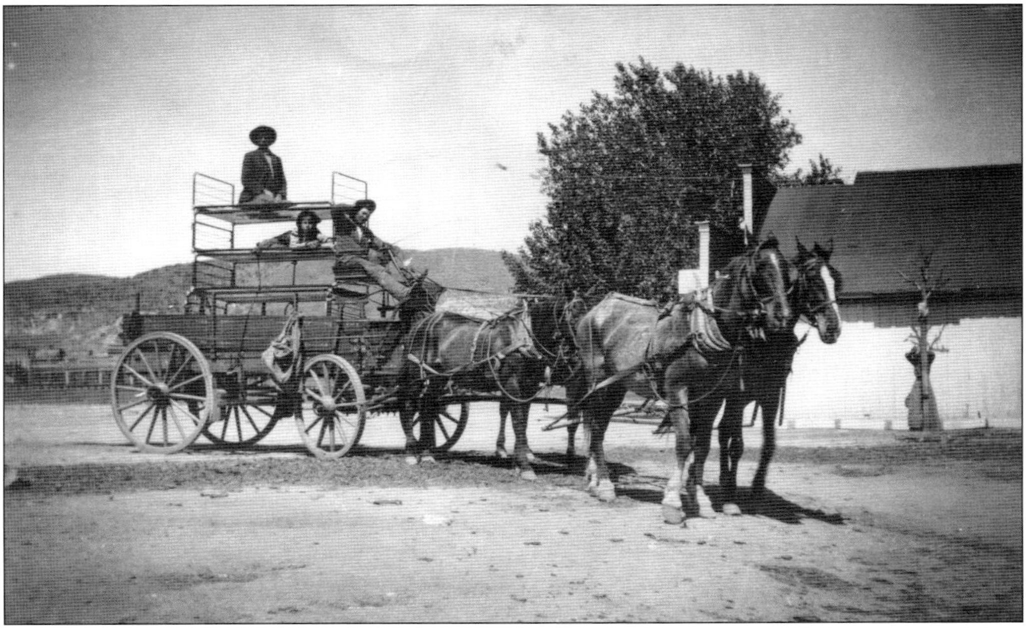

The caption on this c. 1910 photograph says volumes about the recreational lives of local miners: "Freight wagon converted with iron beds to carry workers back to mine 'Monica'—west of Peeples Valley—from Kirkland saloon after wild weekends."

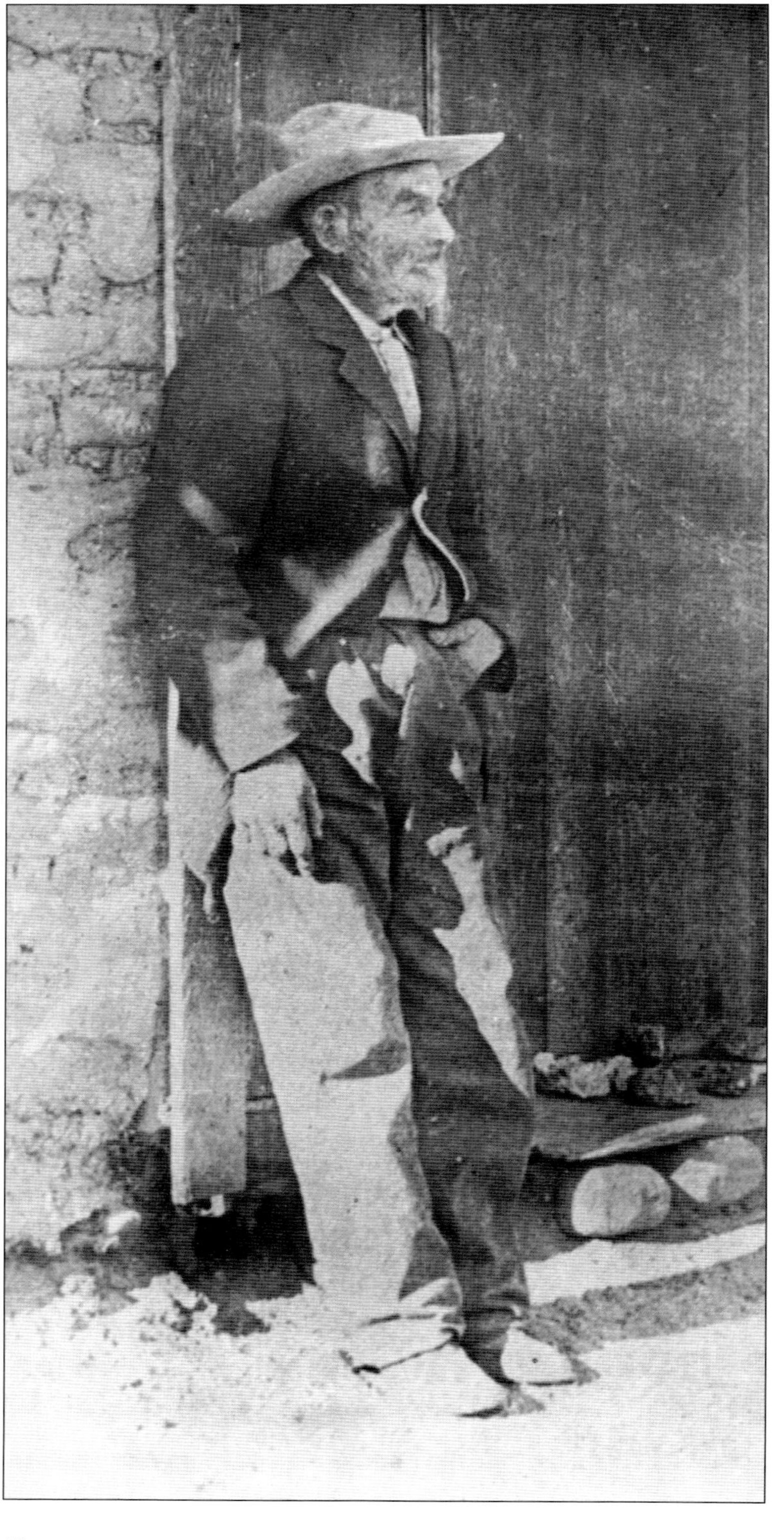

As the end of the 19th century approached, an aging Henry Wickenburg did not slow down. He served as postmaster, a justice of the peace, an election inspector, and in the Arizona Territorial Legislature. He ran a general store for awhile and continued to prospect for gold, holding a number of profitable claims. He was a local elder statesman and was often profiled in Arizona newspapers, including the *Mohave County Miner*, which called him a "brave old pioneer" in 1887. He often traveled to Phoenix on business, and his presence was noted in the *Arizona Republican*.

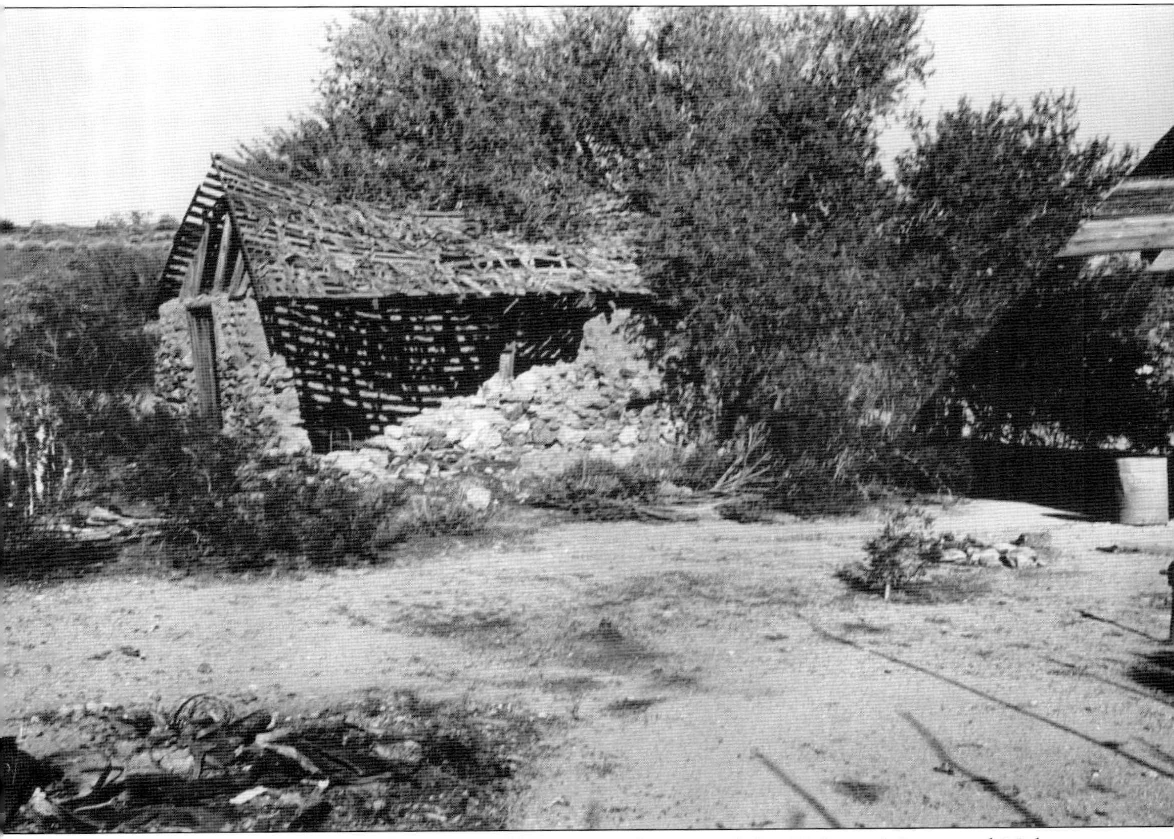

Henry Wickenburg built and kept a small home at the site of the Vulture Mine, and Vulture City grew up around it. It had small, round apertures for windows, possibly made from cans or containers of carbide used for lighting in mines. This house still exists at the Vulture Mine in the crumbled state shown in this 1970s photograph.

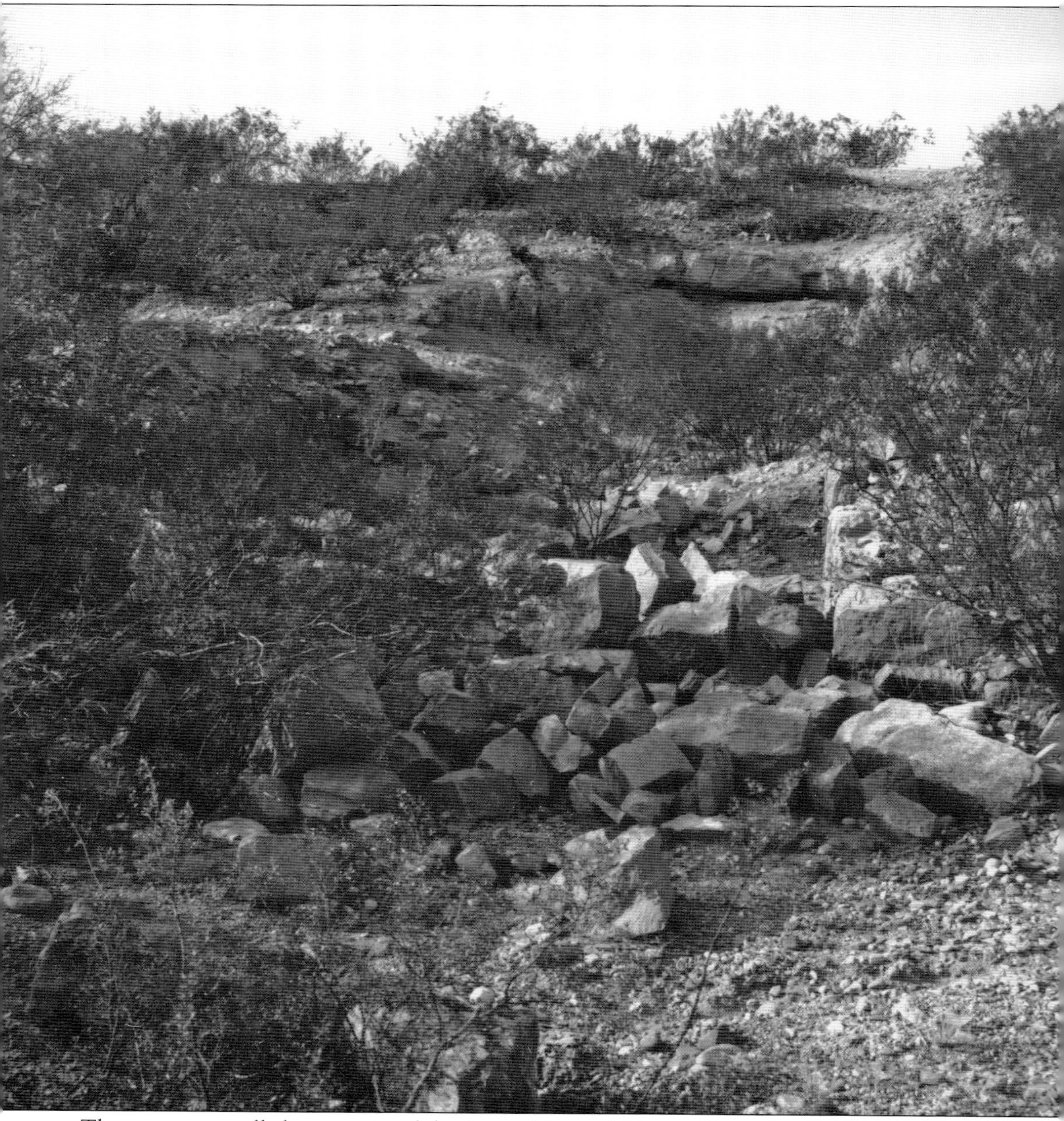

These ruins are all that remain of the "tunnel house," Henry Wickenburg's home at his farm just south of town (he also kept a house at the Vulture Mine). The tunnel was hidden at the back of the home as a place to keep cool in the summer heat and as an escape route in case the house was burned in an Indian attack (which never happened); Wickenburg's early years in the territory taught him to be prepared for any eventuality. The tunnel house was well known to (and explored by) young people up through the 1960s, but the tunnel itself was filled in at the request of nervous parents.

Four

Growing Pains and the Promise of a New Century

Twenty-five years after Henry Wickenburg's discovery of the Vulture lode, the town now named for him was home to farmers and ranchers, in addition to miners. The Yavapai had cultivated the rich soil of the Hassayampa Valley, and now men like Wickenburg began to plant plots of fruits and vegetables in an area dubbed "The Pumpkin Patch." Small ranches were also established, and Wickenburg kept goats, selling their milk in town.

The town's prosperity came to an end in 1890 when the Walnut Grove Dam, located about 30 miles northeast of Wickenburg, burst on February 22, roaring between cliffs all the way into town and killing untold numbers of people. Wickenburg's farm was destroyed, along with the farms and ranches of nearly everyone in the area. Wickenburg sued the Walnut Grove Water Storage Dam Company but lost.

The disaster made the town of Wickenburg even more dependent on mining, but it still had a lot to offer the Arizona territory. Stage companies regularly ran people and mail through town, and the new Santa Fe, Prescott & Phoenix Railway began service through Wickenburg in 1894. The townsite was officially recorded in 1897, a sure sign that the locals intended to stay.

The Vulture Mine also had its ups and downs. The dam break destroyed the pipeline that ran water to the mine from the Hassayampa at Seymour, but the area was still being worked. In 1901, Pres. William McKinley stopped in Wickenburg on his way to Phoenix after seeing the Congress Mine. The same year, a meteor crashed to earth near the Colorado River and the impact was heard more than 100 miles away at the Vulture.

Four years later, Henry Wickenburg appeared in newspapers for the last time when the old pioneer died at age 85 by his own hand in a grove of trees near the last of his several homes. Although some thought he was murdered, most scholars acknowledge that his death was, sadly, suicide.

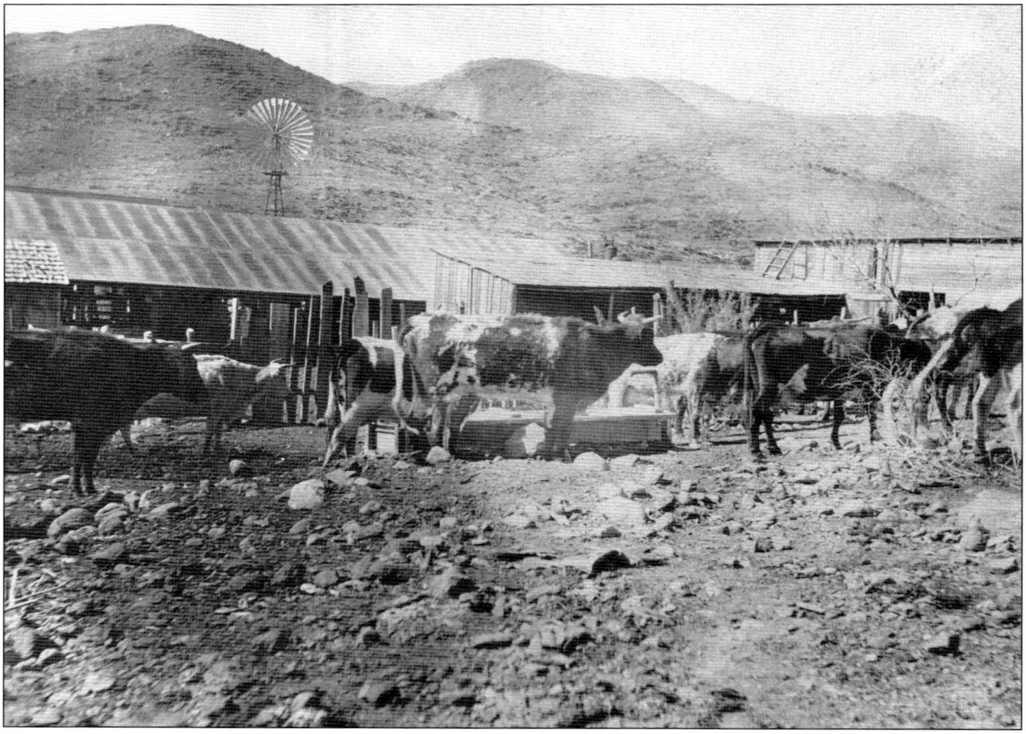

The cattle business was a profitable alternative for the people of Wickenburg. Frederick Brill, James Roark, and others described as "cattlemen" made a good living running herds in the area. Others, like John C. Egloff, combined ranching with other jobs. Egloff, who died in 1890, also worked in the E.O. Grant & Co. general store.

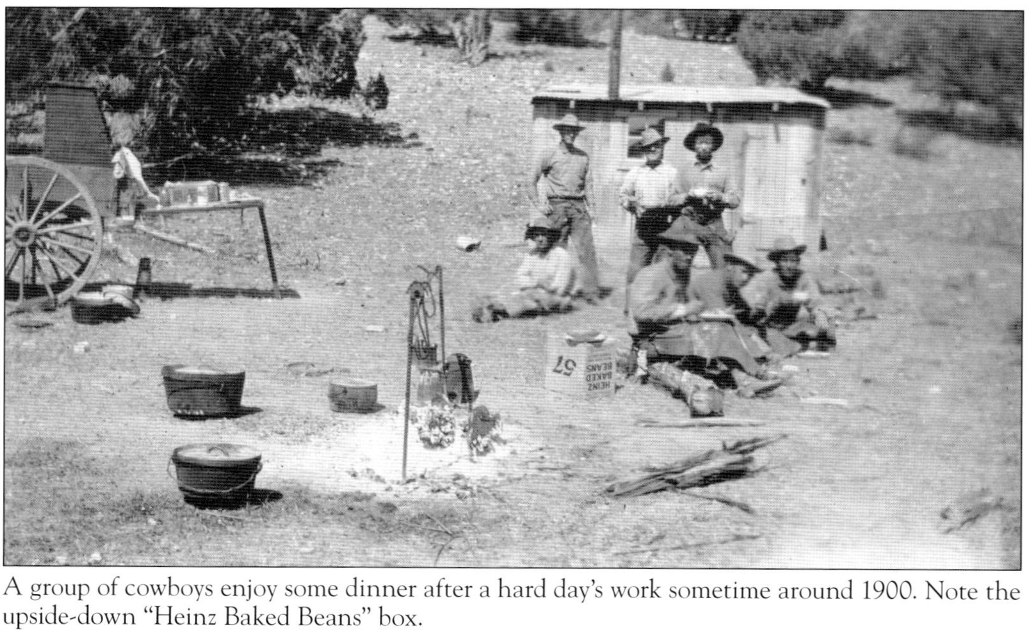

A group of cowboys enjoy some dinner after a hard day's work sometime around 1900. Note the upside-down "Heinz Baked Beans" box.

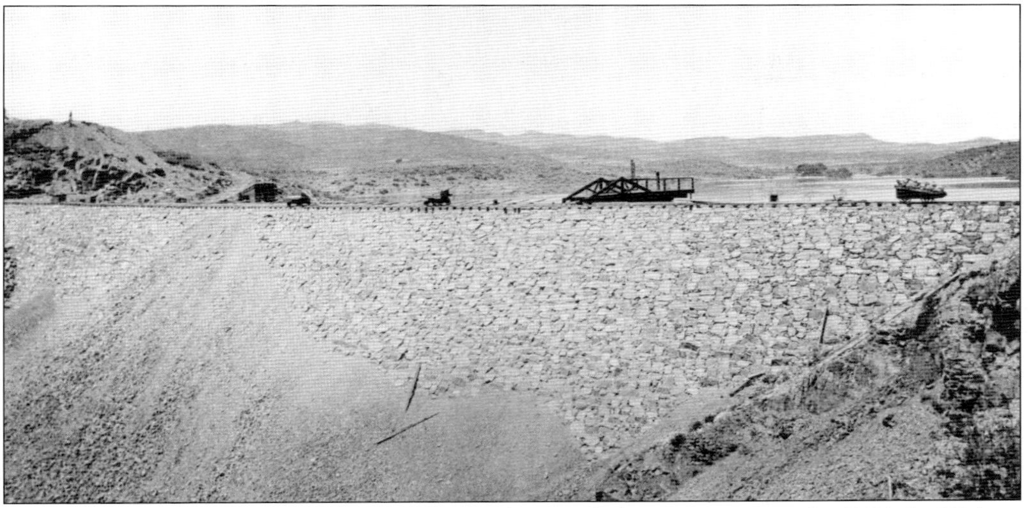

Mines were not the only commercial concerns that needed water to survive. In 1885, the Walnut Grove Water Storage Company was formed in New York with the goal of building a dam across the Hassayampa River at Walnut Grove, about 40 miles northeast of Wickenburg. The site was chosen because of its high cliffs, and the dam would not only provide water for mining but also irrigate hundreds of acres of farmland in the surrounding area. It was completed in 1887, forming a reservoir; a second dam, 12 miles downstream, was begun in 1888. It seemed that modern engineering had come to Wickenburg, but it was not to last. The unusually wet winter of 1890 brought heavy rains to the valley, and on February 21, water began to pour over the first dam. At about 1:00 a.m., the entire structure exploded, sending water, rocks, and steel cable careening through the canyons toward Wickenburg.

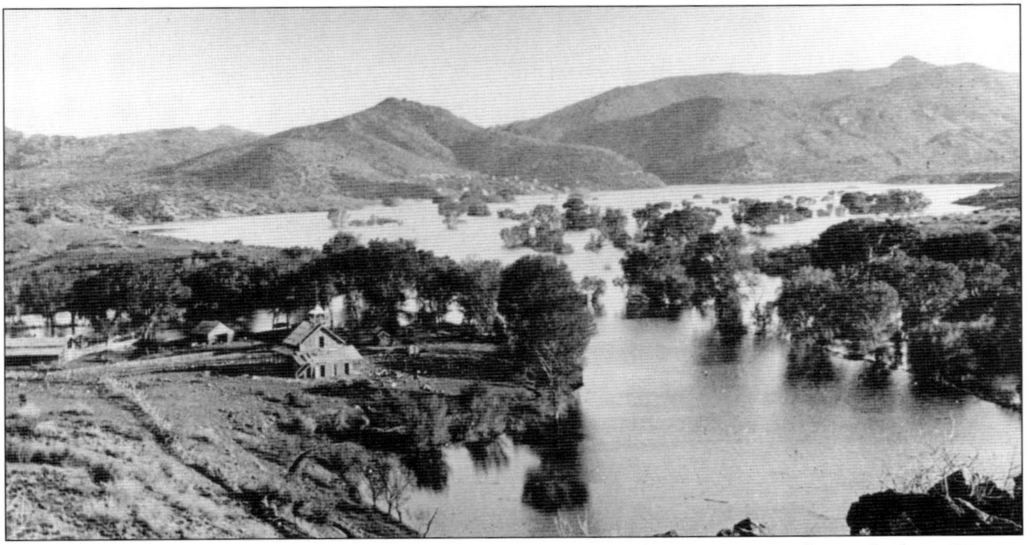

When the floodwater reached town, it tore apart everything in its path, including Henry Wickenburg's farm. Before subsiding, the water was 40 feet high in some places. Next in the path of destruction was the vital pipeline at Seymour, which served the Vulture Mine. When the flood's force was spent, dozens of people were dead—the exact count will never be known. Although faulty construction was considered the cause of the disaster, Wickenburg lost the lawsuit that he filed against the Walnut Grove Water Storage Company; his farm never recovered.

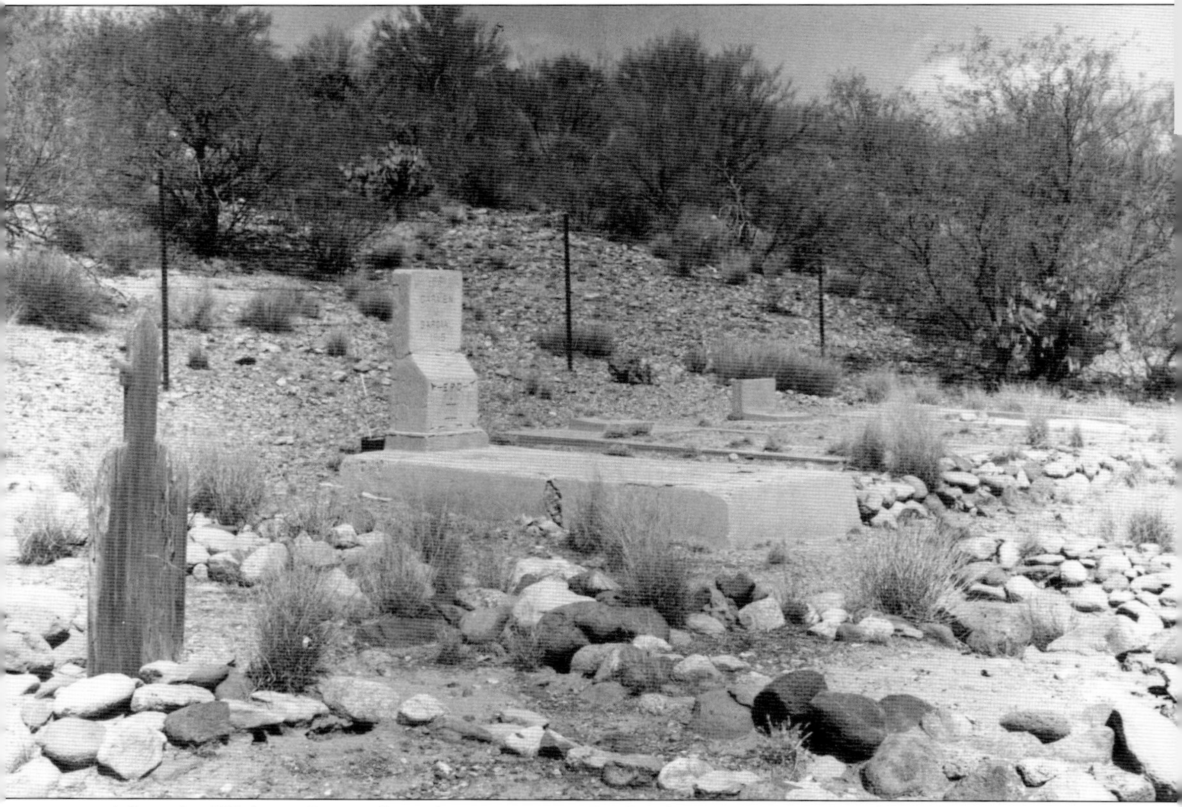

After the Walnut Grove dam disaster, some Wickenburg citizens refused to allow the burials of Mexican and Chinese residents who died in the floods in the local cemetery. Ignacio Garcia, a native of Mexico who arrived in Wickenburg in 1876, came to the rescue. By 1890, he and his family had a substantial ranch near present-day downtown Wickenburg, and he donated a few acres of his land to create a cemetery for the disaster victims. Today, the Garcia Cemetery is a local landmark and the resting place of many of Wickenburg's Hispanic residents.

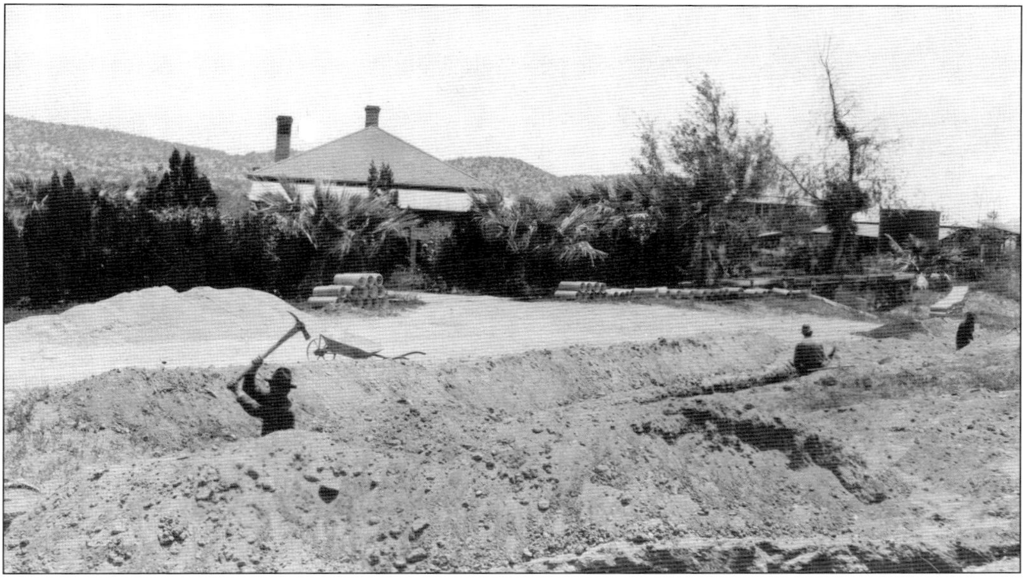

The destruction of farmland around Wickenburg meant the city was even more dependent on mining. Francis X. O'Brien (1848–1926) was a prosperous local mining man and one of the owners of the Gold Bar Mine in the 1890s. He also owned substantial property in and around town and married Mary Patricia Hutchinson, the daughter of a Vulture Mine engineer. O'Brien's home and property, pictured in this early-20th-century photograph, would play a big part in Wickenburg's future as a tourist destination.

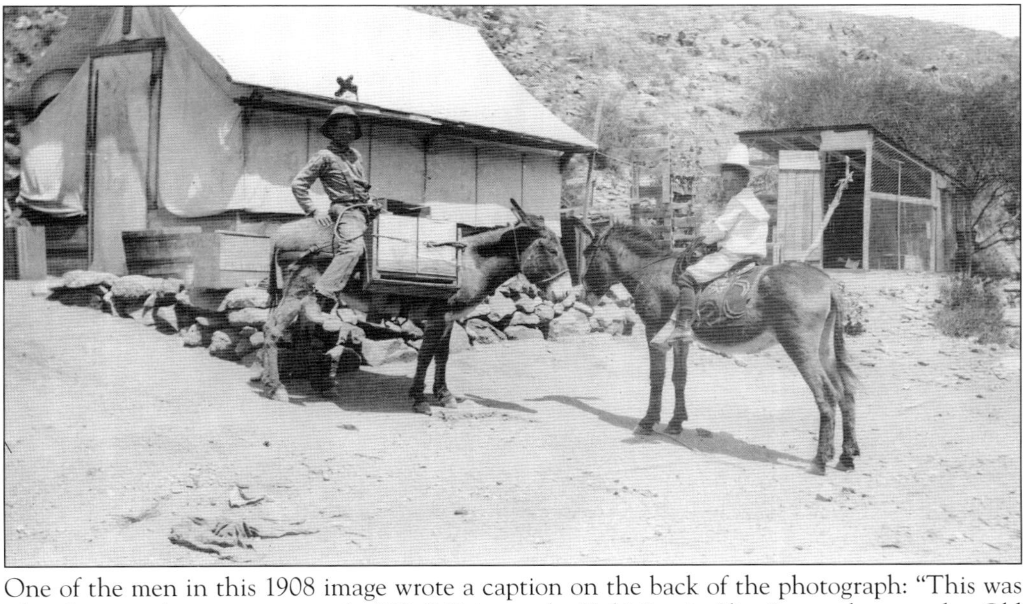

One of the men in this 1908 image wrote a caption on the back of the photograph: "This was when I was packing camp water for F.X. O'Brien at the Hal Mine in Slim Jim wash on road to Old Constellation. 50¢ per day for me and the other Jackass." The Constellation area is northeast of Wickenburg and was home to a number of mines near the Monte Cristo, Gold Bar, and others.

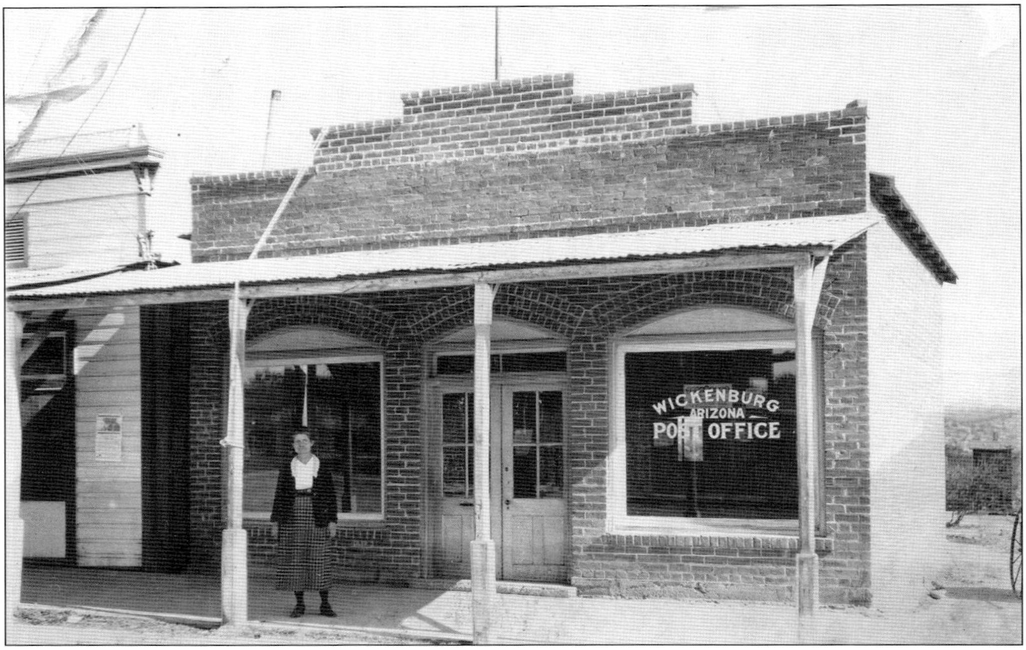

The Wickenburg Post Office was established in 1865, and the first postmaster was B.F. Howell. Henry Wickenburg served as postmaster from 1874 to 1877. Mattie J. Howell, pictured here, was the postmistress from 1920 to 1925. Postal records show that until 1894, the town name was spelled "Wickenburgh."

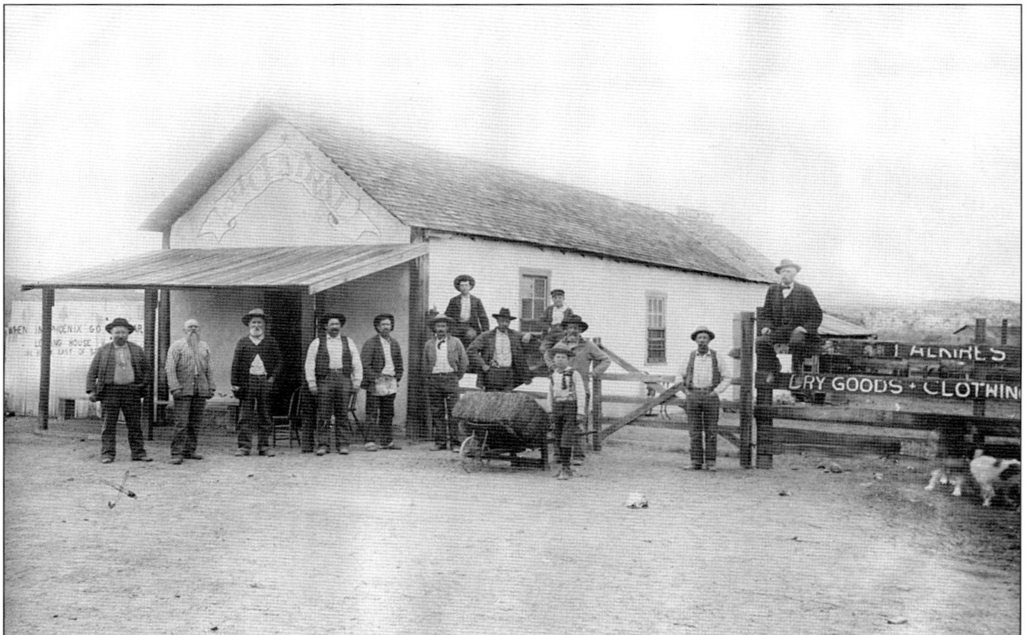

According to an 1881 Wickenburg business directory, the town had a blacksmith, general merchandise dealer, two hotels, a saloon, a feed yard, and a Wells Fargo express agency. By 1902, there was one saloon for every 20 men in Wickenburg.

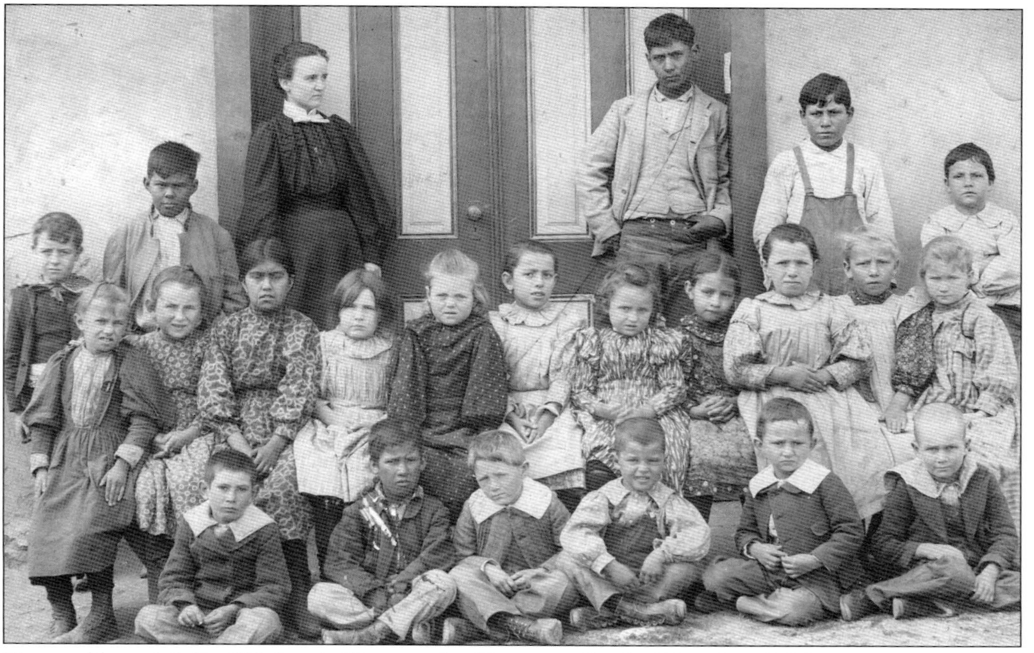
Pictured here is Miss Wickam's Class at the Congress Grade School in 1896.

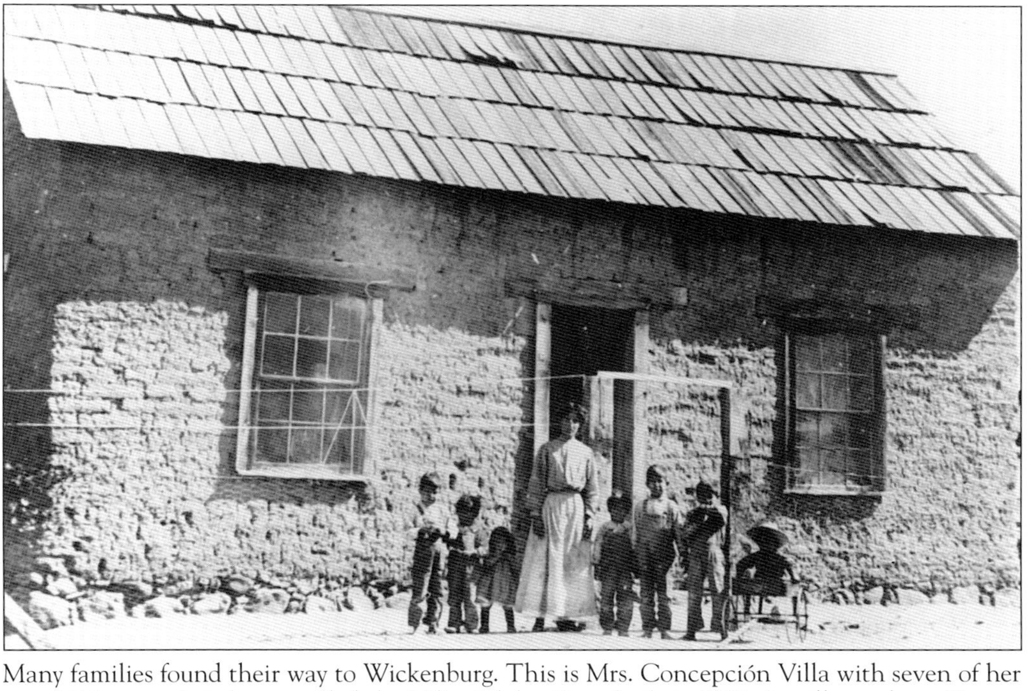
Many families found their way to Wickenburg. This is Mrs. Concepción Villa with seven of her ten children at their home called the Villa Adobe Casa, built in 1896. It still stands on Tegner and Apache streets in town today.

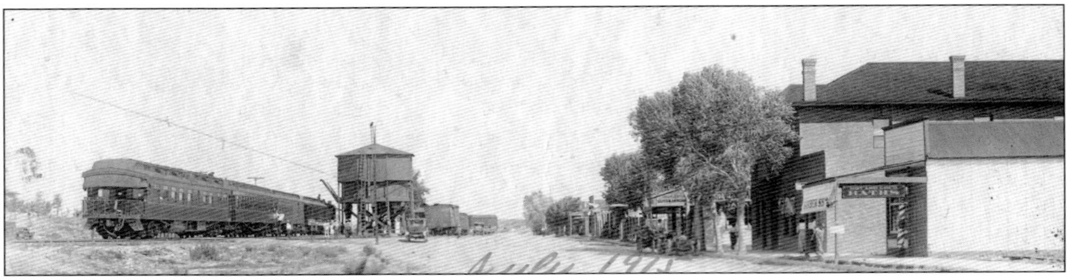

This 1915 Wickenburg street scene shows a train pulling into town alongside—appropriately—Railroad Street. Frank Murphy, owner of the Congress Mine, built the Santa Fe, Prescott & Phoenix Railway in 1891. By 1895, the line from Ash Fork to Phoenix—nicknamed "The Peavine" because of its loopy, winding route—included a stop in Wickenburg. The railroad brought jobs into town, a depot (later acquired by the Santa Fe Railway) was built in 1895, and the local ranch economy got a boost from being linked by rail to major markets.

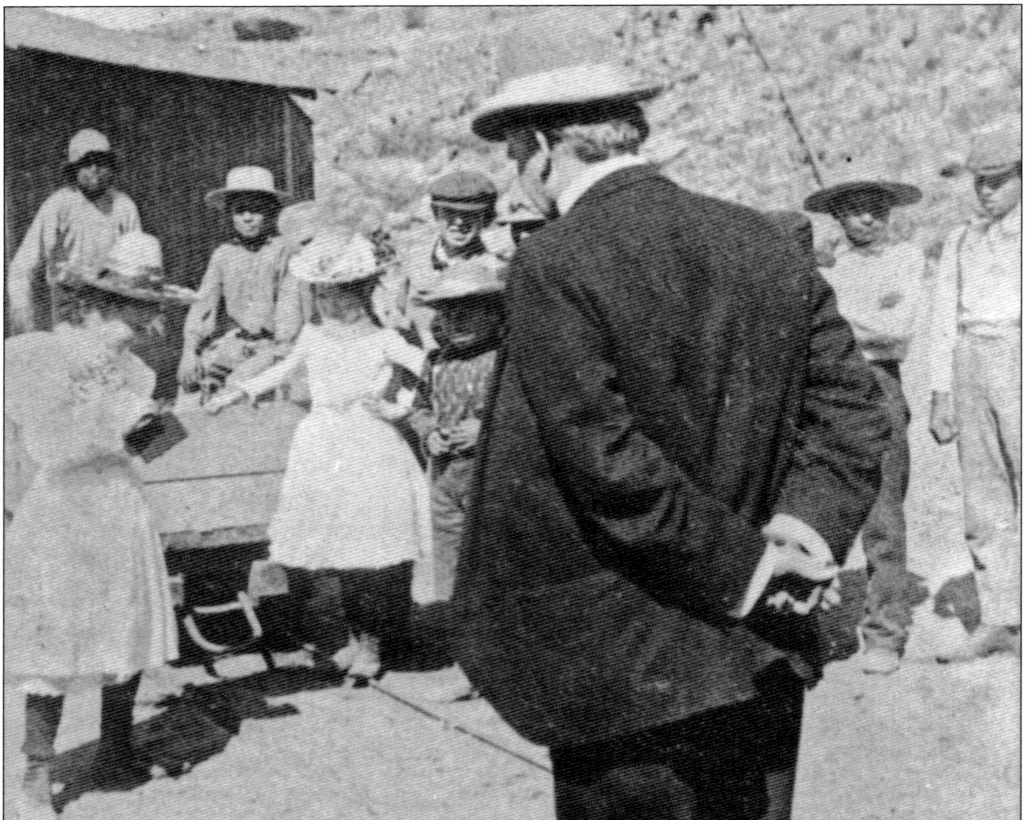

On May 7, 1901, Pres. William McKinley visited the Congress Mine during a rail trip from New Orleans to Portland. On the return trip to Phoenix, his train's engine developed wheel trouble. As it limped along, waiting for a replacement engine, the railroad made its planned stop in Wickenburg, where the president met with a group of schoolchildren. They gave him a "cabinet of specimens," and he thanked them on behalf of his wife, then gave a short address: "I have been glad to note that in your Territory broad and ample provisions are made for education. The schoolhouse is the university out of which come good citizens, and it is on good citizenship we must rely not only for the present but for the future good and glory of the republic."

By the beginning of the 1900s, members of the Yavapai tribe moved off local reservations and entered the market economy, turning to agriculture and ranching. Others sold baskets; this group of visitors near the Congress Mine watches women at work on this traditional task.

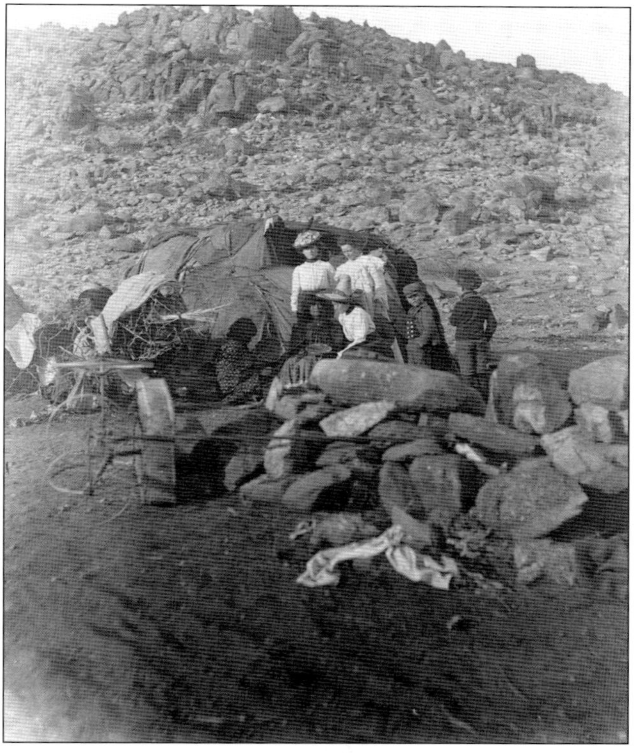

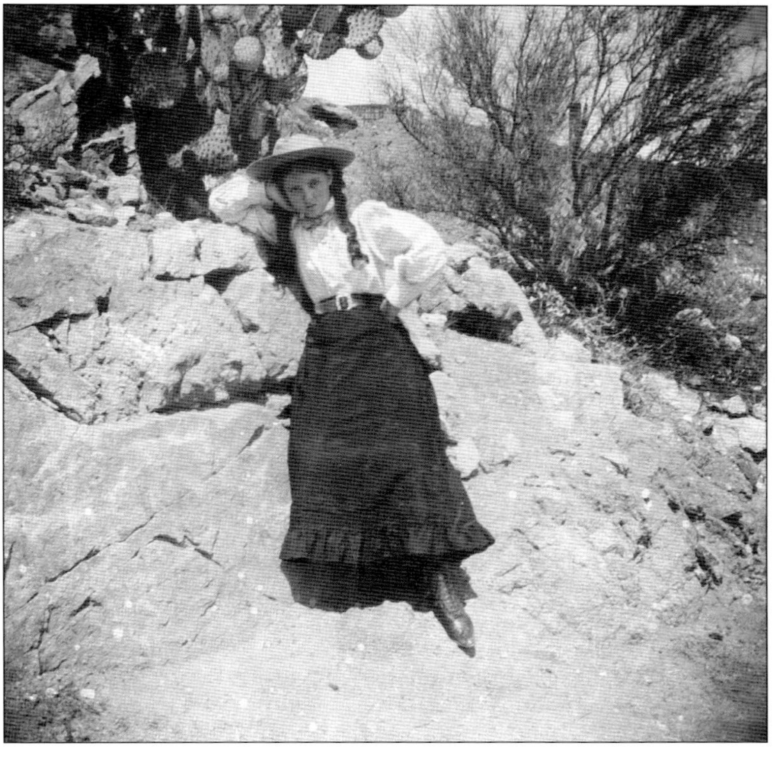

A visitor or new resident poses in a classic desert setting in this undated photograph.

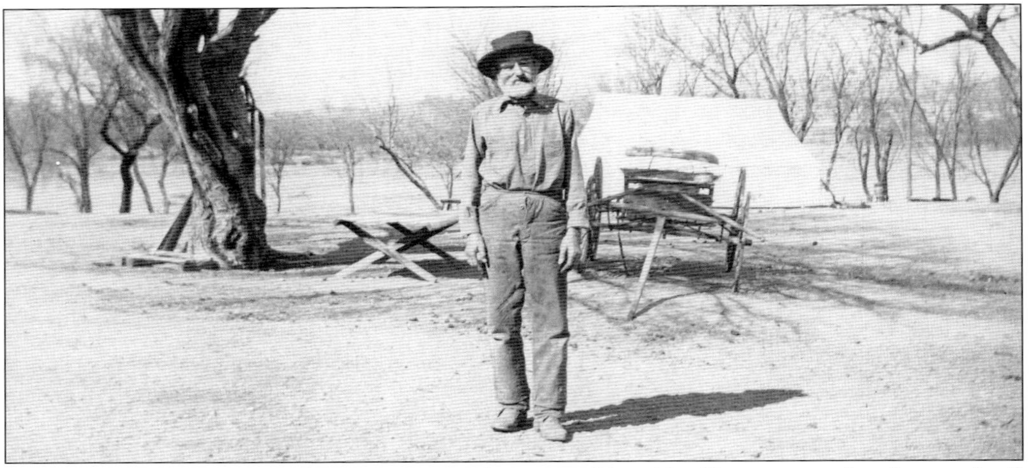

Henry Wickenburg was still active even as he entered his 80s. He continued to buy and sell real estate, was reported to be sinking a new well, and was interviewed and profiled in Arizona journals. In an unnamed newspaper published in February 1899, Wickenburg said: "Wickenburg is my home, is my town, and there is where my body will rest when life's troubles are over. I love that old town, it contains all that is dear to me, and while I rejoice at the growth of Phoenix, I think the old town in the mountain foothills has no equal on earth." *The Prospect*, a mining paper published in Prescott, wrote in 1902 that Wickenburg was "hale and hearty, with chances in favor of his becoming a centenarian." But he did not make it.

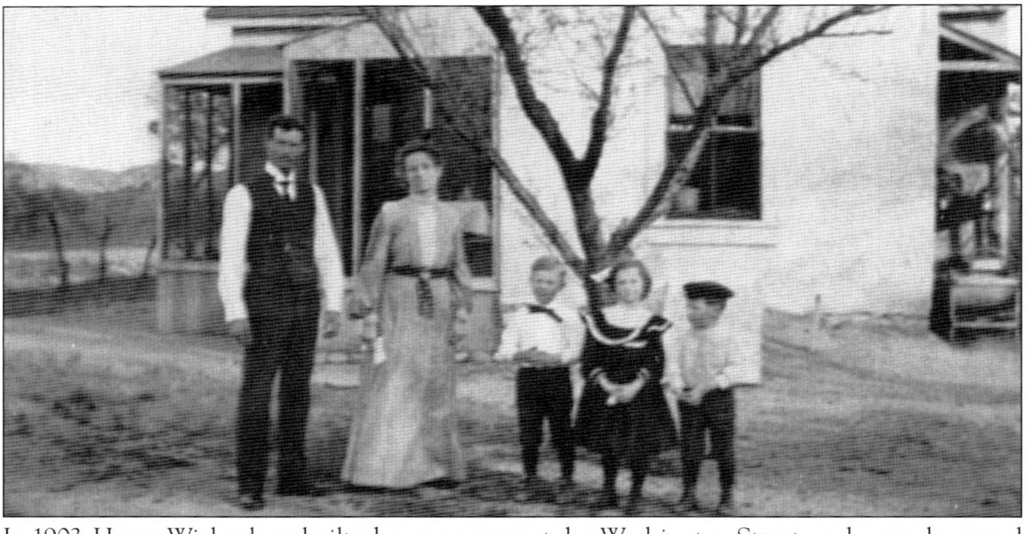

In 1903, Henry Wickenburg built a house on present-day Washington Street, and a couple named Holland helped him with the everyday tasks of living. The Etter family, shown here, lived nearby, with a home separated from Wickenburg's by a grove of trees; Etter and his brother owned a general store in town. On May 14, 1905, the Etter children found Wickenburg's body among the trees between the houses. The Hollands, Angela Hammer (owner of the local newspaper), and others were summoned, and the news was spread throughout town. An inquest determined that he had taken his own life. Some people said he had been despondent over money, but no one knows, or will ever know, the reason for his suicide. He was mourned by many and memorialized in papers as a "sturdy frontiersman" and a man who made "the afternoon of life pleasant for brother pioneers who pass his way."

Five

Officially on the Map

Everything was new for Wickenburg in the new century. Between 1900 and 1920, the town grew in myriad ways: incorporation and the first mayor, the first bank and first two newspapers, the first bridge on the Hassayampa River, and water and electrical service. Thanks to the opening of newly discovered mines and the continued stream of men and material, Wickenburg enjoyed a permanence that eluded it in previous decades. When a growing population of children made a new schoolhouse necessary in 1905, the land was donated by one of Wickenburg's most generous Hispanic residents, Ignacio Garcia. A Catholic and a Protestant church were built by the faithful in 1902 and 1905 respectively. Hotels like the Vernetta and stores like the Brayton Commercial Co. opened. Public picnics were held in Wickenburg, and special trains were chartered to bring revelers into town.

The Vulture Mine continued to be the most well known of the local mining concerns, and its fame meant that any change in status—for good or bad—was covered in Arizona newspapers. Mines in the Constellation area northeast of town as well as the Octave and Congress continued to pay well, too. In fact, when people spoke of Wickenburg, it was usually with mining in mind.

Word began to spread beyond Arizona's borders about the beauty of the landscape and the fine amenities in town. Bridges were built across the Hassayampa between 1914 and 1926 to make automobile travel more convenient for residents and visitors—successive storms meant rebuilding more than once—and federal highway programs brought Highways 60 and 89 through town.

A sense of civic life began to take hold, with Boy Scout troops, a library, and holiday observances becoming part of the fabric of local life. In 1934, Wickenburg's history was celebrated with *The Pioneer Play*. It now had a past, and its future looked bright.

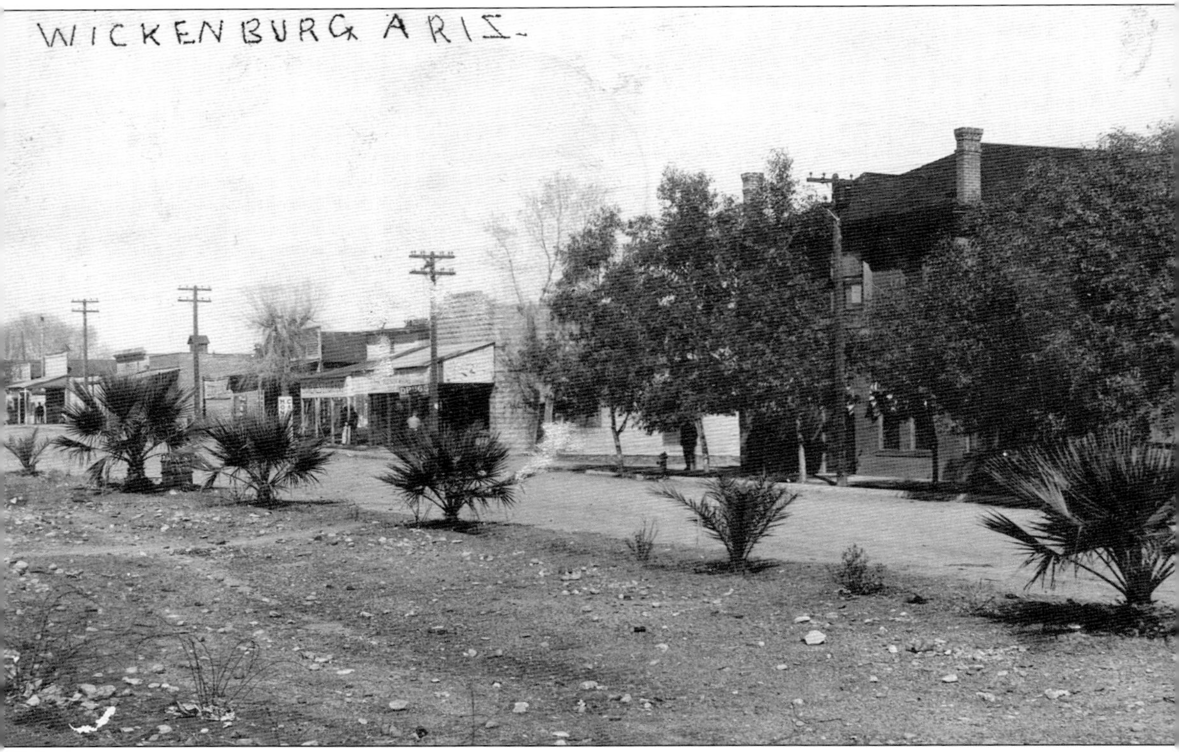

This street scene from the early 20th century shows how the mining town of Wickenburg grew into a fully functioning city in the space of just a few decades. Mature trees, sturdy storefronts, telephone service, regular railroad service, a diversified economy, and a fairly steady population meant that Wickenburg's days of depending on the fortunes of gold- and silver-seekers were over.

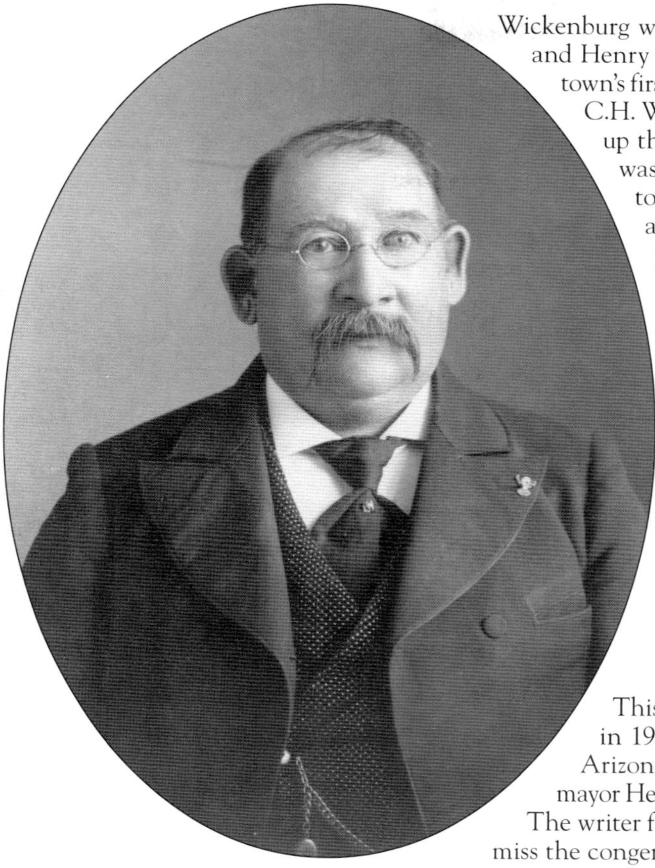

Wickenburg was officially incorporated in 1909, and Henry Cowell (pictured) was elected the town's first mayor. Felipe Garcia, R.W. Baxter, C.H. Widmeyer, and John Bachtiger made up the town council; Edward L. Garcia was named marshal; T.J. Prescott the town attorney; Ike B. Wood served as constable; and John Riggs was the justice of the peace.

This postcard, mailed from Wickenburg in 1928 to a Mrs. Hunter in Glendale, Arizona, gave a detailed account of former mayor Henry's Cowell's last illness and death. The writer finished up her note with, "We will miss the congenial old fellow."

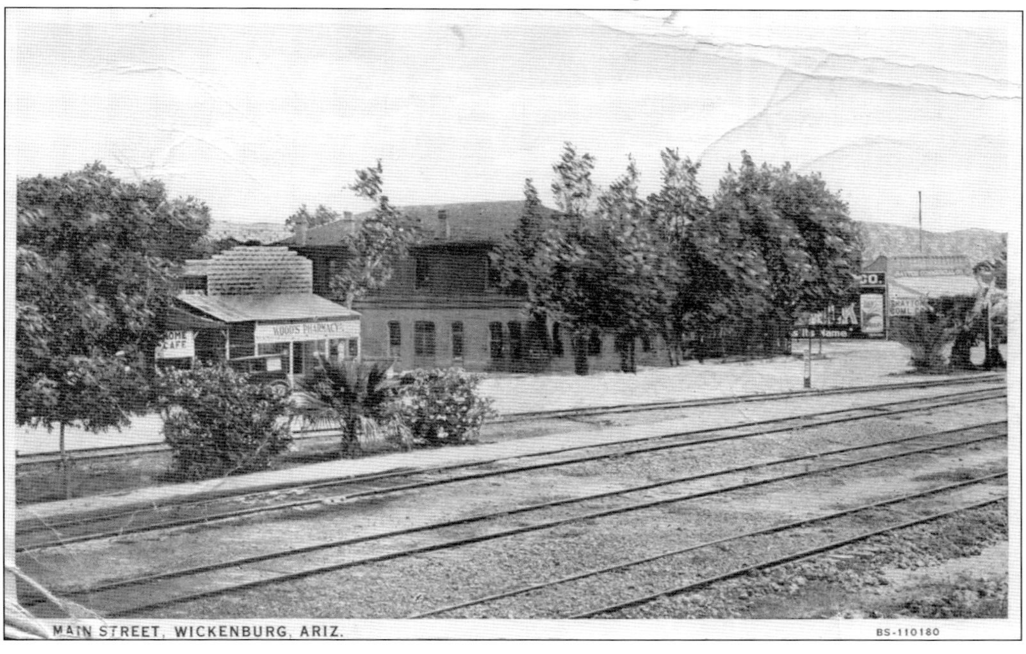

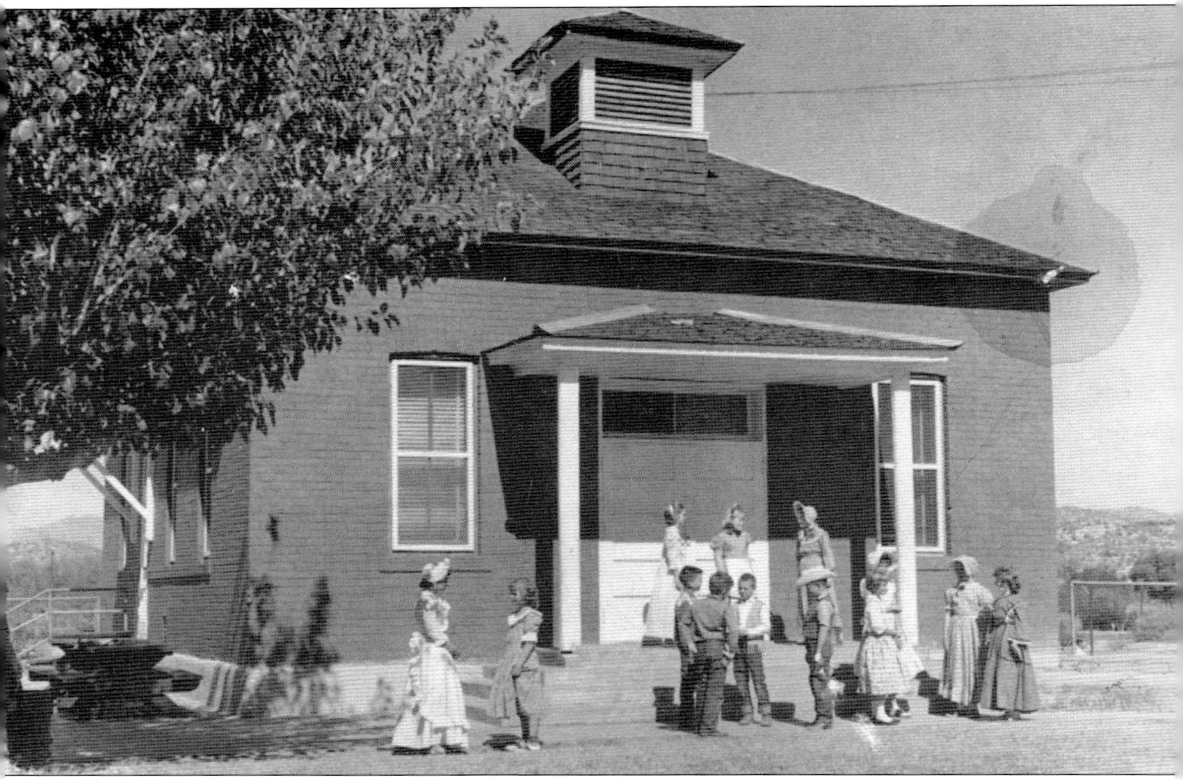

The school building erected on a town lot donated by Ignacio Garcia in 1895 needed replacing at the beginning of the 20th century. The Wickenburg school district passed a bond and built a new schoolhouse in the same place, which opened in January 1906. Originally called Wickenburg Elementary School, the name was changed to Garcia School in 1972 in honor of the man whose land went to help educate the city's children. Today, the Garcia Little Red Schoolhouse serves as the office of the Wickenburg Children's Cultural Organization and houses an exhibition about early Wickenburg education. The building is also in the National Register of Historic Places.

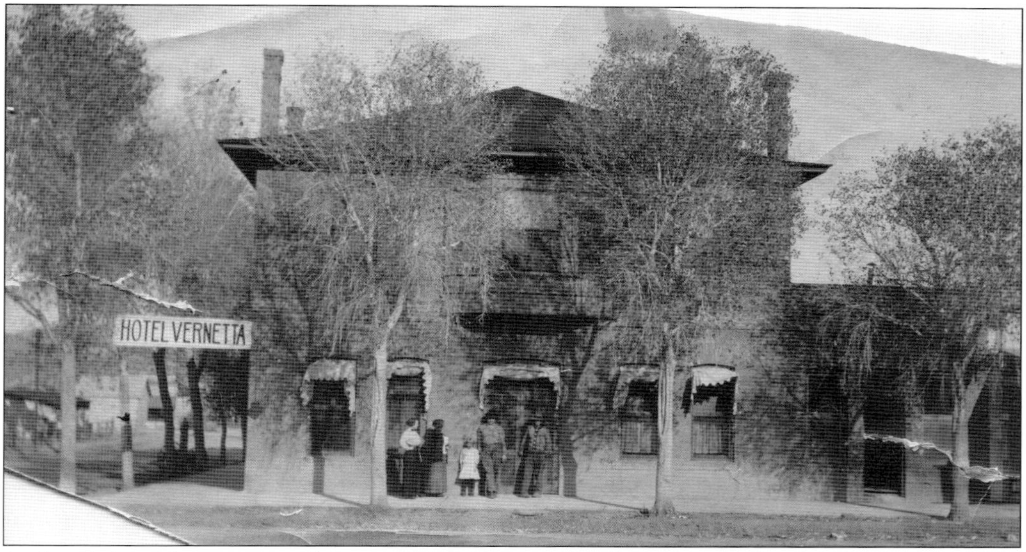

Railroads brought more people to Wickenburg, and in 1905, the Vernetta Hotel was opened on Railroad Street by Elizabeth Smith and her husband, Bill, the town's first African American citizens. They had arrived in 1897 and managed the Baxter Hotel but were then asked by Santa Fe Railway officials to open a new, modern facility near the depot. The Vernetta—named for Bill Smith's mother—opened in 1905. The couple was also among the founding members of the first Presbyterian Church. Elizabeth spoke fluent French and participated in some social functions. However, racism did exist, and she experienced some social ostracism. Nevertheless, Elizabeth continued to work at the hotel, despite separating from her husband in 1912, and she remained there until her death in 1935. She is buried in the Garcia Cemetery, and the building is in the National Register of Historic Places.

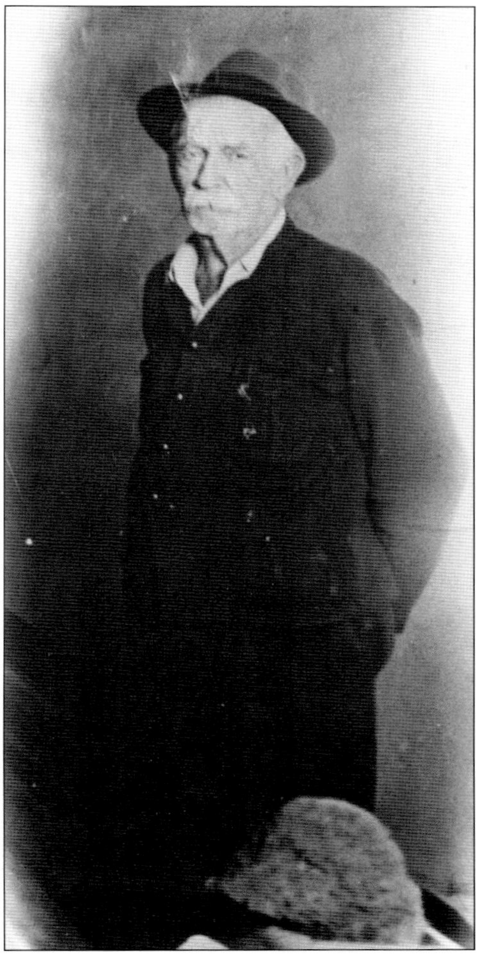

John Grace was one of Wickenburg's local characters. He arrived in town in 1917 and worked as a miner and a goat farmer. The caption on the back of this photograph reads, "John was sleeping off a drunk on the Little Big Horn. When the big battle was fought between Custer & Sitting Bull was wounded in the ankle by a stray bullet." The Old West was fertile ground for tall tales.

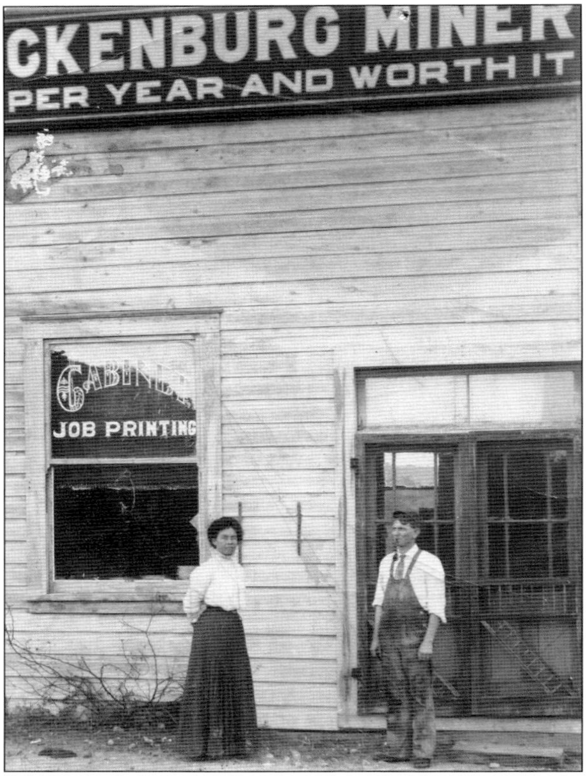

Wickenburg's early newspaper history is a bit convoluted. In 1901, J.O. Dunbar started up one paper at the same time that brothers DeForest and E.R. Hall launched the *Wickenburg News*. Dunbar sold out and the Halls renamed their paper the *News-Herald*. Sometime before 1905, the Halls sold the paper to Eli Perkins, and DeForest Hall later became known as the Salome, Arizona, humorist "Dick Wick" Hall. Angela Hammer (1870–1952), who had acquired *The Miner*, a Unida copper company sheet used to court investors, also bought the *Wickenburg Miner* from Perkins. Born in Nevada, Hammer had visited Arizona as a child, and when her father found work as a mining engineer at the Vulture Mine in 1885, the family relocated to Wickenburg. Divorced from her husband and with children to raise, Hammer operated the *Wickenburg Miner* to support her family. She left Wickenburg in 1911, but she went on to a storied career in journalism and Arizona politics.

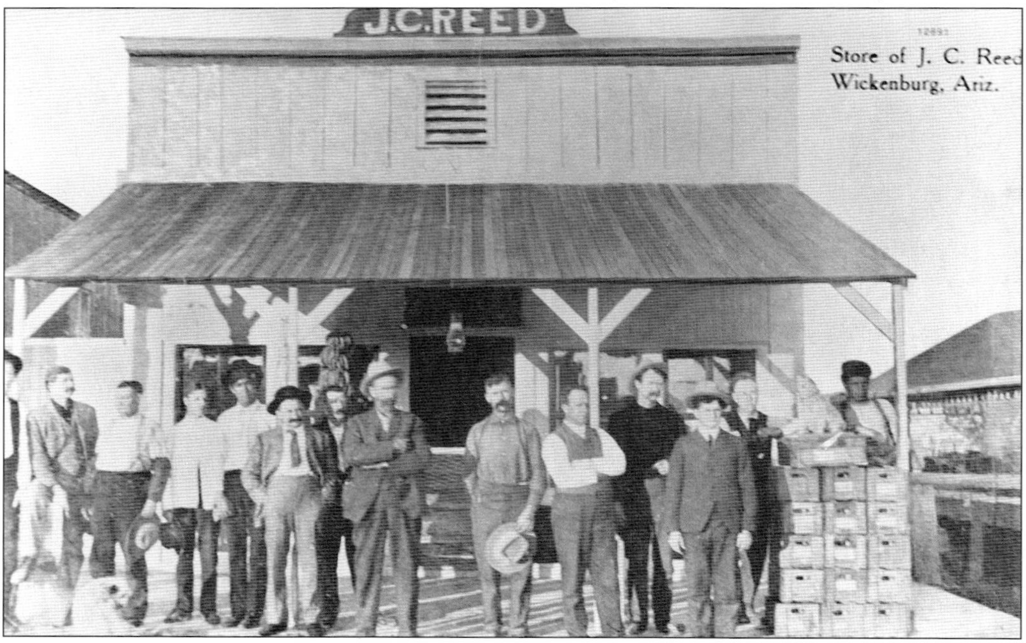

The J.C. Reed store, on present-day Frontier Street across from the old Vernetta Hotel, was conveniently located near the railroad depot. "Reed the Outfitter" advertised that he had "Everything for Home and Camp."

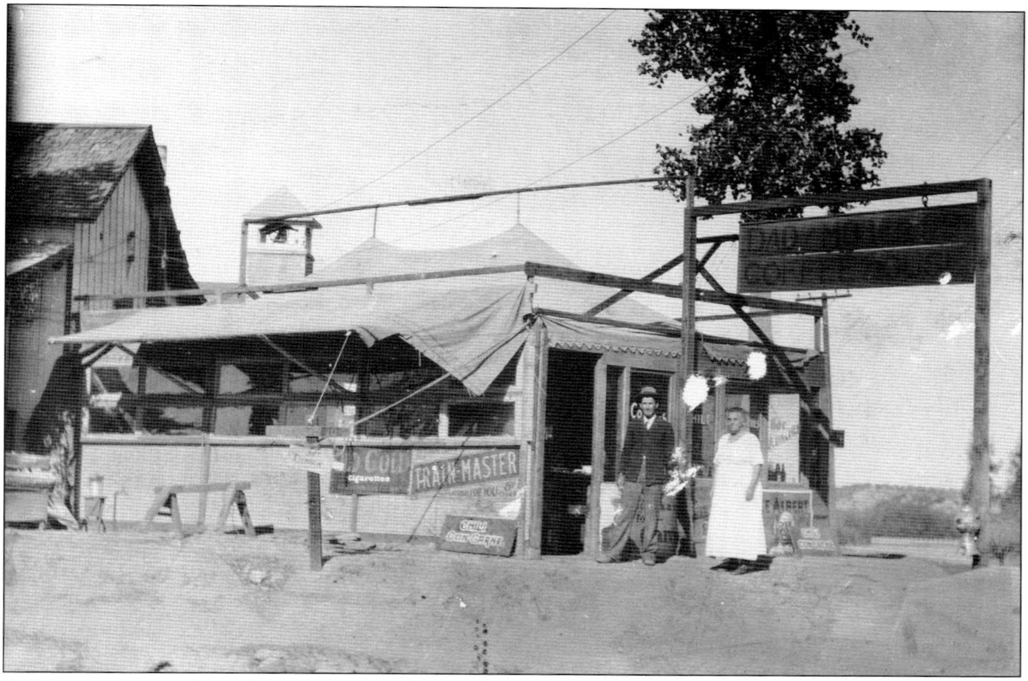

Restaurants were highly prized in early Wickenburg. In 1901, the *Tombstone Epitaph* reported that, "The editor of the *News-Herald* at Wickenburg records with glee that a new restaurant is to be opened in that town. All the old timers are evidently 'onto' the editorial curves, for he announces that he will board at the new gastronomical emporium as long as his credit is good." These c. 1907 photographs are of Dad & Mother's Coffee House.

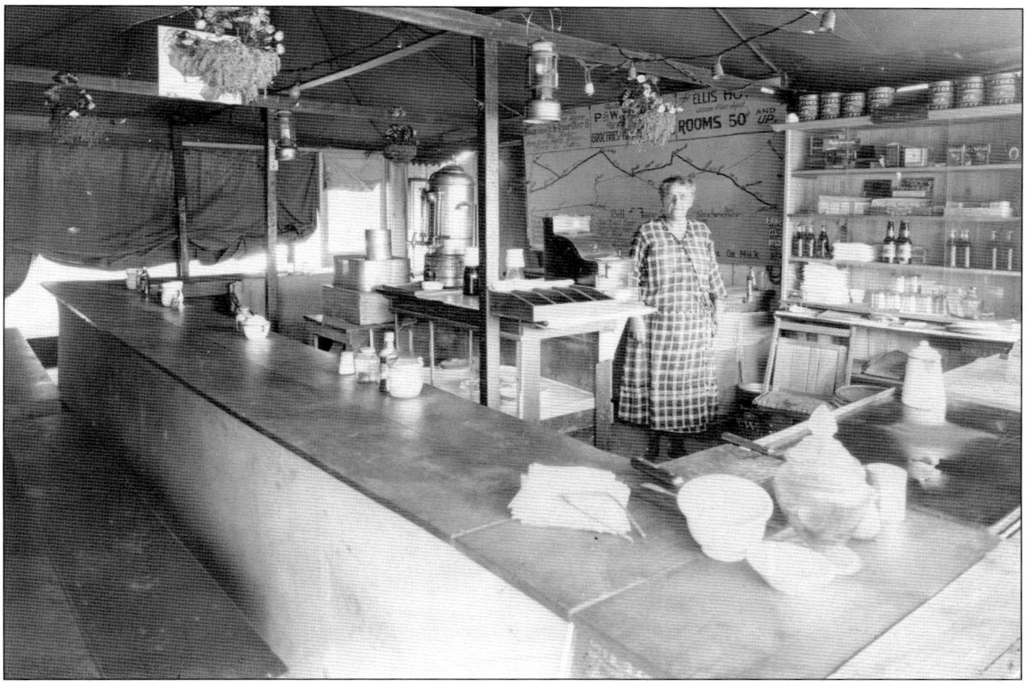

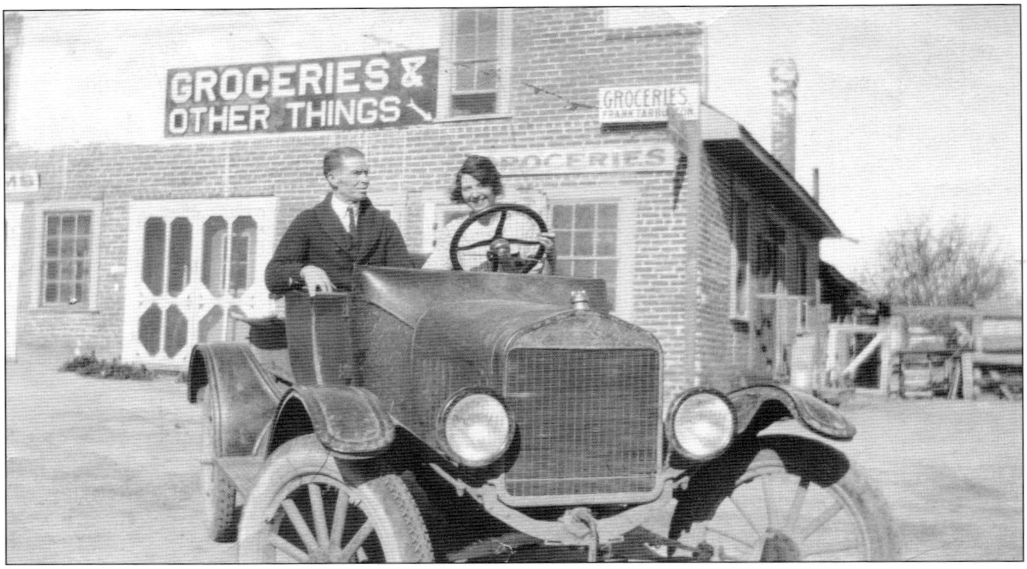

Frank Tarburton, pictured here, owned a local store behind the Cowell Building, owned by the former mayor, where he offered "Groceries & Other Things."

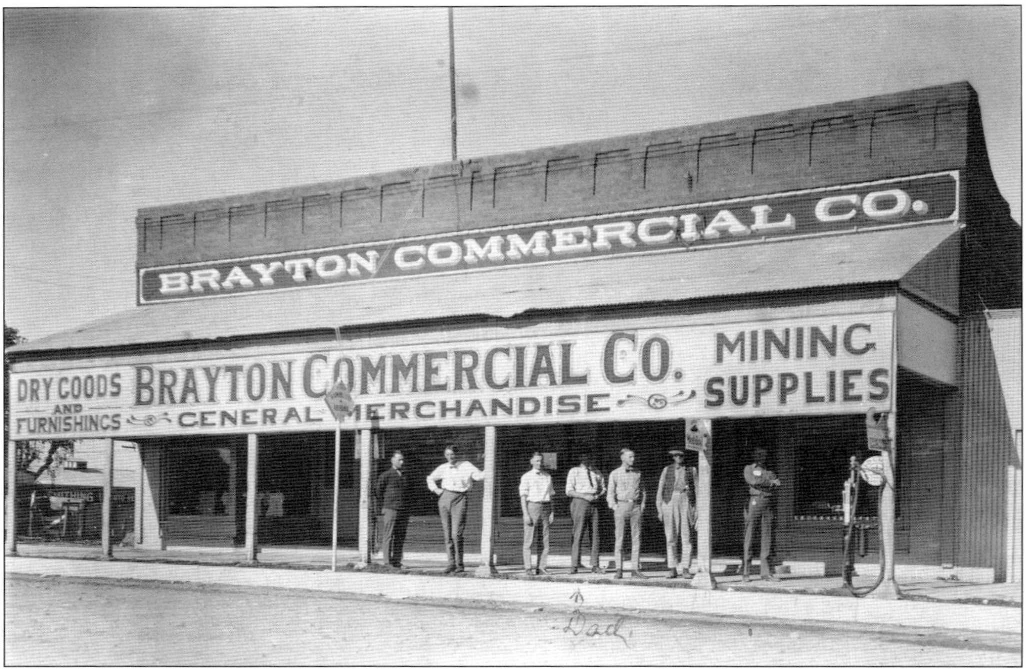

Brayton Commercial Co. opened in 1906 and quickly became indispensable to local residents, to whom it offered everything from "dynamite to diapers, and hay to hairpins."

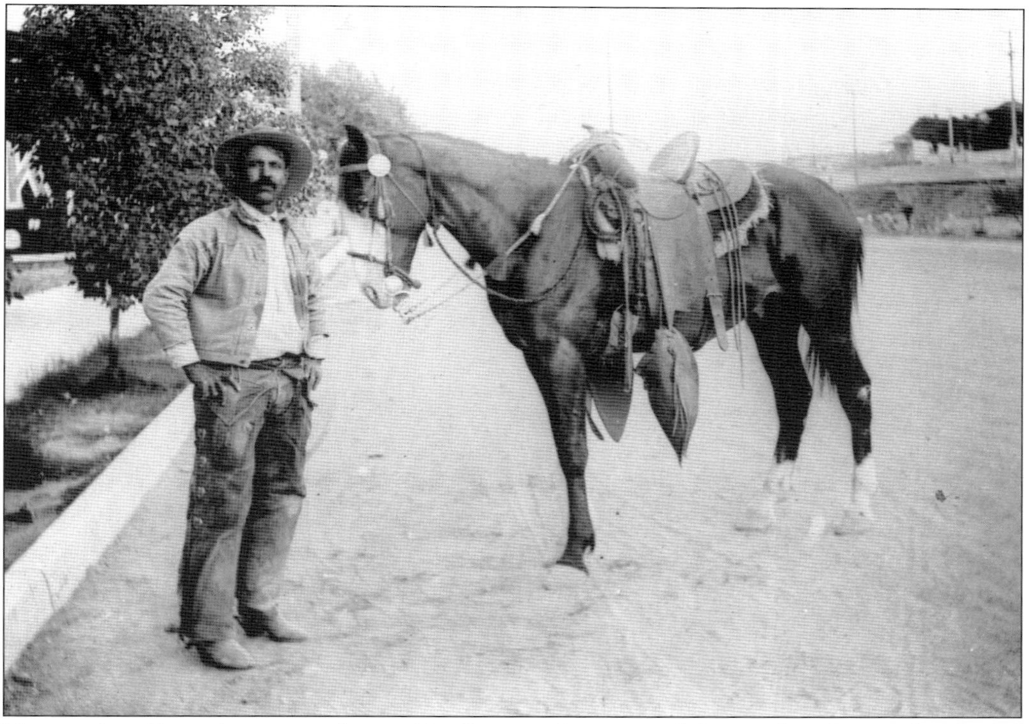

Vaquero Jose Quesada poses in front of the Brayton Commercial Co. in 1911, the year he arrived in Wickenburg. Quesada was a member of one of the many multigenerational Hispanic families that called Wickenburg home, and his descendants still live in the area.

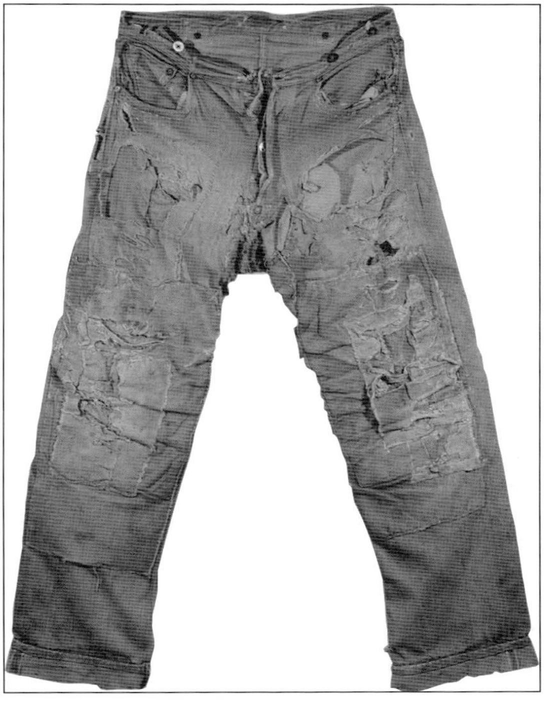

In 1917, hard rock miner Homer Campbell bought a pair of Levi's® jeans at Brayton Commercial Co. and went back to work in the mines in the Constellation area. Three years later, he mailed his jeans back to the company, complaining that they had "gone to pieces." The company sent him a new pair, and the original jeans are now in the Levi Strauss & Co. corporate archives. Close study revealed that the jeans were actually in good shape; it was the denim patches that Campbell sewed onto the thighs and seat that fell apart. Campbell died in 1944 and is buried in the Walnut Grove Cemetery near Wickenburg. (Courtesy Levi Strauss & Co. Archives.)

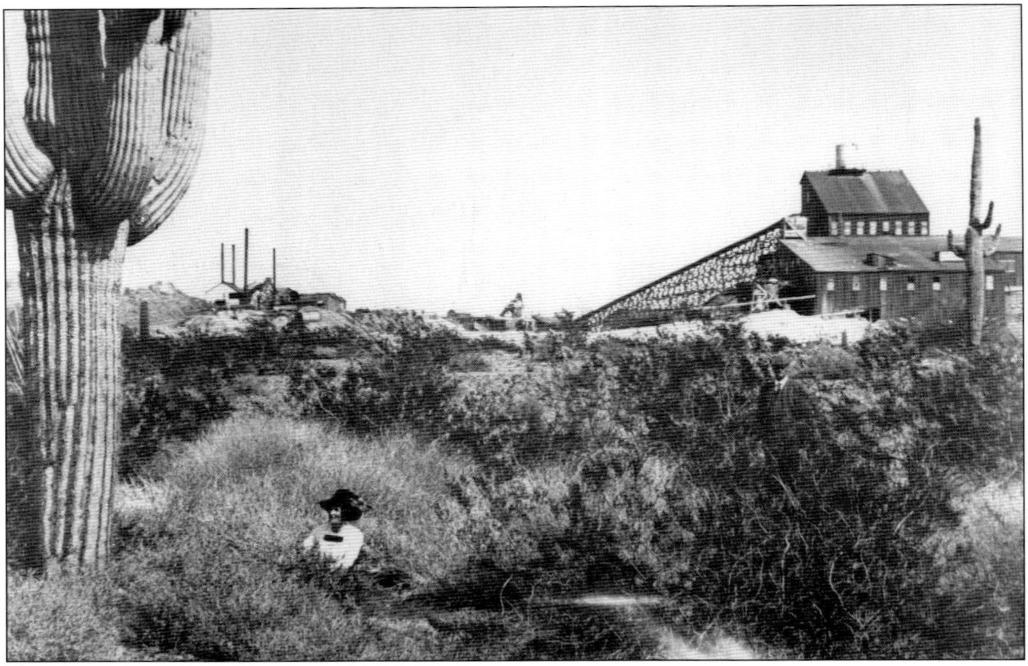

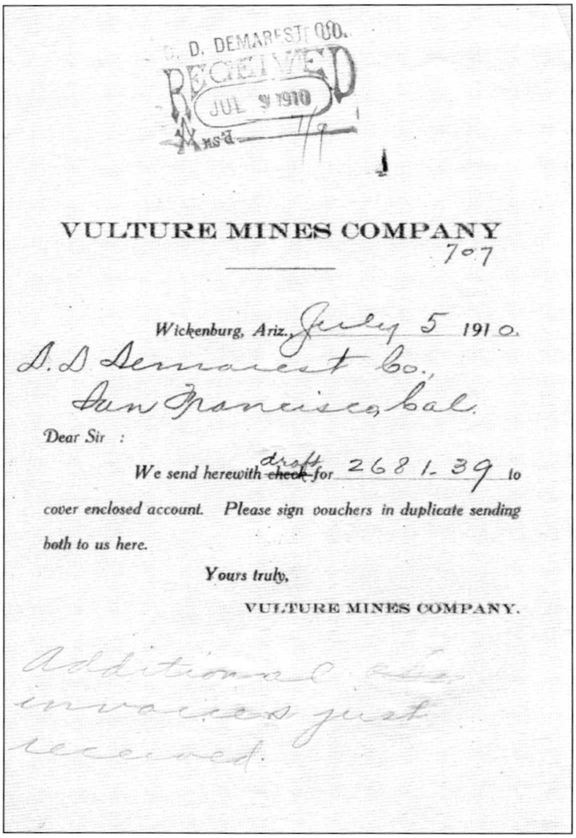

D. D. DEMAREST CO.
RECEIVED
JUL 9 1910

VULTURE MINES COMPANY

707

Wickenburg, Ariz., July 5 1910.

D. D. Demarest Co.,
San Francisco, Cal.

Dear Sir :

We send herewith ~~check~~ draft for 2681.39 to cover enclosed account. Please sign vouchers in duplicate sending both to us here.

Yours truly,

VULTURE MINES COMPANY.

Additional invoices just received.

The fortunes of the Vulture Mine varied widely as the old century gave way to the new. Closed, reopened, passing through a series of owners—the mine's potential still dazzled investors and local miners. A cyanide plant was constructed in 1903 to process the tailings—ore left over after metal extraction, sometimes called waste rock. Articles about the discovery of new veins continued to make the papers with headlines such as this one from the September 13, 1909, edition of the *Los Angeles Herald*: "Old Vulture Mine a Treasure Vault."

Davie Durie Demarest's iron works firm supplied equipment to mines from Mexico to the Klondike, including the Vulture.

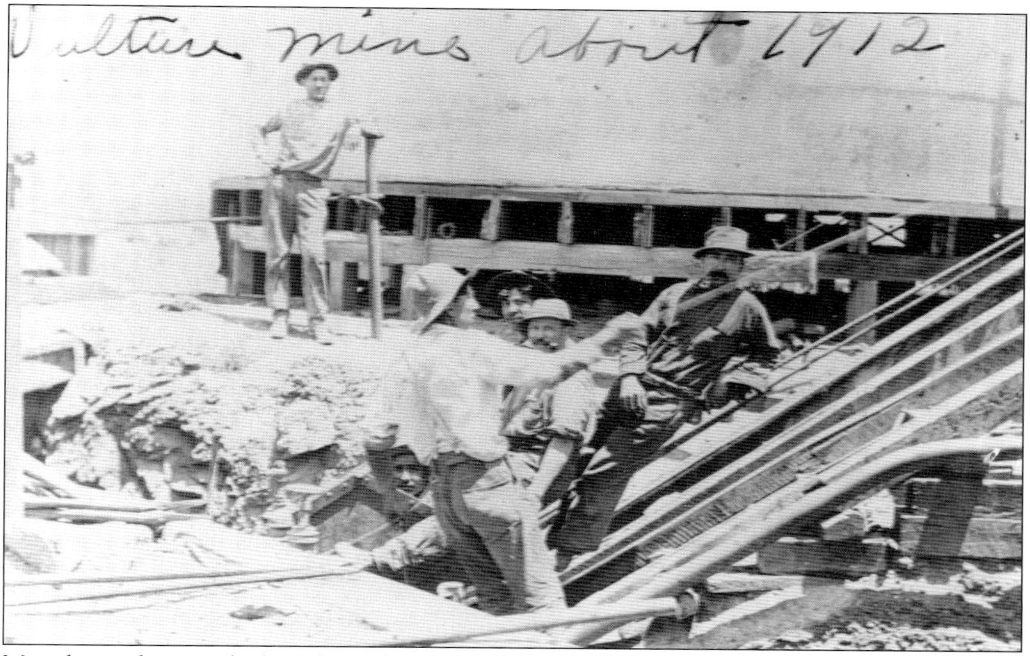

Men descend into a shaft at the Vulture in 1912.

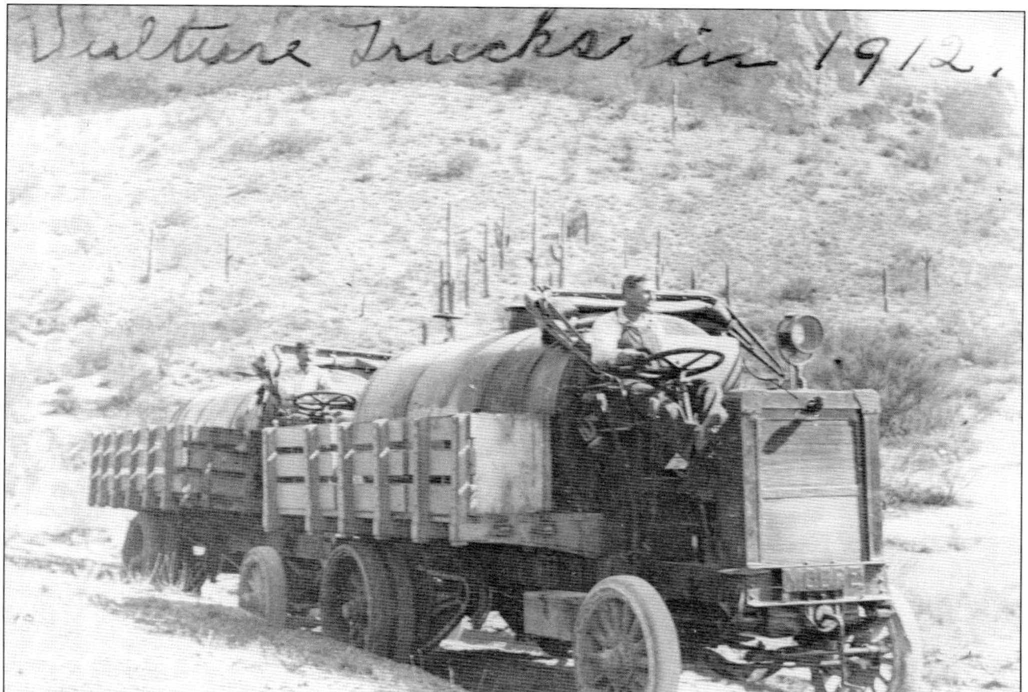

John Wisdom hauls distillate, used to start the smelting process, to the Vulture Mine in 1912. The mine's owners employed local men at the site, but this did not keep some from doing what was called "high grading" after hours—working the mine on their own to find leftover gold in order to augment their regular wages.

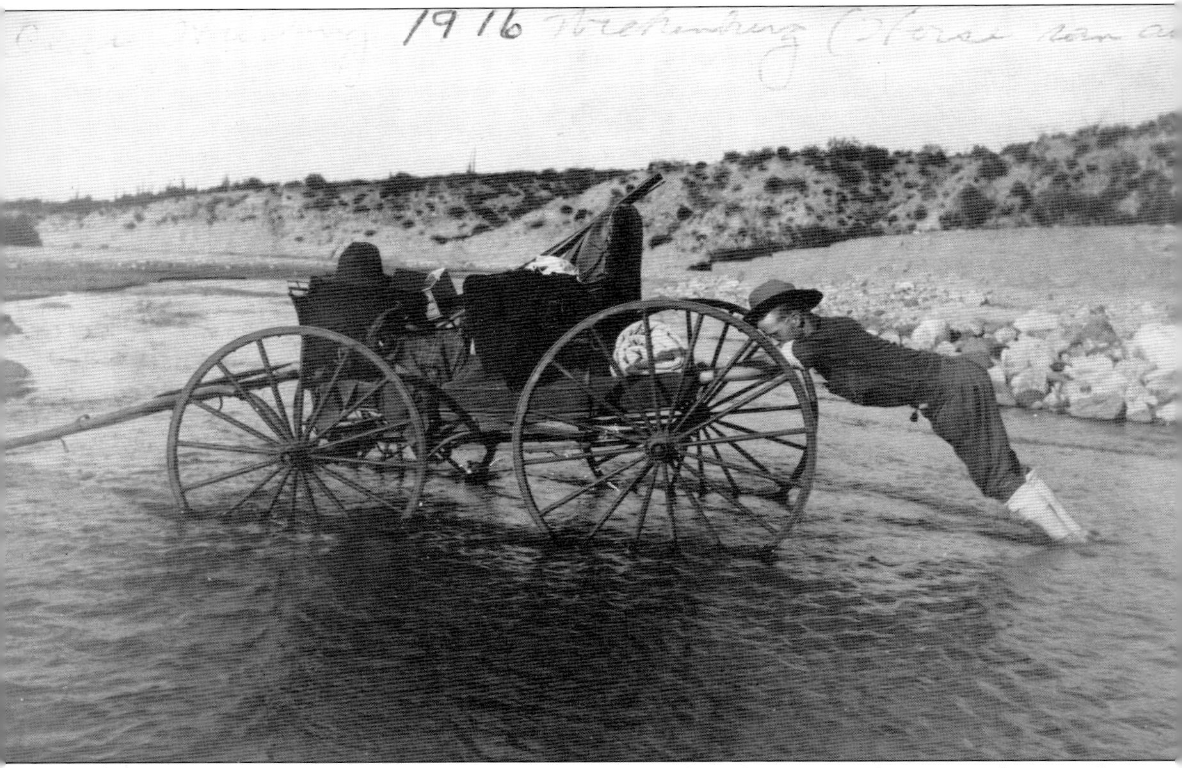

The Hassayampa River may disappear underground in the course of its 100-mile meander, but in years of heavy rains (such as 1890) floods are all too common. Even crossing the river during times of modest rainfall was a struggle, as seen in this scene from 1916. The first bridge at Wickenburg was built across the Hassayampa in 1914, but it washed away in 1916. A cable suspension pedestrian bridge went up in 1918, followed by automobile bridges in 1926 and 1937; the latter was replaced in 2009.

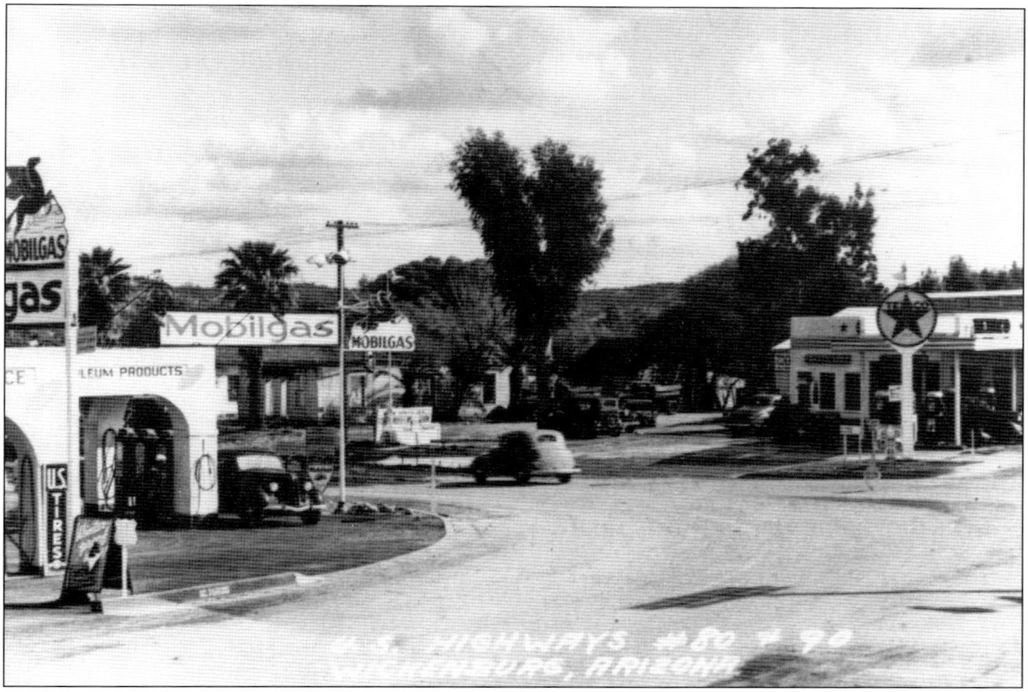

Federal highway programs in the 1920s and 1930s brought new roads—and more gas stations—to Wickenburg. The Phoenix-Prescott road through town was designated as part of north/south US 89, and the eastbound/westbound Phoenix-Ehrenberg road included Wickenburg on the new US 60.

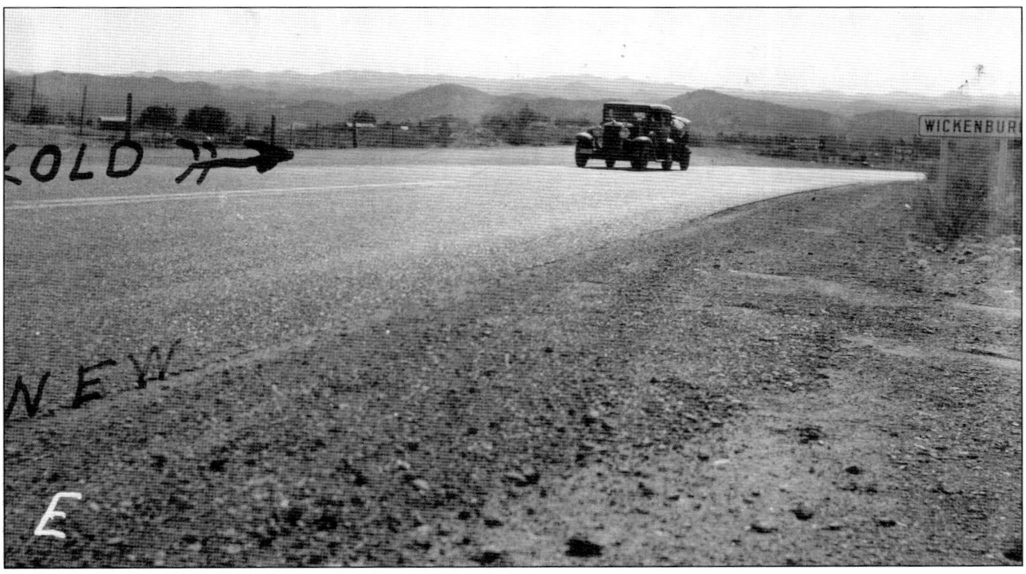

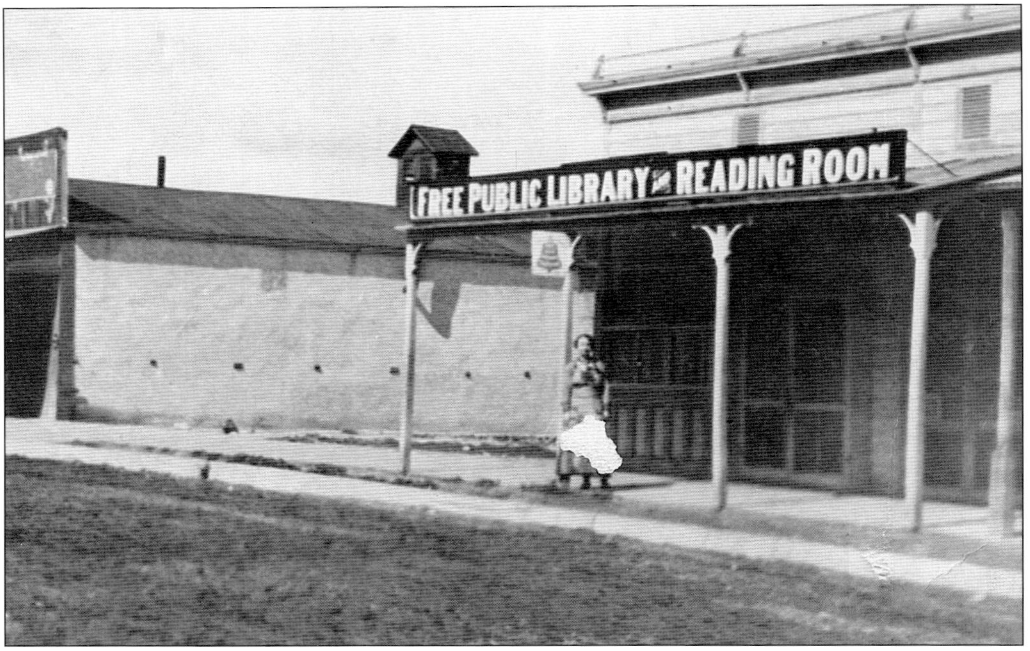

The Wickenburg Free Library was established in 1908, and this photograph dates to the 1920s. The library was eventually dissolved and then reopened as the Wickenburg Public Library in 1942.

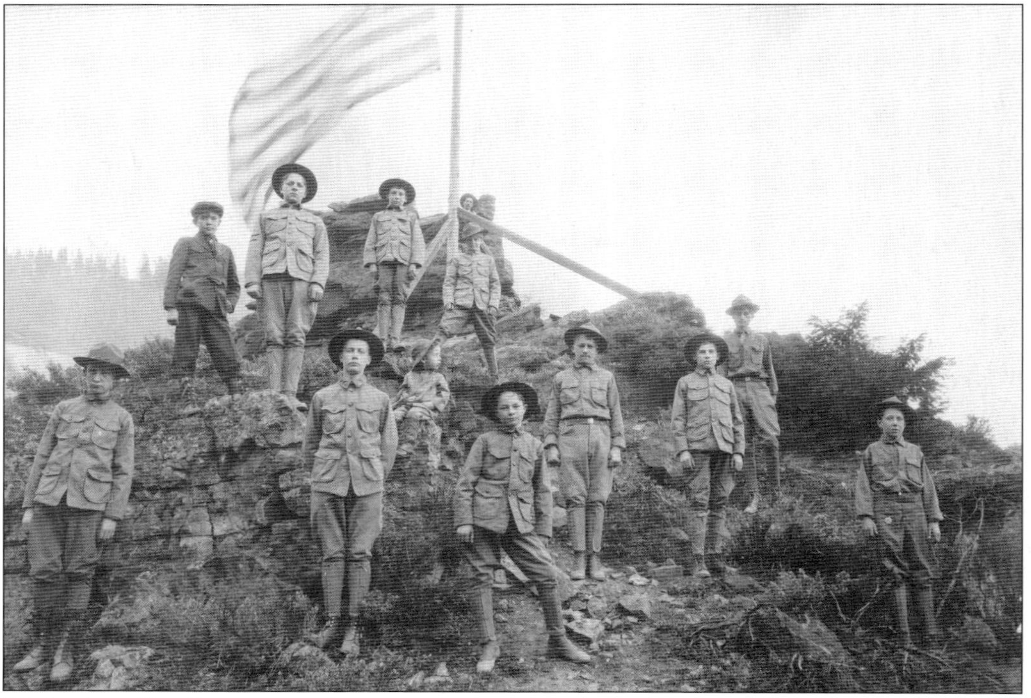

Wickenburg Boy Scouts pose during an outing in 1915.

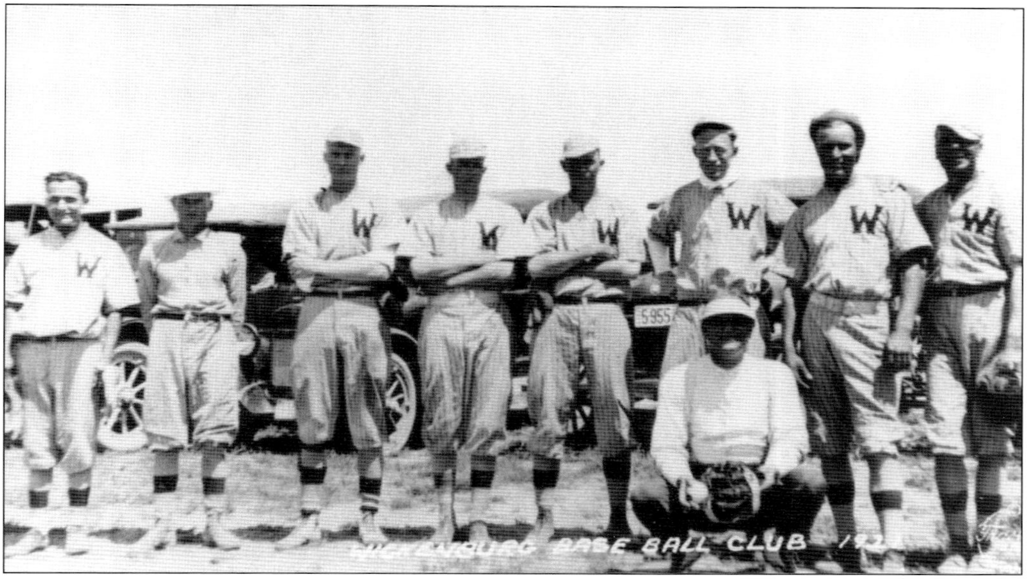

This image shows the Wickenburg "Base Ball" Club in 1921. Note the caption on the photograph with baseball written as two words.

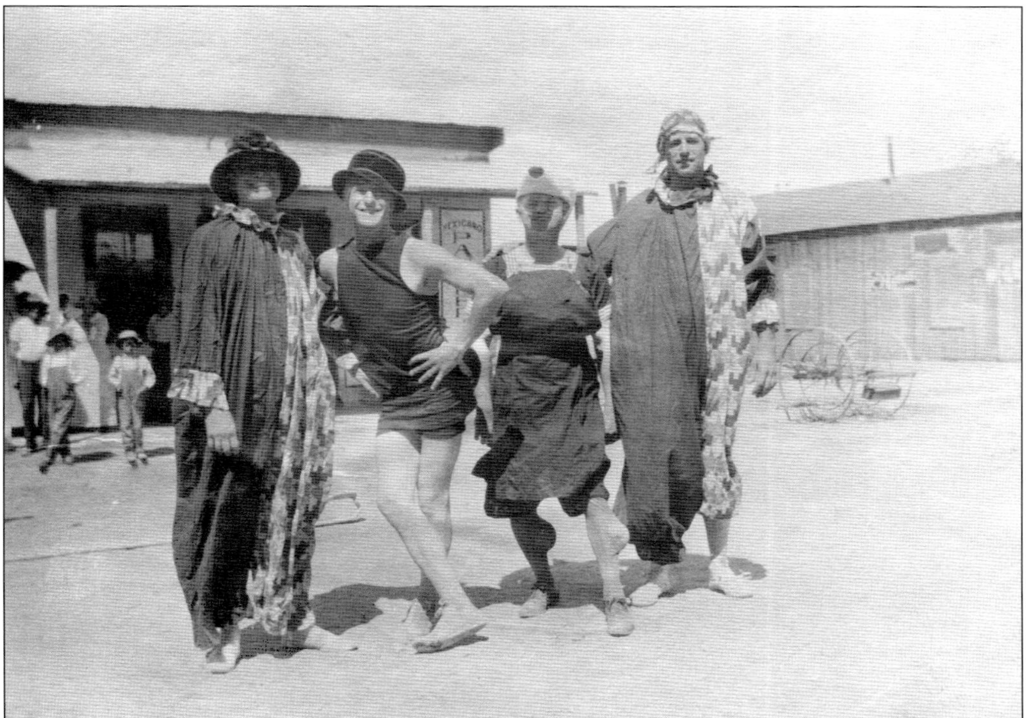

This group of residents clowns around near the public library on Independence Day in 1916.

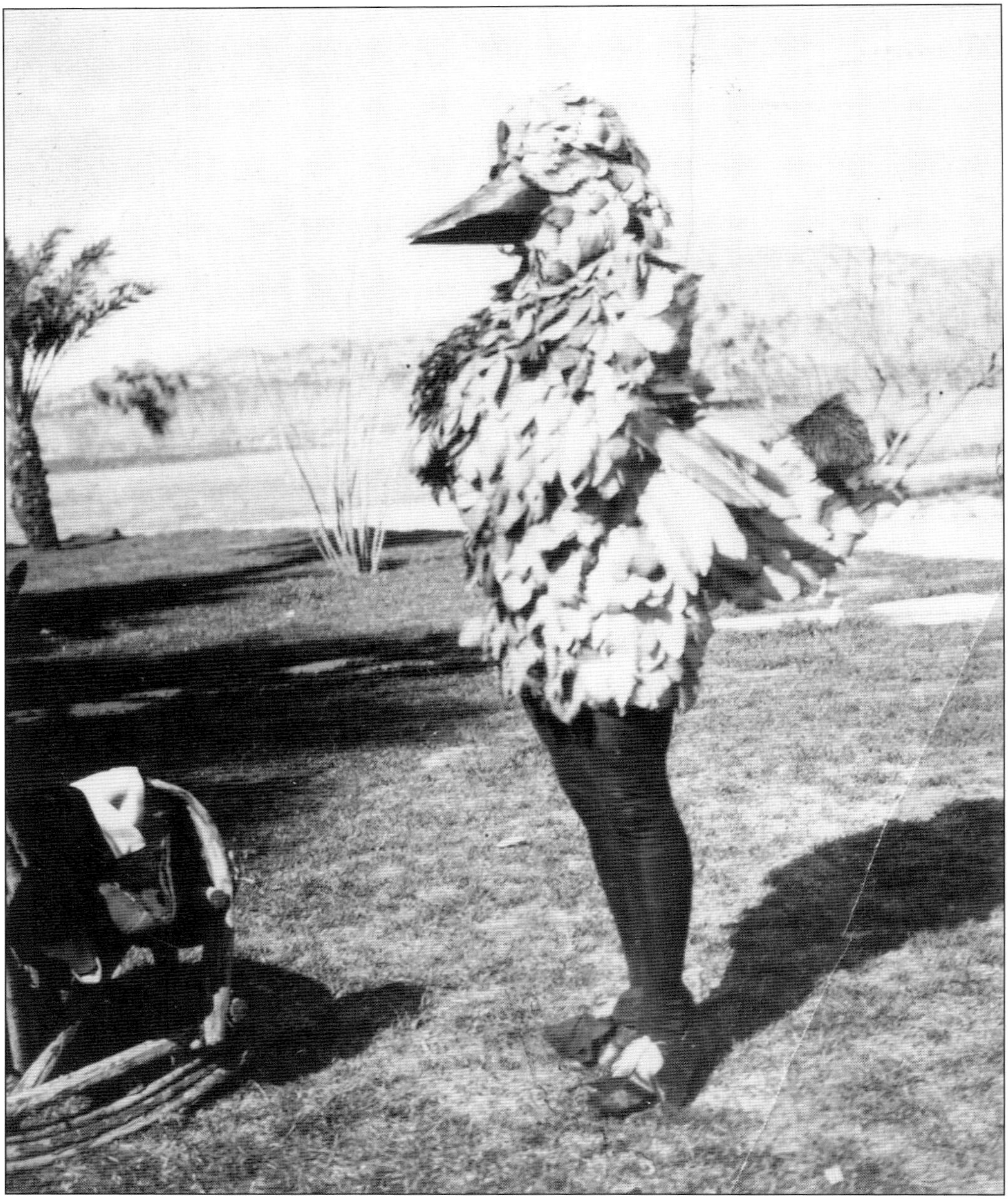

In 1934, a group of citizens got together to plan a pageant in order to lure tourists to town and help cement some of the commercial rivalries between the new guest ranches. The result was *Wickenburg: The Pioneer Play*, written by former newspaperwoman Angela Hammer, who still had relatives in town. In four acts, it told Wickenburg's story through tales of "Apache" Indians, Henry Wickenburg and the Vulture Mine, Jack Swilling, Inocente Valenzuela, and a number of anonymous highwaymen and frontiersmen. It was performed at the Ah-ha-say-ampa Bowl, made especially for the event near F.X. O'Brien's ranch. Many of Wickenburg's prominent citizens and business leaders had roles in the play, including members of the Echeverria, Hutchinson, O'Brien, Quesada, Burden, White, and Garcia families. Pictured here is the most unusual member of the cast: "The Hassayampa Bird."

Six

A Trickle of Tourists

Many who passed through town on the railroad or by car on one of the new highways considered Wickenburg merely a mining and ranching town. To be sure, mining still fueled much of Wickenburg's business, though investment in local mines often came from speculators who lived elsewhere. Ranching also supported the local economy, especially at round-up time. But the town would soon acquire another source of income: tourism.

Many wealthy easterners, eager to trade winter weather for some desert sun, traveled to Castle Hot Springs, a resort east of Wickenburg that opened in 1896. If those visitors ever ventured into town, it was usually to watch the rodeo, sponsored by local businesses, or to catch a glimpse of some authentic gold miners. Then, in 1912, the Garden of Allah, a longtime stage stop on the Hassayampa to the southeast, was officially opened as a guest ranch, and the tourism industry was born.

Wickenburg had the appearance of a classic "Western" town, and in the 1920s and early 1930s, this had great appeal for people who enjoyed the many Western films being cranked out by Hollywood studios. Once automobiles became more affordable and highways easier to navigate, Americans began to hit the road. Some traveled for the sake of the journey itself, and others made pilgrimages to Arizona and other western states in search of an authentic experience that included riding, fishing, and other outdoor activities (not to mention food cooked outdoors over an open fire).

Guest ranches, started by real ranchers who needed extra income, slowly sprung up around Wickenburg. Auto camps and early versions of motels also appeared in town, and local businesses saw an opportunity in the making.

In 1931, the first Wickenburg Chamber of Commerce organization was opened and called the Round-Up Club. It was the beginning of a new chapter in Wickenburg's story, one that would last for over 40 years.

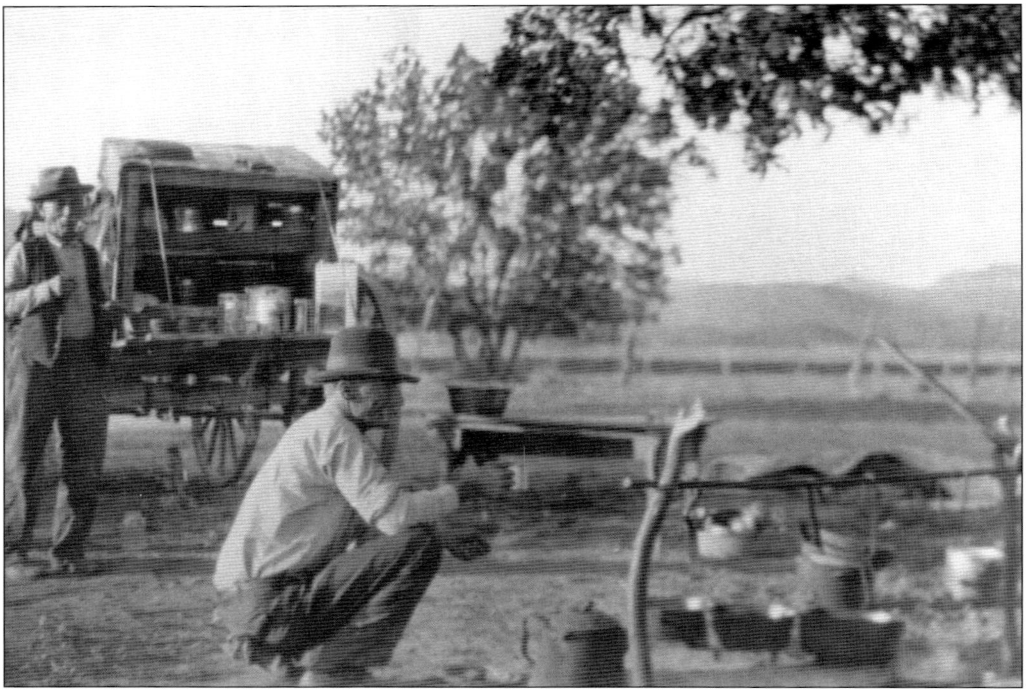

Local ranchers take time out for a meal near their chuck wagon in the spring of 1927.

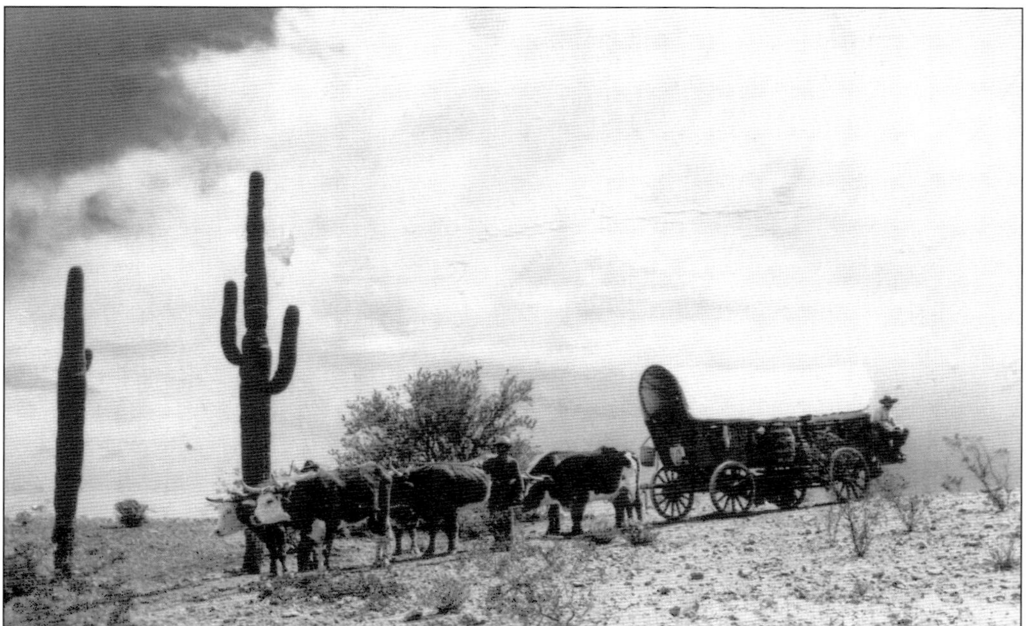

This undated photograph of a ranching wagon is captioned, "I don't know where this came from, there were several of these outfits around when we first landed here."

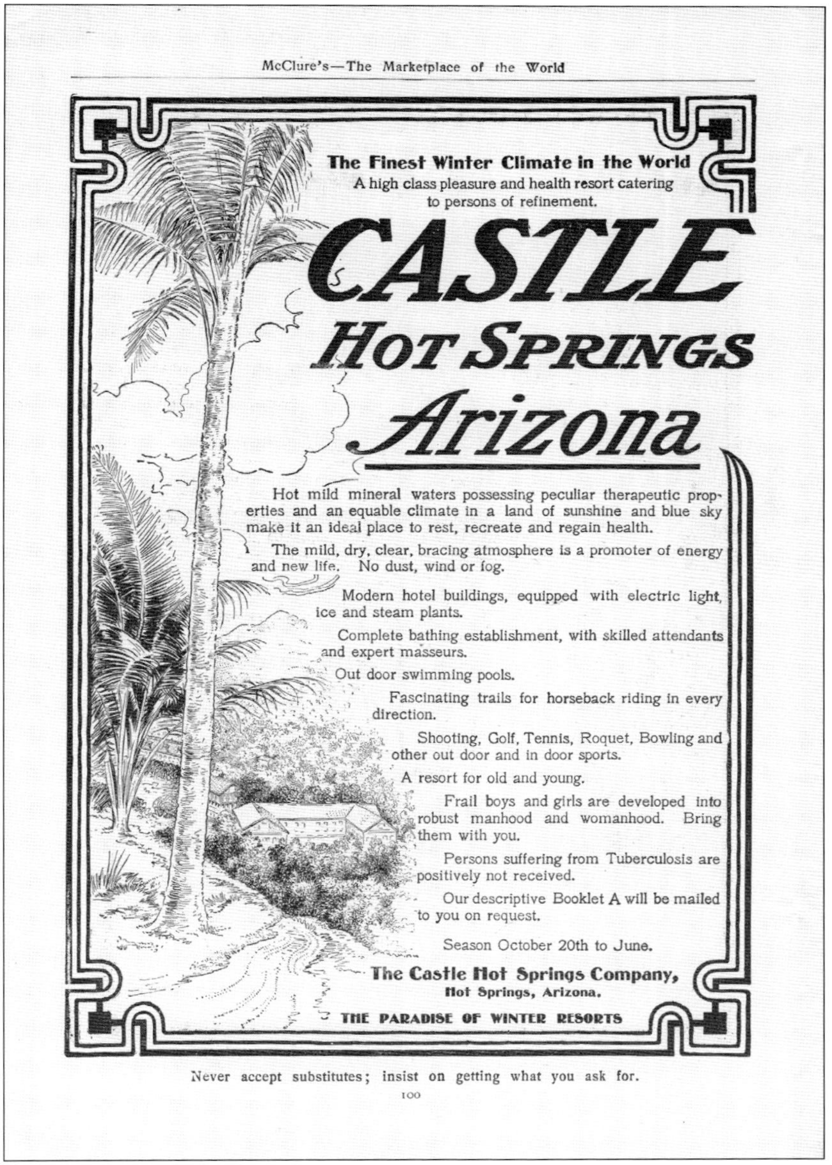

Native Americans first discovered the healing waters of a valley in the Bradshaw Mountains, 55 miles from present-day Phoenix, and white settlers later took advantage of the site. In 1896, Frank Murphy built a lavish resort for wealthy tuberculosis sufferers and others in need of a rest. In later years, the ill were not encouraged to visit, and Castle Hot Springs became a destination for tourists only. Visitors took the train from Phoenix to Morristown, about 10 miles east of Wickenburg, and then suffered a bone-rattling five-hour stagecoach ride to the resort. It was easily spotted from a distance thanks to the lavish collection of palm trees surrounding the buildings. Castle Hot Springs hosted many of America's wealthiest families, including the Rockefellers, the Carnegies, and the Wrigleys. Writer Zane Grey also stopped there. During World War II, Castle Hot Springs was leased to the military to treat injured pilots, including future president John F. Kennedy. After a destructive fire in 1976, the site went through a number of owners and is currently under private ownership. (Collection of the author.)

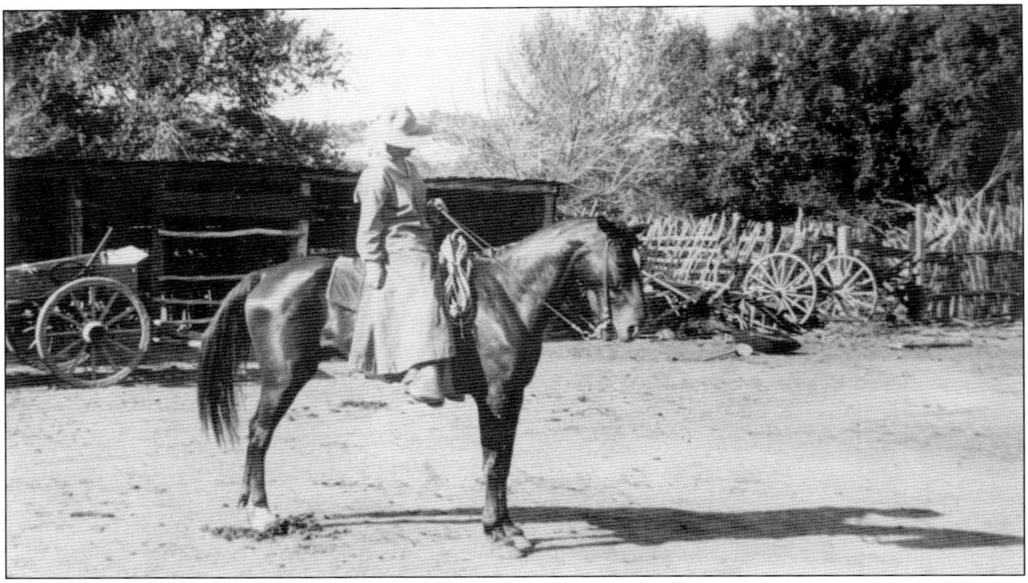

Rancher and farmer Frederick Brill developed his property south of town, on the Hassayampa River. There, he grew fruits and vegetables and experimented with fish farming in a nearby pond. In 1913, he sold his land to Dr. John Sanger, who, along with Leb Chapman, opened a resort named the Garden of Allah. Following the completion of the Santa Fe Railway line from Wickenburg to Los Angeles, visitors looking for a desert resort experience could get to town more easily. Cottages were built, and the original Brill home was turned into the main guesthouse. Children rode around the property on burros, and ranch hands rode into Wickenburg daily to get the mail. In this 1912 photograph, a woman prepares for a trail ride.

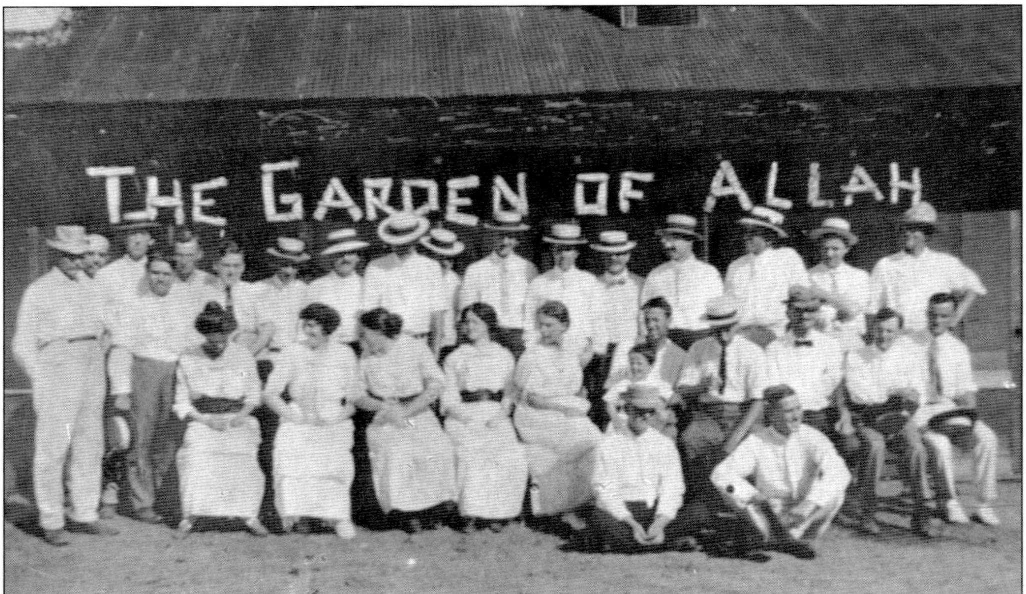

In 1913, the Phoenix Ad Club posed for a photograph during a visit to the Garden of Allah. In 1916, Alden K. Thomas leased the property, and in the following decades it was run as a cattle and guest ranch. Today, the property is part of The Nature Conservancy's Hassayampa River Preserve.

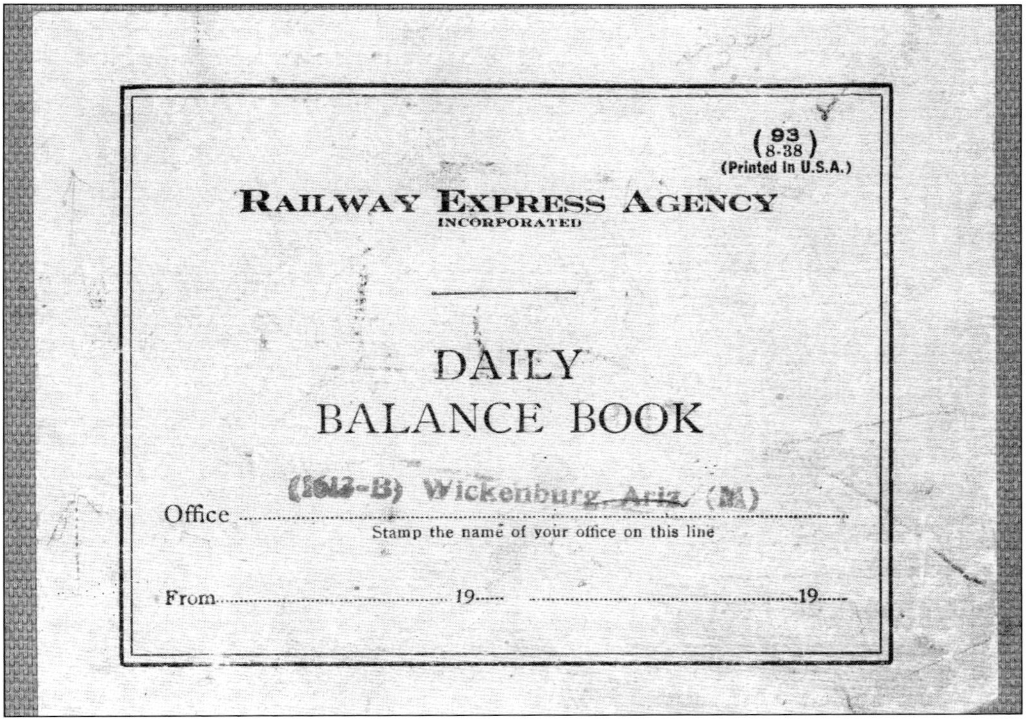
(93 8-38)
(Printed in U.S.A.)

RAILWAY EXPRESS AGENCY
INCORPORATED

DAILY
BALANCE BOOK

Office (1612-B) Wickenburg, Ariz. (M)
Stamp the name of your office on this line

From 19 19

The railroad changed everything. With connections to major cities throughout the West in place, it was easier to get to and from Wickenburg. This brought jobs as well as tourists into Wickenburg and spurred a variety of entrepreneurs to open up guest ranches. This railroad express book from the 1930s–1940s has entries detailing the many packages shipped to and from Wickenburg in the 1920s, a vital source of commerce that increased with the decades. (Collection of the author.)

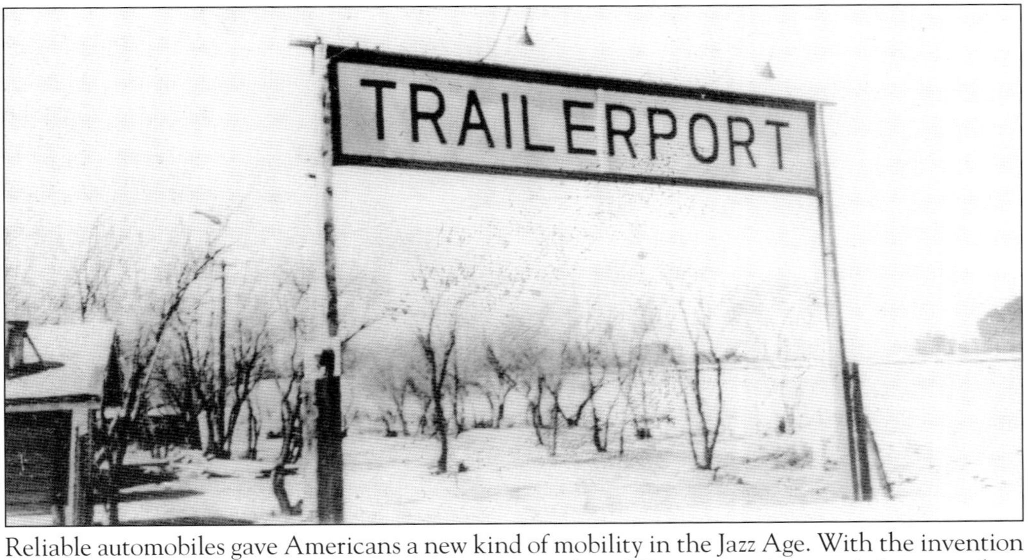

Reliable automobiles gave Americans a new kind of mobility in the Jazz Age. With the invention of the camping trailer in the 1910s, inexpensive travel out West was within reach for more than just the wealthy. "Trailerports" like this one near Wickenburg opened in the 1920s to serve these early road warriors.

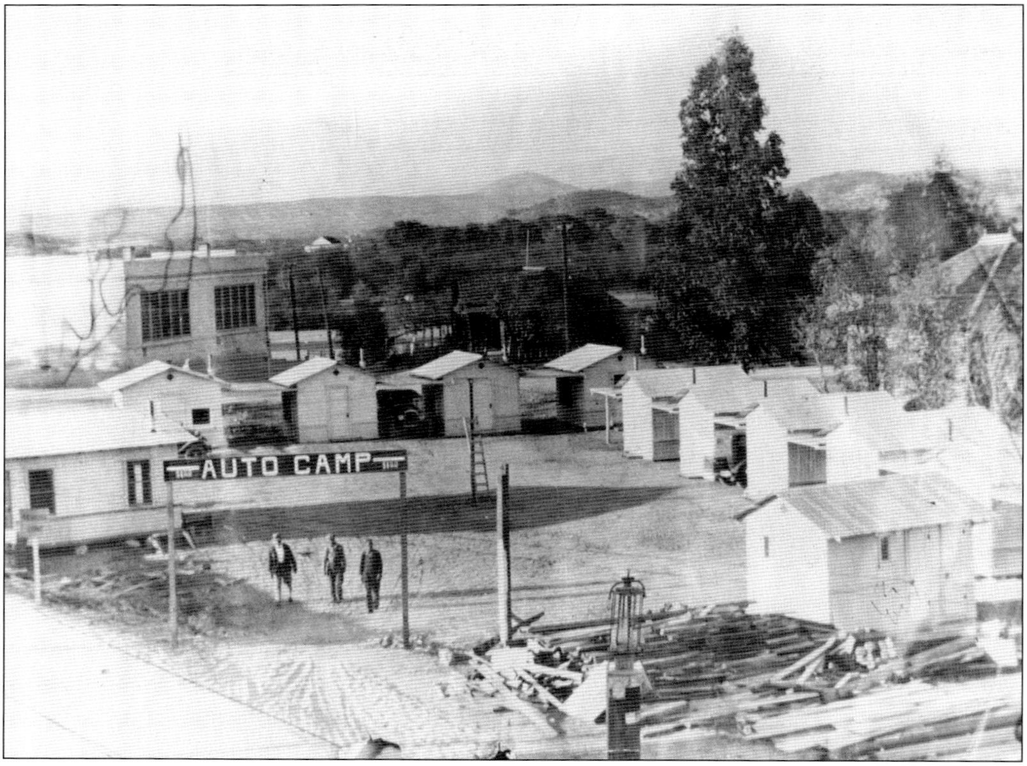

Before the motel, there was the auto court. Tourists who could not afford hotels could pull up to these hastily constructed shacks and, for just a few dollars, have a roof over their heads and a mattress to sleep on (though not much more). This October 1929 photograph shows the Wickenburg Auto Camp.

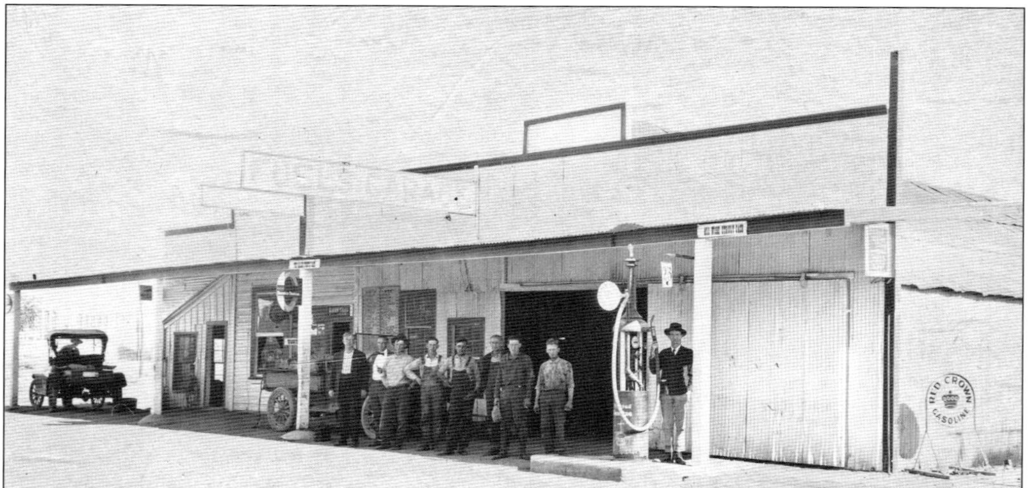

More cars created a need for more gas stations. Fuels Garage in Wickenburg is pictured here in the 1920s.

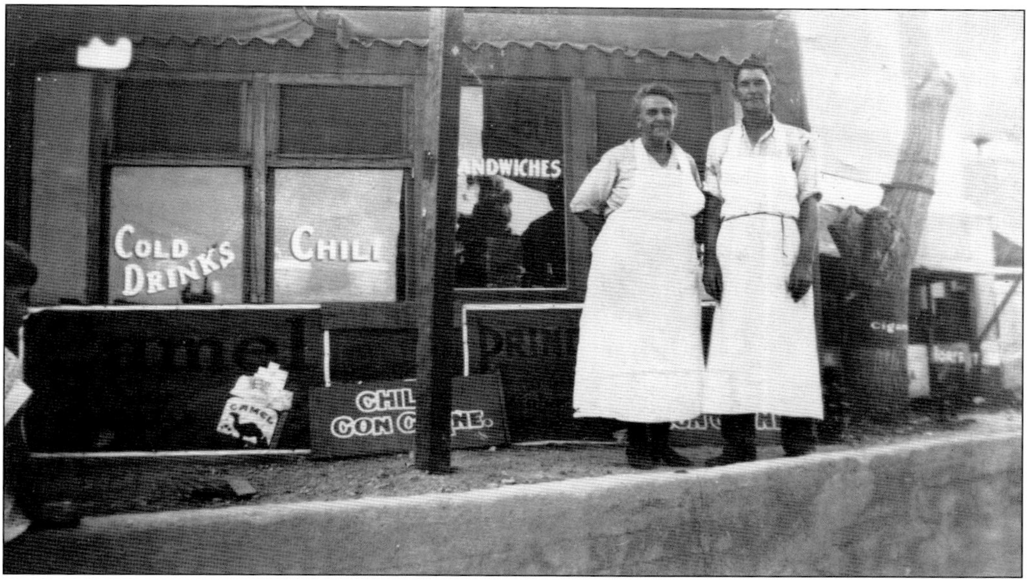

New restaurants opened as more tourists began streaming into town in the 1920s and 1930s. Chili con carne was an exotic food to many eastern visitors.

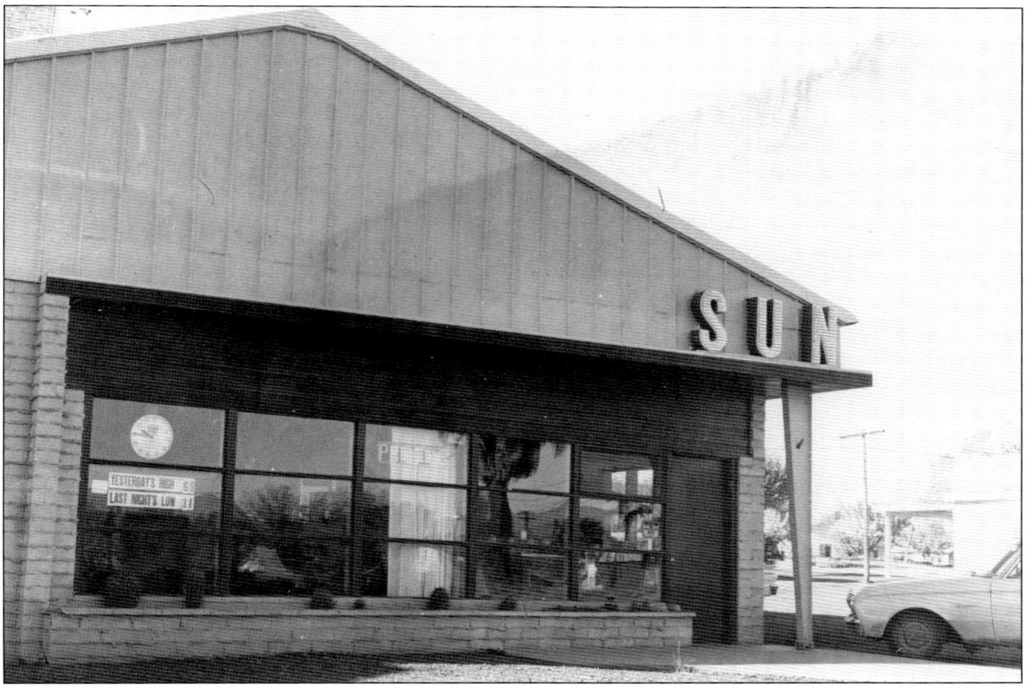

The *Wickenburg Sun*, founded in 1932, reported on both local and national happenings and is still published in town today.

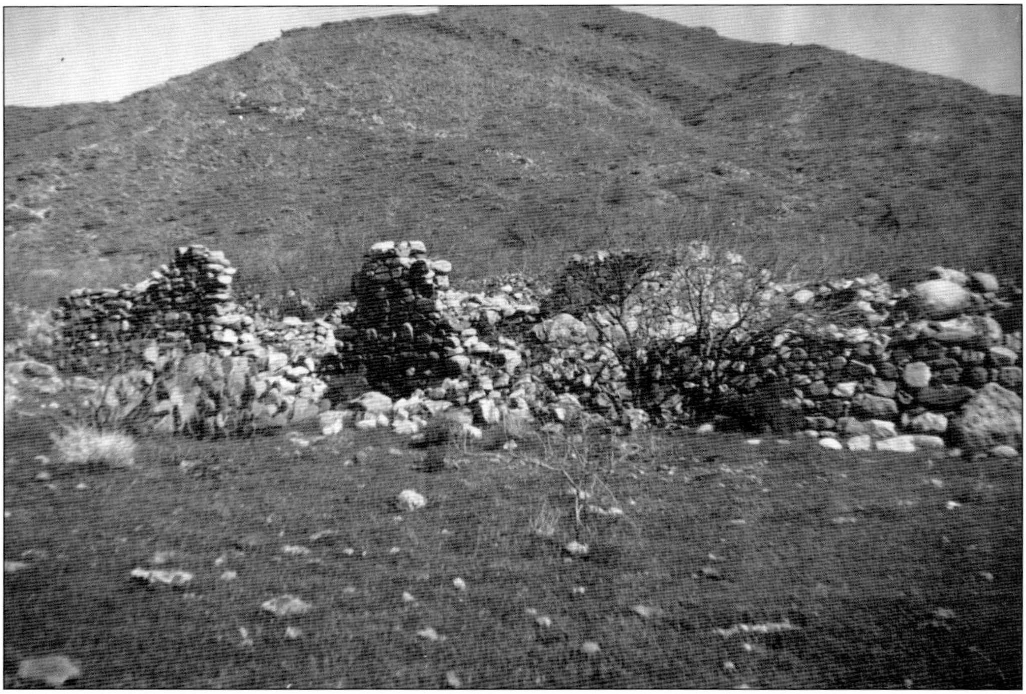

This photograph is captioned, "Only one stone house remains standing in the little ghost town of Weaver." Tourists often ventured outside of Wickenburg to see the former mining camps.

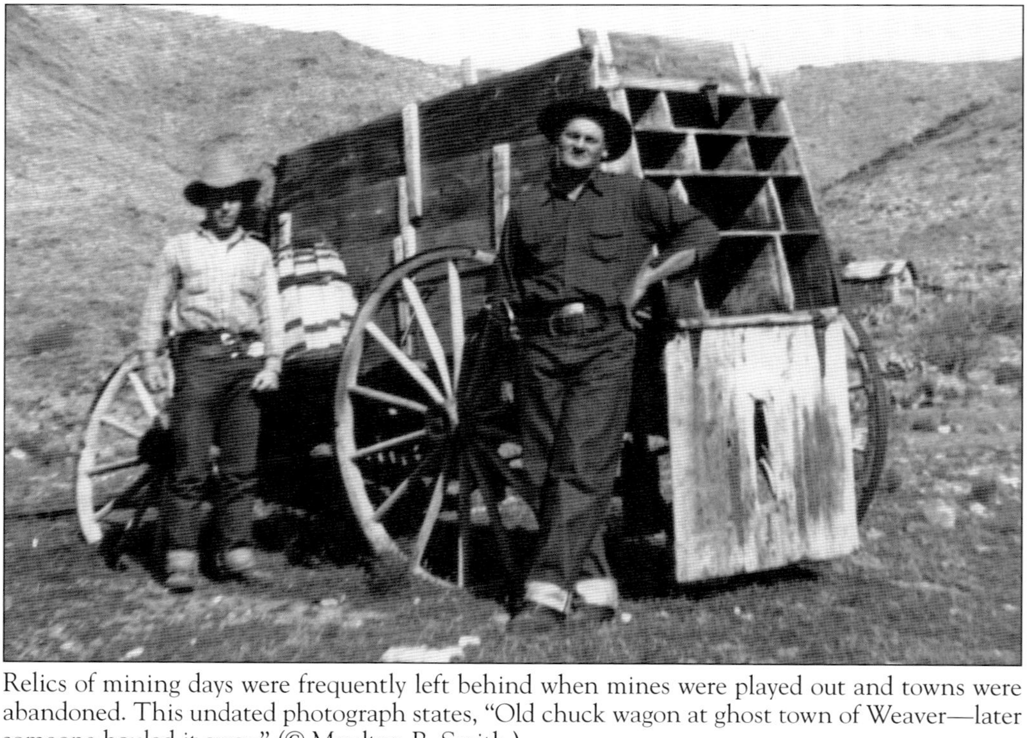

Relics of mining days were frequently left behind when mines were played out and towns were abandoned. This undated photograph states, "Old chuck wagon at ghost town of Weaver—later someone hauled it away." (© Moulton B. Smith.)

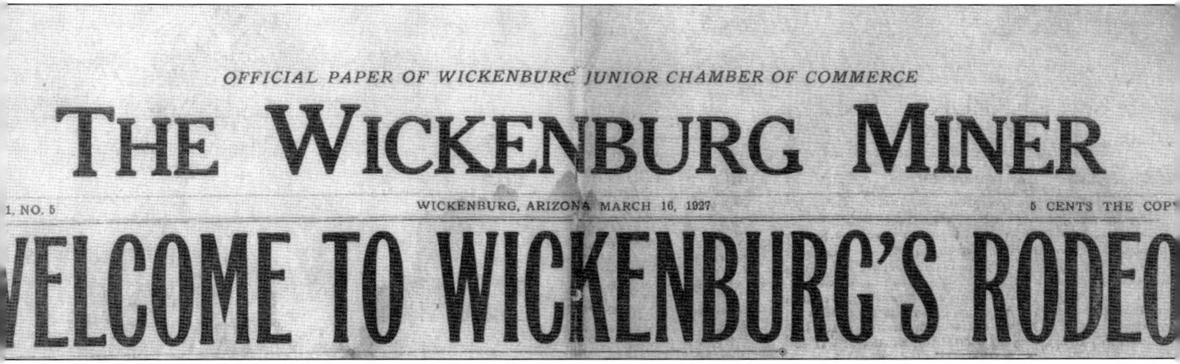
OFFICIAL PAPER OF WICKENBURG JUNIOR CHAMBER OF COMMERCE

THE WICKENBURG MINER

1, NO. 5 WICKENBURG, ARIZONA MARCH 16, 1927 5 CENTS THE COPY

WELCOME TO WICKENBURG'S RODEO

Local businesses started putting on rodeos in the 1920s. And although Wickenburg was fast becoming a town known more for its cowboys and rodeos, the local newspaper was still called the *Wickenburg Miner*, a nod to the town's founding industry.

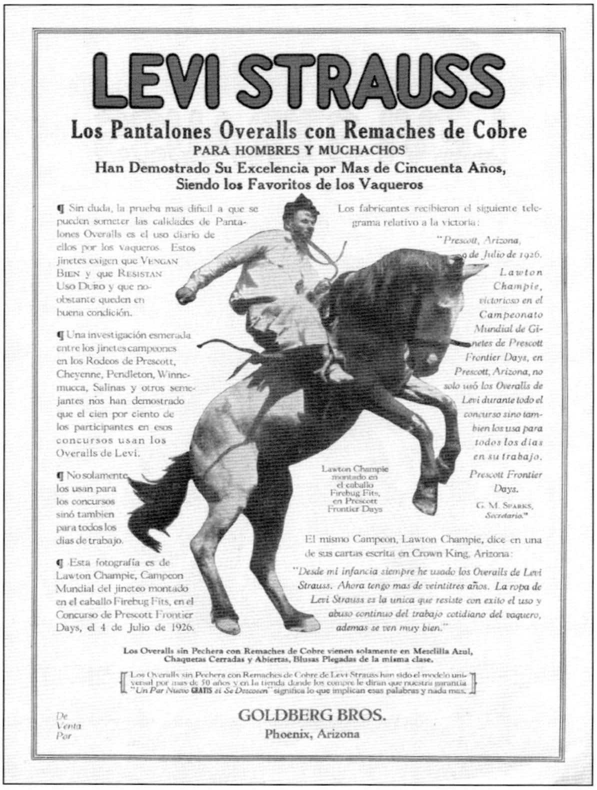

Local rodeo champions became big stars in the 1920s through events in Wickenburg and elsewhere, such as the Prescott Frontier Days. San Francisco's Levi Strauss & Co. frequently used images of Lawton Champie on flyers advertising its jeans. These flyers were printed in English, Spanish, and Portuguese and featured the names and locations of stores that carried the company's products. This 1926 item was created for Goldberg Bros. in Phoenix. (Courtesy Levi Strauss & Co. Archives.)

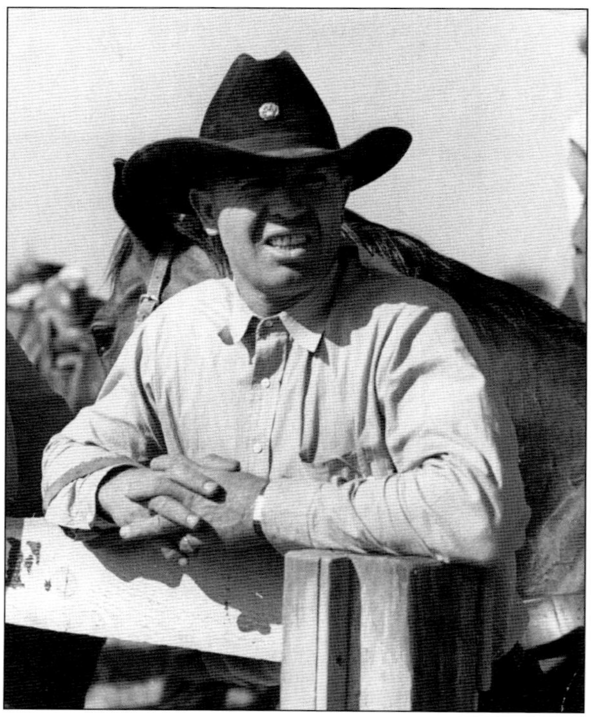

Everett Bowman (1899–1971) is sometimes called "the cowboy's cowboy." He started on the rodeo circuit in 1924 and claimed winning buckles and championship titles in a career that spanned 19 years. He was a founder of the Cowboy Turtles Association, the precursor to the Professional Rodeo Cowboys Association, which aimed to help improve working conditions and pay. He was the head wrangler at the Flying E Ranch in Wickenburg from 1960 to 1962; the ranch has a spot on one of its riding trails named for him. Bowman died in a plane crash in 1971, and a monument to his memory was erected in town in 2002. The local rodeo grounds are named in his honor. (Courtesy Levi Strauss & Co. Archives.)

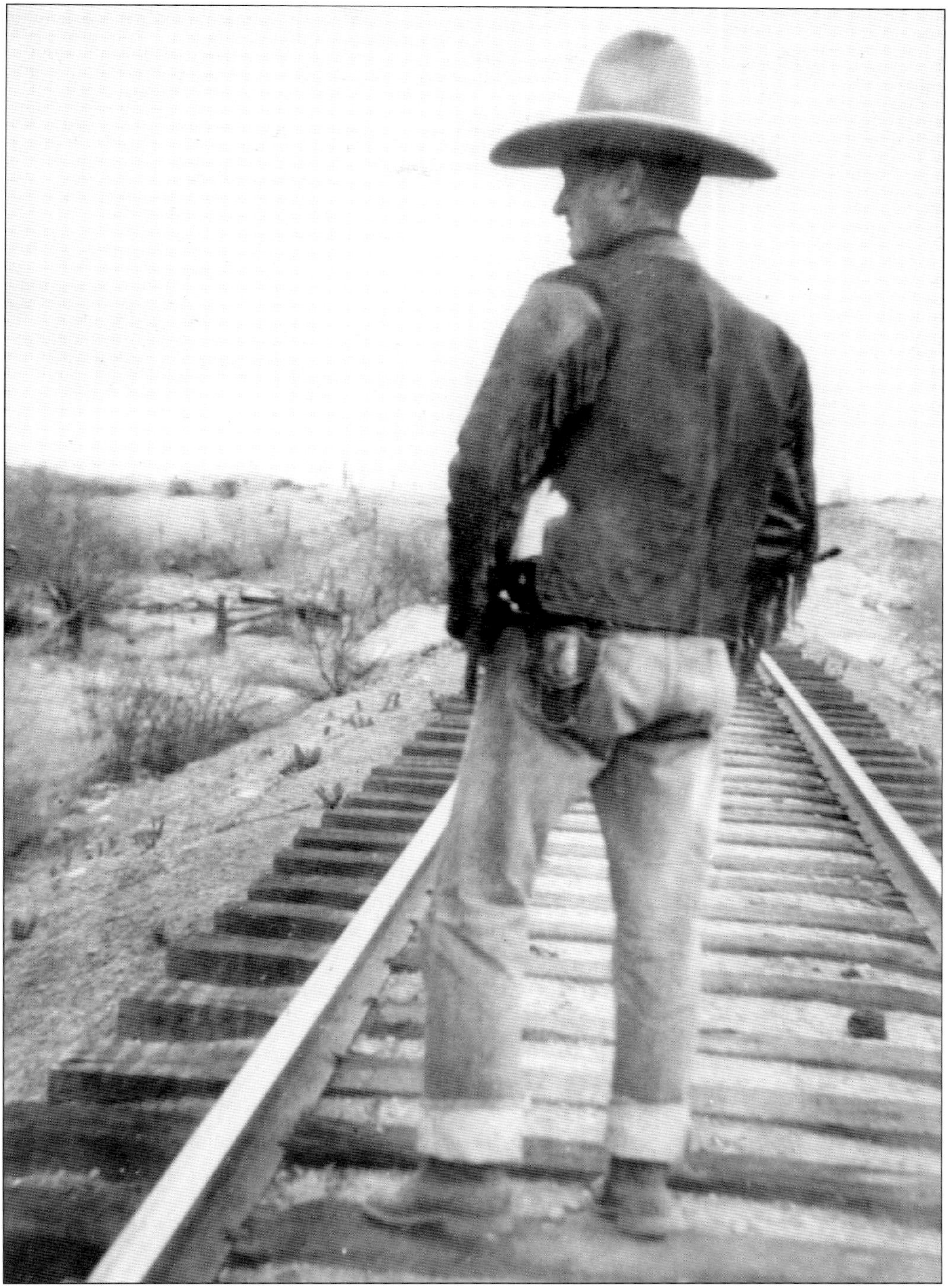

Leo and Nell Weaver leased the working Bar FX ranch from F.X. O'Brien in 1923 to open a guest ranch, which they named the Circle Flying W. They left the property one year later and leased the old Garden of Allah land from Alden Thomas in 1925, reopening the Circle Flying W as a cattle and guest ranch. Leo Weaver is pictured here around 1924.

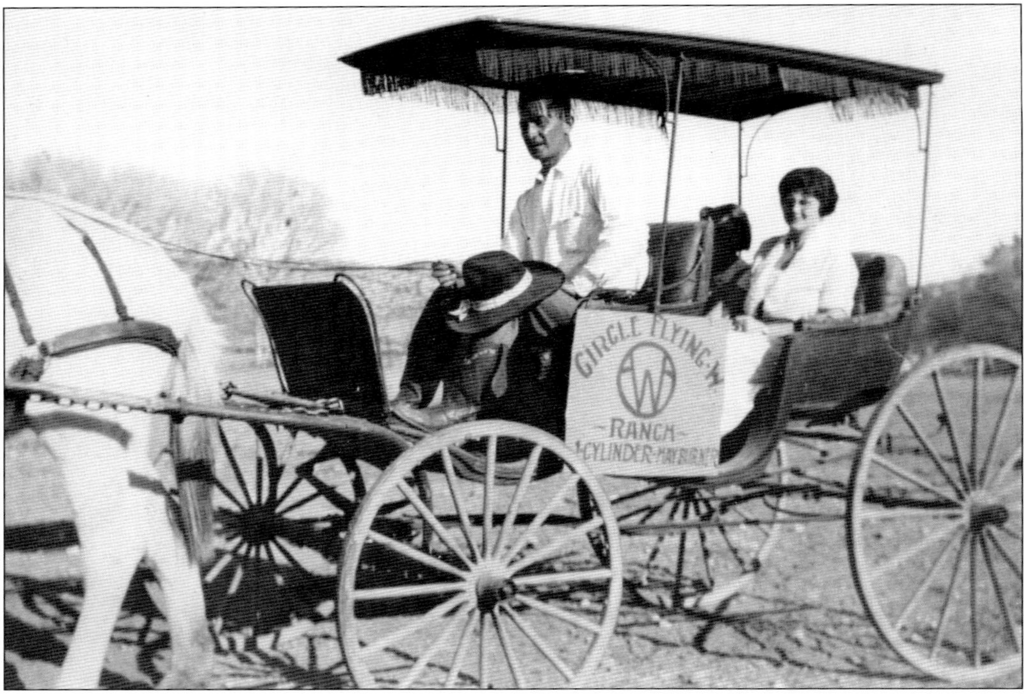

Visitors to the Circle Flying W were met at the Santa Fe Railroad station in Wickenburg and then driven out to the ranch in automobiles. A surrey, pulled by a "One-Cylinder Hay Burner," was also used to chauffeur guests around. A Santa Fe brochure about local guest ranches said that visitors would find "scenery for the artist, game for the hunter and sport for all." Other attractions included "clock golf, hunting, camping, trail trips, swimming, mountain climbing, visits to cave dwellings, petrified forests and canyons."

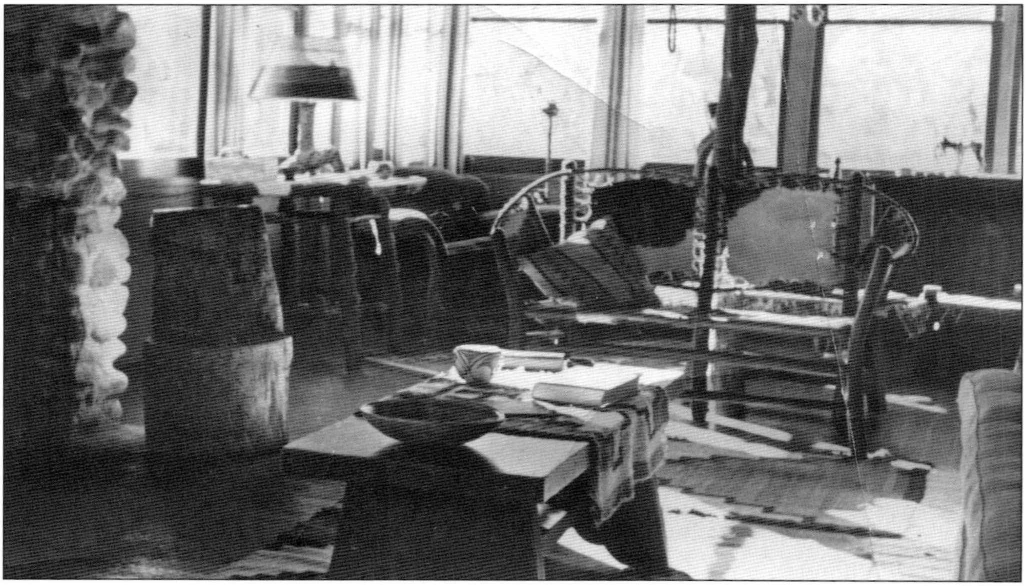

In 1930, Leb Chapman bought the Circle Flying W and changed the name to the Lazy RC, which is pictured here. Later operated by the Corwin family, it closed in 1944.

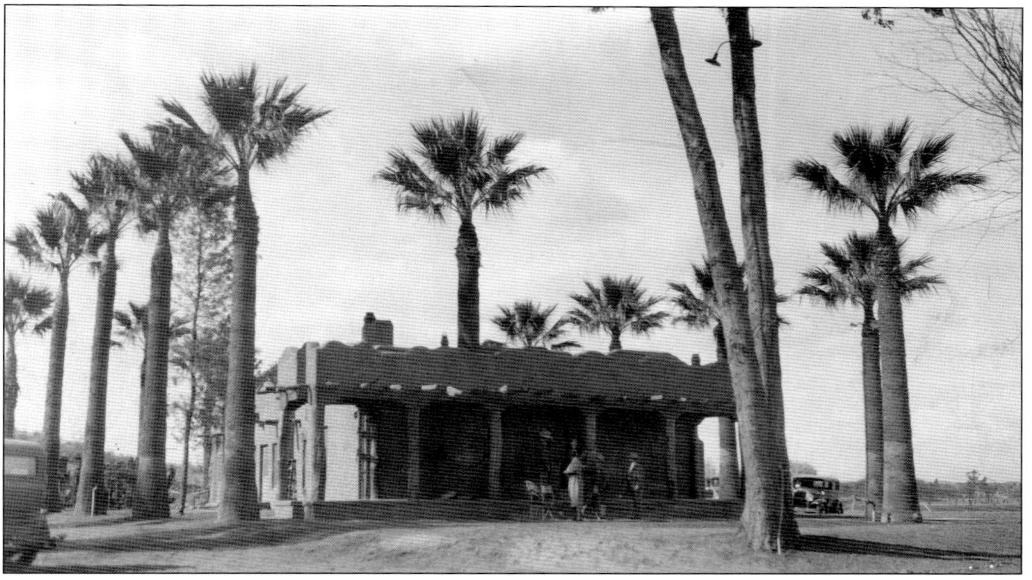

After Leo Weaver left the Bar FX Ranch in 1924, the property was leased by Bob White and Jack Burden, who operated a guest ranch that they named the Remuda. F.X. O'Brien died in 1926, and his widow, Mary, repossessed the land and buildings in 1928, reopening it as a farm and later a dude ranch called the Bar FX Ranch. A 1930s tourist brochure stated that rooms were equipped with steam heat, private bath, and electricity. Activities included horseback riding, badminton, tennis, croquet, target practice, and polo. Today, Bar FX is known as the Simpson Ranch, and the building pictured here still stands on the property.

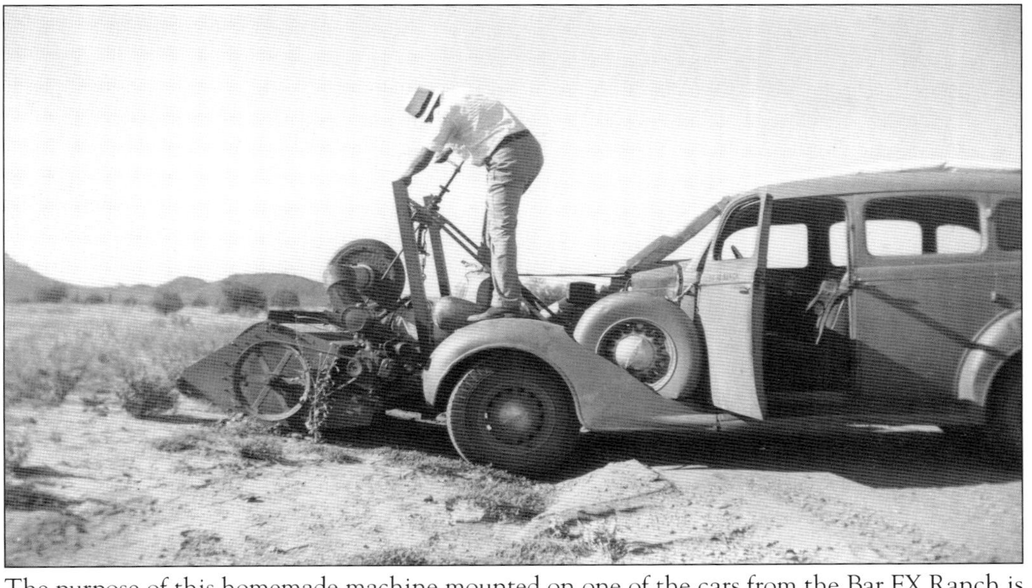

The purpose of this homemade machine mounted on one of the cars from the Bar FX Ranch is a mystery.

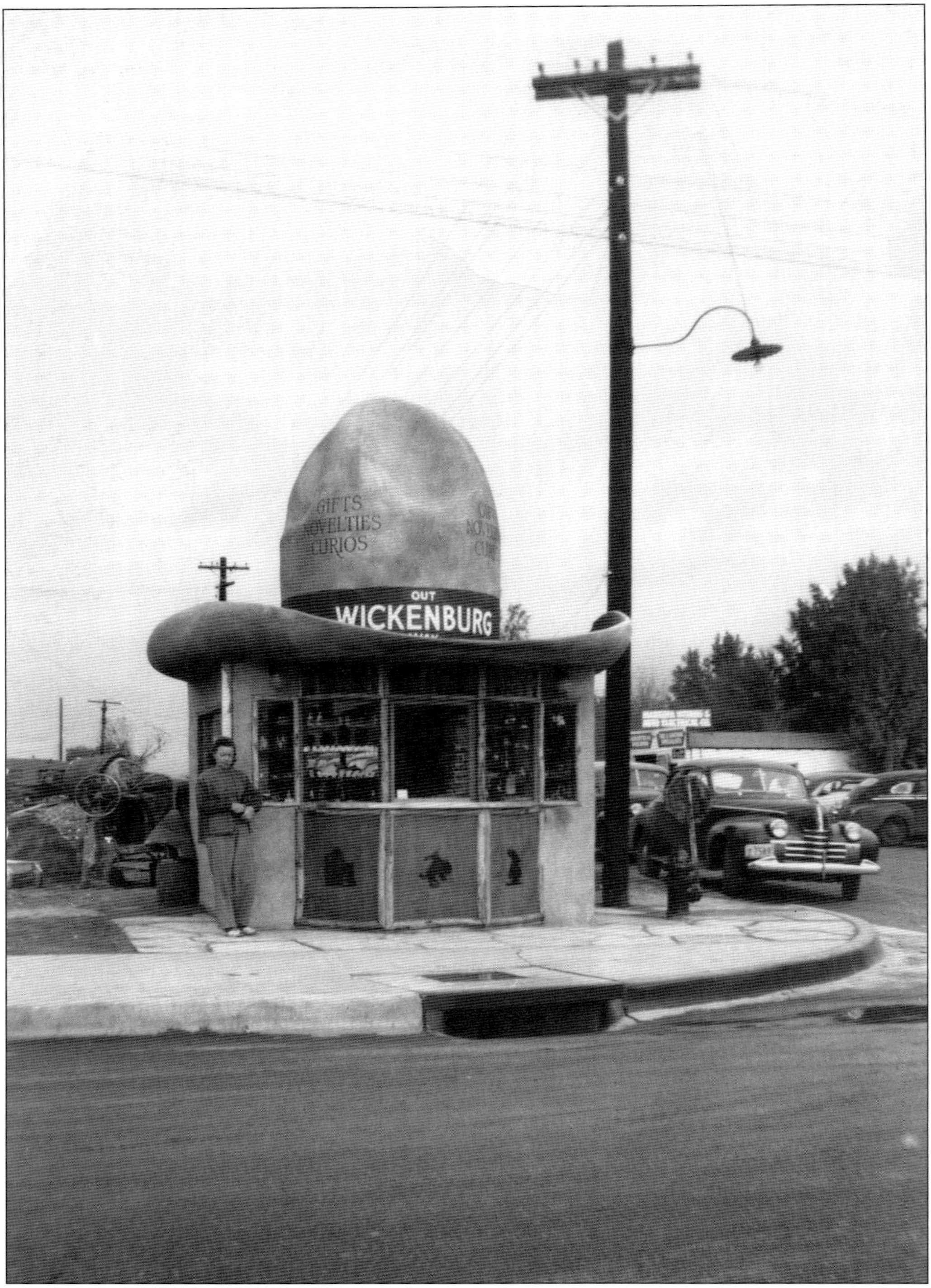

In the late 1930s, the Round-Up Club built this souvenir shop at the intersection of Valentine and Center Streets. "The Big Hat" was a popular local landmark until the 1960s, when it was demolished after enduring the ravages of time and too many encounters with speeding cars.

Seven

Dude Ranch Capital of the World

The first American guest ranches were created in the Rocky Mountain West in the late 19th century and catered to the wealthy of the United States and England who wanted guides for hunting trips. By the 1920s, however, these ranches also saw regular tourists, and by the 1930s, the word "guest" had been replaced by the word "dude."

There seems to be no agreement about the origins of the word "dude"—when it was first used or what it originally meant. Some say it simply meant a visitor to a Western ranch who paid for meals, accommodations, and a guide. Others define dude as a derogatory description of a "tenderfoot" who plays cowboy at a real ranch. (The terms "dudette" or "dudine," the female forms of "dude," have an even murkier past.)

However the phrase came about, by the 1930s a number of new ranches opened in quick succession in and around Wickenburg. Many early visitors were wealthy easterners who sometimes spent an entire season at one locale. Some were famous, such as English writer J.B. Priestley, who spent the winter of 1935–1936 at the Remuda Ranch. However, the middle class was also on the move and taking short stays at local dude ranches.

Although visits to the ranches dropped during the Depression, mining and cattle ranching were still viable sources of income. Many locals made a little extra money by working old mine tailings and dry washes to find gold.

The Round-Up Club watched the influx of tourists and by the mid-1930s was handing out sophisticated brochures about Wickenburg, calling the town "The Land Without Winter." Aimed at both transients and potential year-round residents, these booklets touted local services such as a doctor and a well-equipped hospital, a film developing service, mining suppliers, a fire department, and a dance pavilion.

By the end of the 1930s, the phrase "Out Wickenburg Way" was the city's official motto, succinctly expressing the optimism and opportunities available in what was soon called "The Dude Ranch Capital of the World."

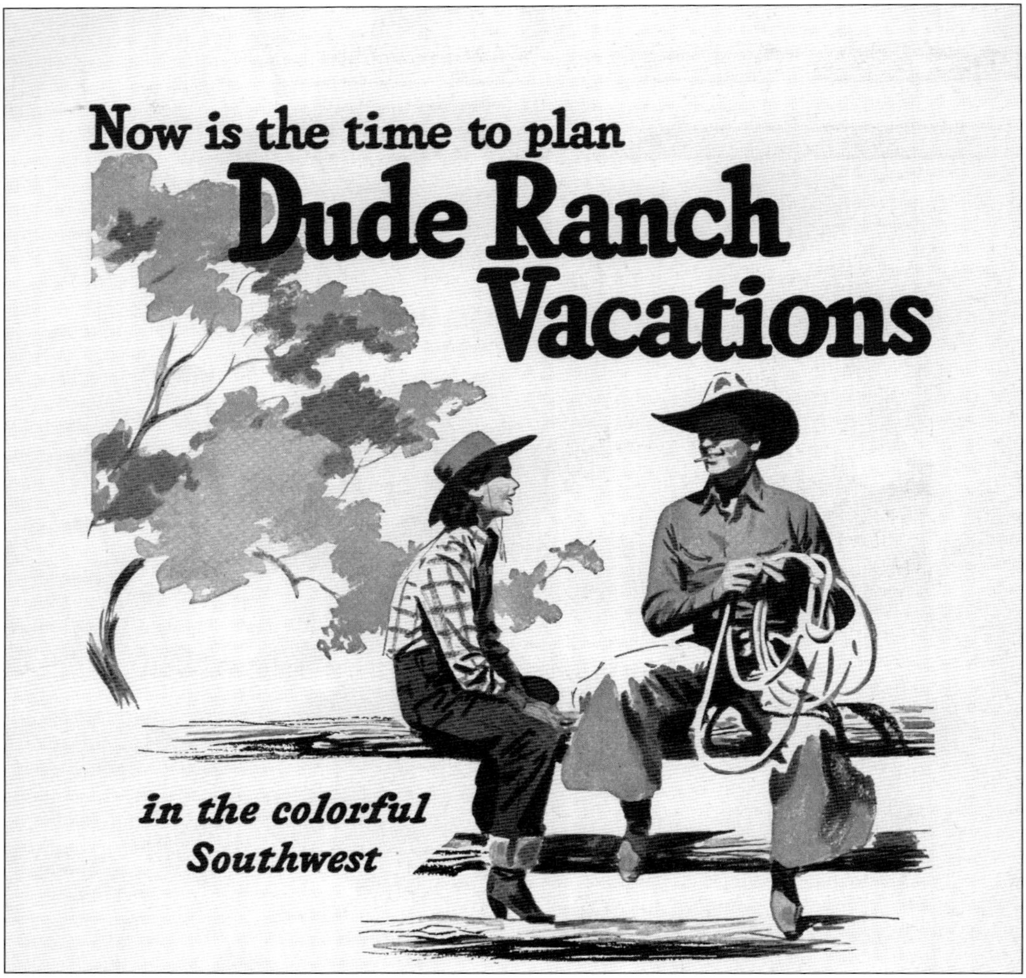

In the 1920s, the Santa Fe and Southern Pacific Railroads began printing up brochures and magazine advertisements about Western dude ranches designed to entice people into traveling out West (on the train, of course). These brochures emphasized everything that was unique or unusual about the West, with language designed to appeal to those back East. "Come to a house party on an old frontier ranch," ran the beginning of one brochure. Information on the climate, activities (including those for women and children), and clothing regularly appeared in these promotional items. "There is little style about a guest ranch and the atmosphere is essentially democratic," states a Southern Pacific brochure from around 1930. "Boots that you care much for should not be worn as they would be scratched in riding or hiking through the brush." This Santa Fe Railroad advertisement dates to the 1940s. (Collection of the author.)

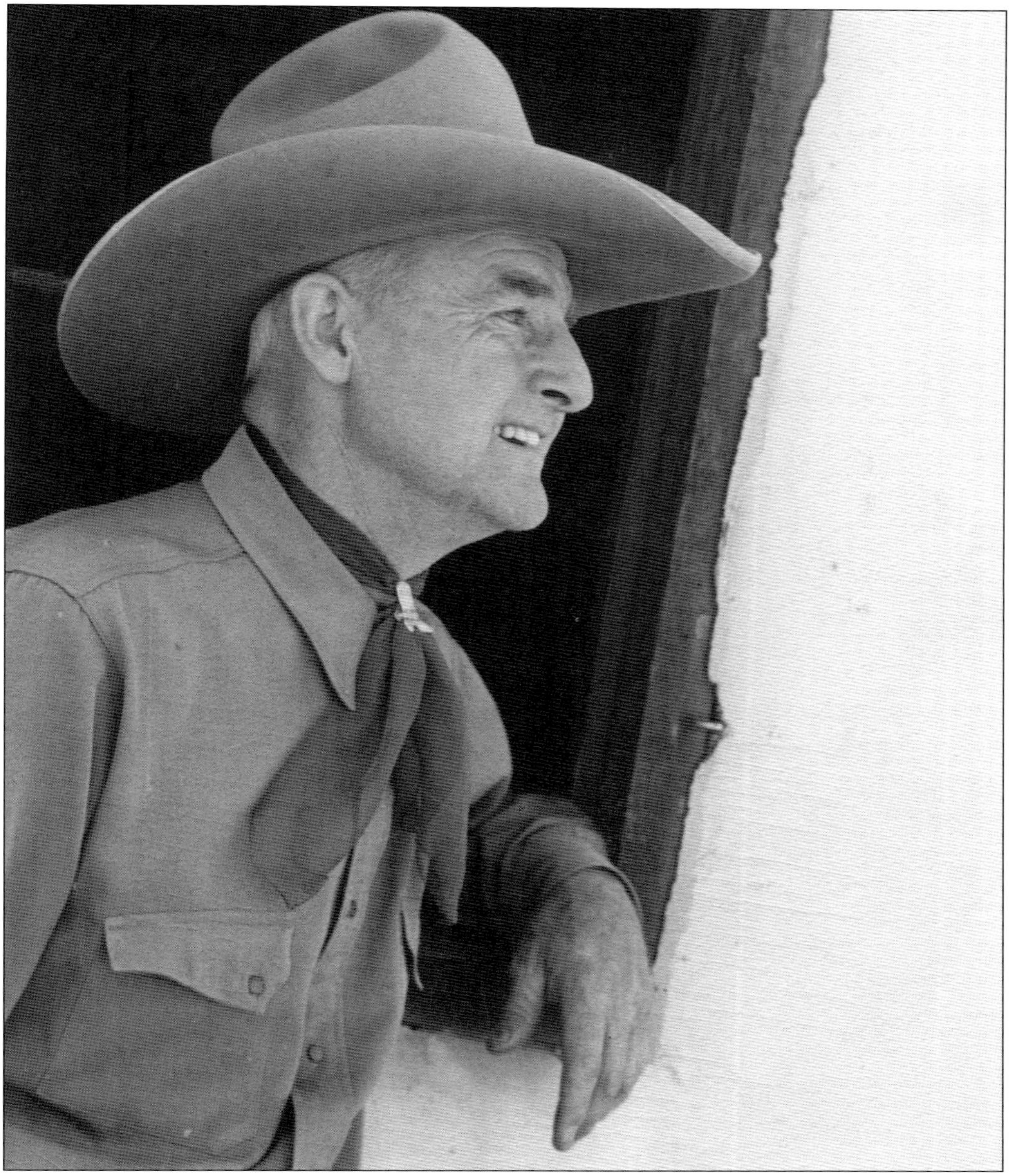

Romaine Lowdermilk was a Kansas-born ranch hand working in Prescott when he decided to homestead 160 acres on the Hassayampa River in 1908. He registered the Kay El Bar brand the following year and had constructed a ranch for himself and his widowed mother by 1910. He had literary and musical talent, writing a column for a Prescott newspaper, and had Western stories published by a variety of magazines. In 1914, he built four adobes, and in 1918, encouraged by visitors, he built another adobe and began to welcome guests. In 1922, he was a singer on a Phoenix radio station, and in 1926, he and Henry Warbasse developed the Kay El Bar as a guest ranch. Lowdermilk sold out to Warbasse in 1927, then worked as an entertainer and wrangler at the Arizona Biltmore and gained fame as a cowboy singer, along with running a number of other ranches in Arizona. Lowdermilk died in Phoenix in 1970. The Kay El Bar is still open today, "an authentic, historic guest ranch in the heart of the Wild West."

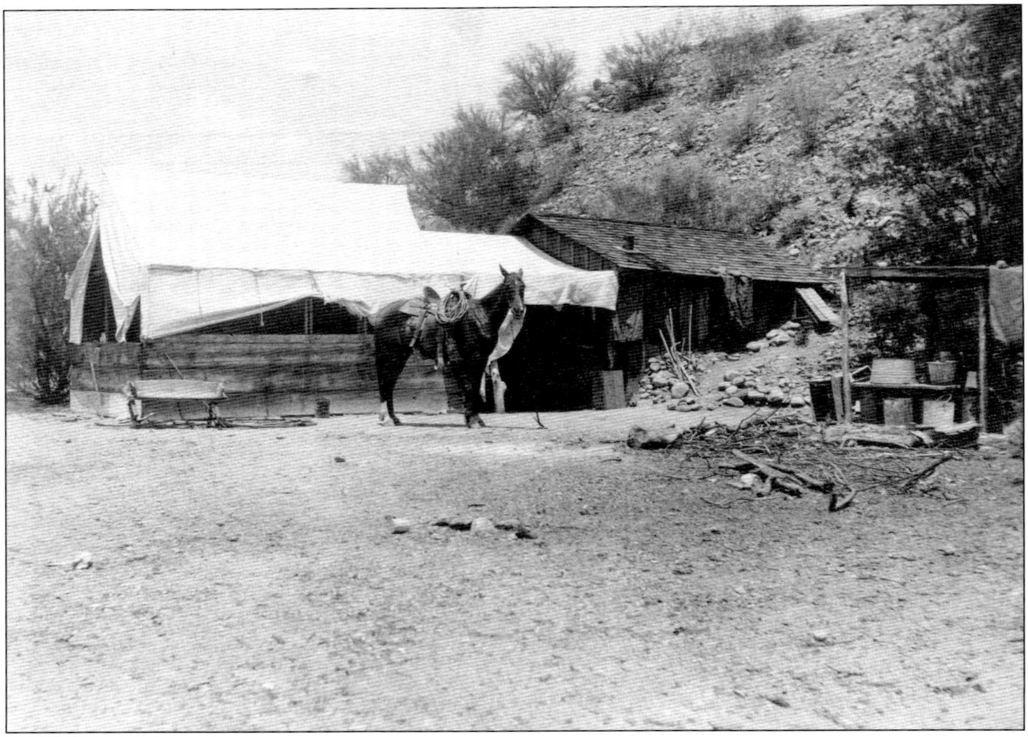

Some of the first buildings on the Kay El Bar were dug into a nearby hill. Early structures were used as toolsheds or places to shoe the horses.

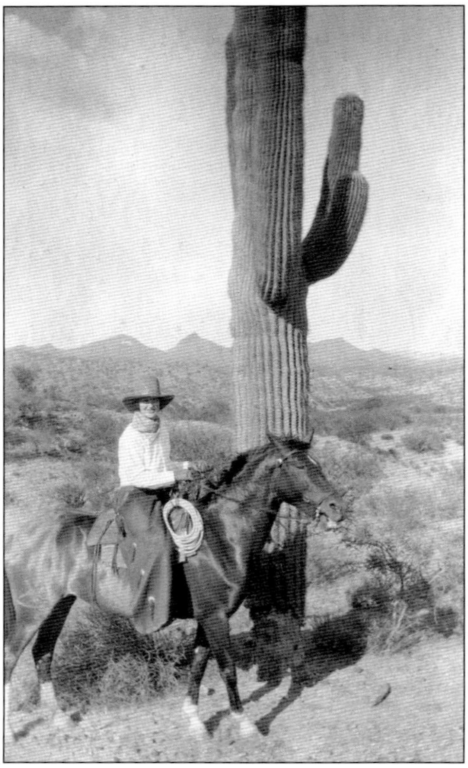

Women were encouraged to visit dude ranches. Although the only activity available at the Kay El Bar in the 1920s was horseback riding, going Western was a novelty for women used to riding English at stables back East. Images like this, in which a rider poses on a horse by a large saguaro cactus, were popular to send to friends back home.

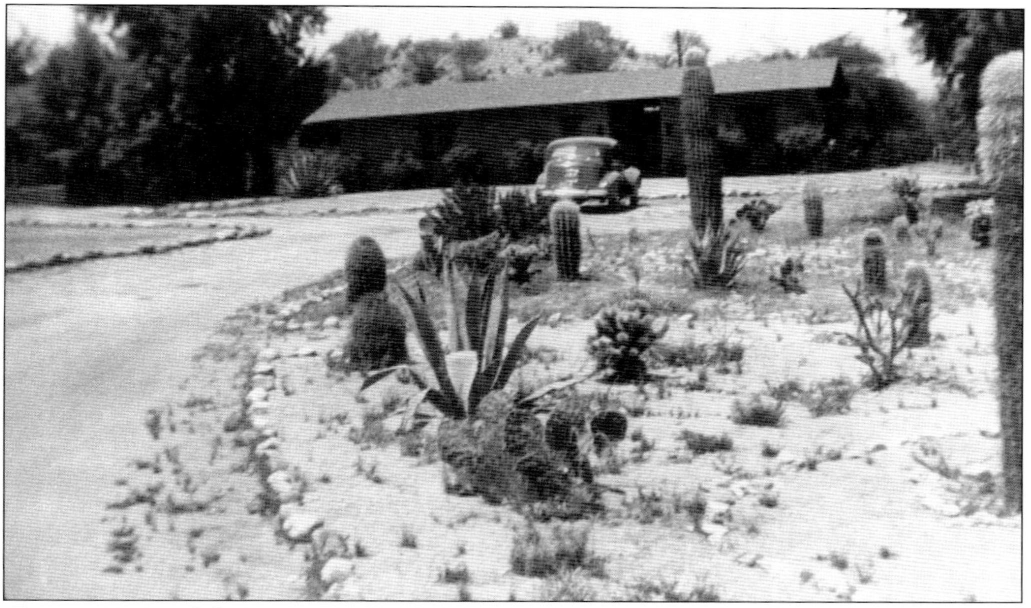

This 1938 view of the cactus garden at the Kay El Bar also shows the car kept at the ranch to transport visitors from the Santa Fe depot in Wickenburg. In 1941, movie star Nelson Eddy and his wife stayed at the Kay El Bar and were rumored to have attended the senior high school play in town that year.

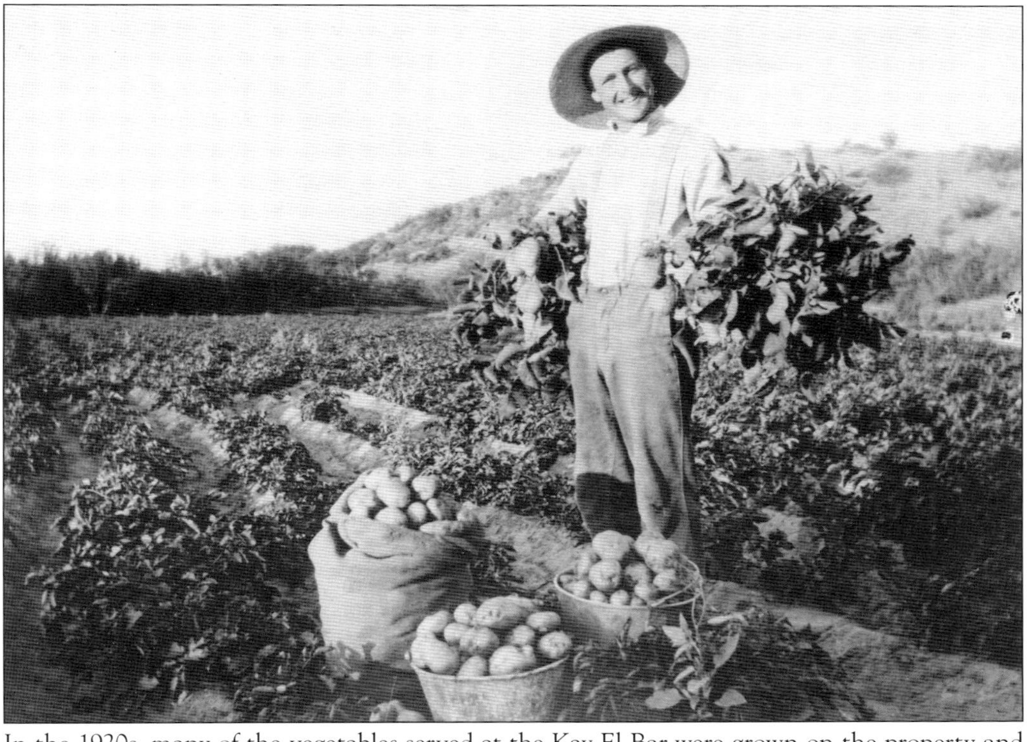

In the 1920s, many of the vegetables served at the Kay El Bar were grown on the property and harvested by staff members, such as this unidentified man.

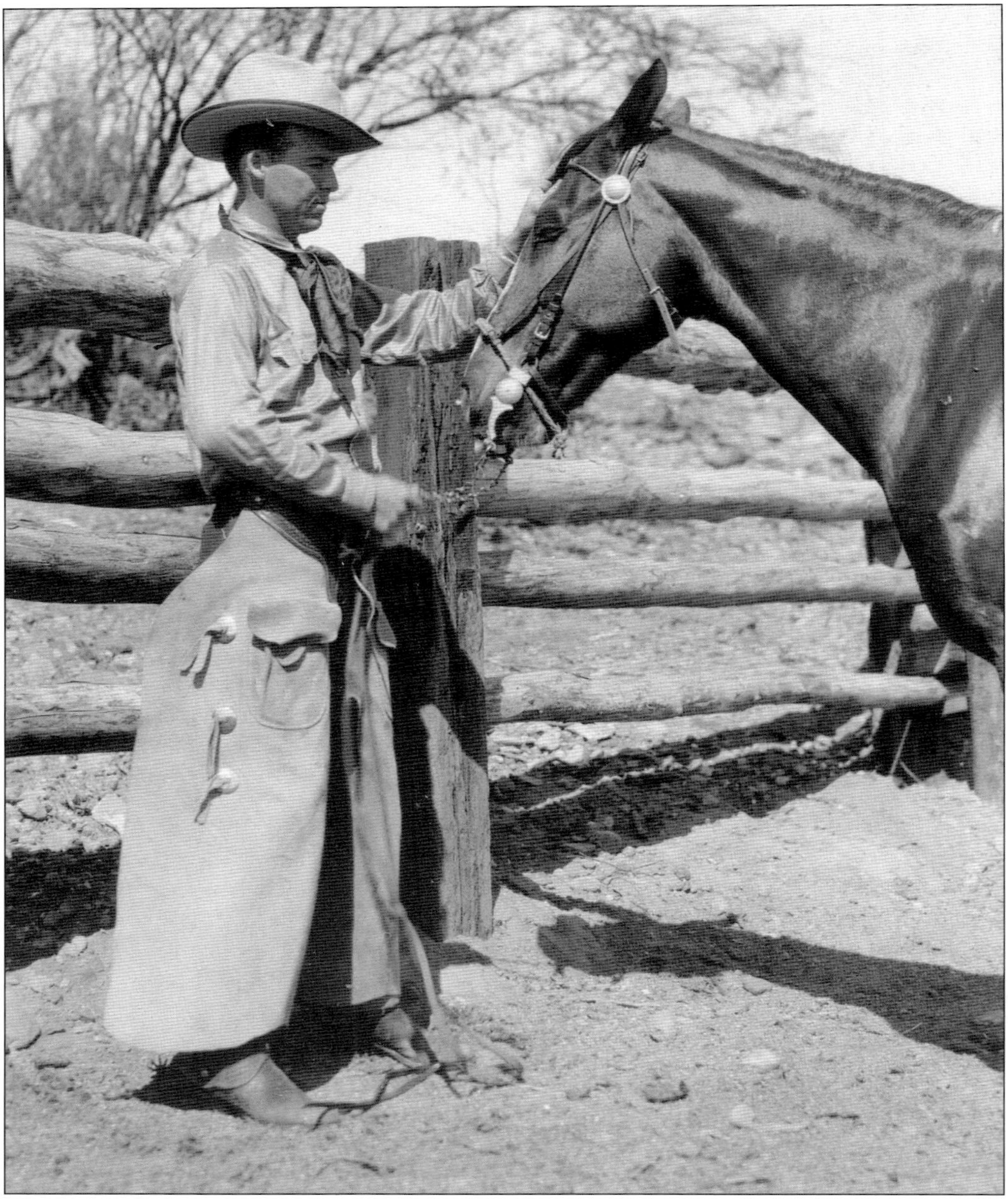

L.C. "Bob" White came to Prescott in 1919 to recover from tuberculosis, and when he was cured in 1922 he found his way to Wickenburg. There, he met Romaine Lowdermilk and agreed to help him run the Kay El Bar. In 1924, White also became the wrangler on the O'Brien ranch, where Leo Weaver was operating the Circle Flying W. After leaving to go to the University of Arizona in 1924, White came back in the summer and met Jack Burden. The two men leased the Circle Flying W and opened it as the Remuda Ranch; White then sold his interest one year later. In 1926, he leased 120 acres from Ignacio Garcia in order to open his own guest ranch. Monte Vista Ranch opened in November of that year, with White and his wife, Edith, as hosts. White, his brother John, and Romaine Lowdermilk entertained guests with Western songs. The Whites sold the ranch in 1940 and retired in 1946.

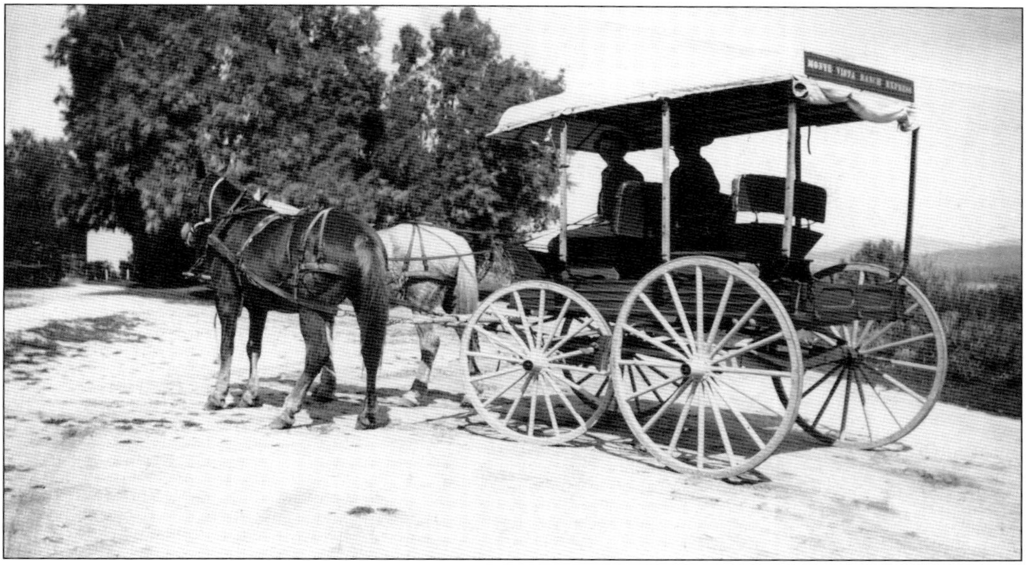

Before the Monte Vista Ranch had a Packard to transport guests, it had a surrey, shown here around 1928.

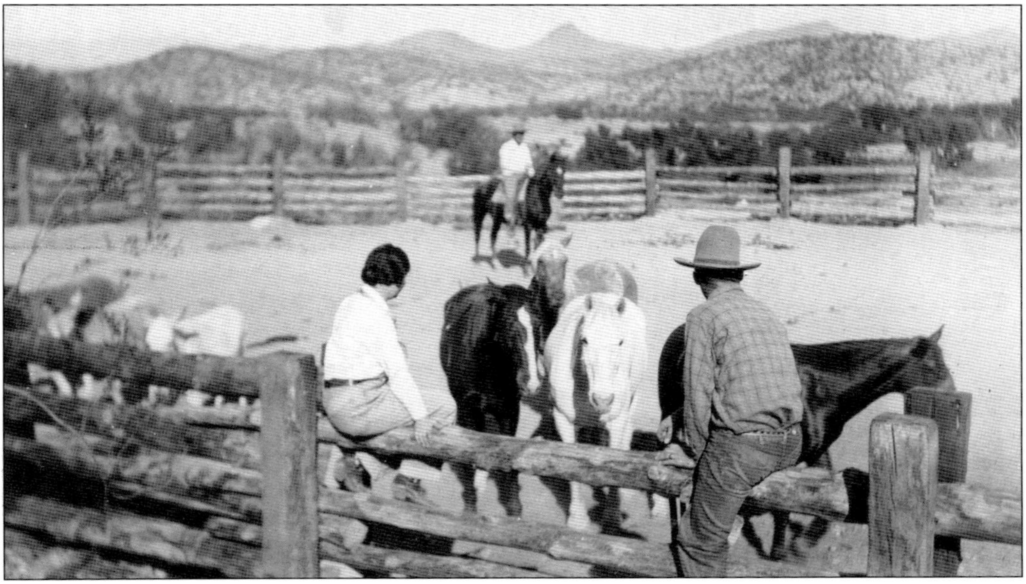

Monte Vista was also a working ranch, though guests could still enjoy horseback riding, rodeos, badminton, tennis, croquet, trap shooting, hunting, and sightseeing.

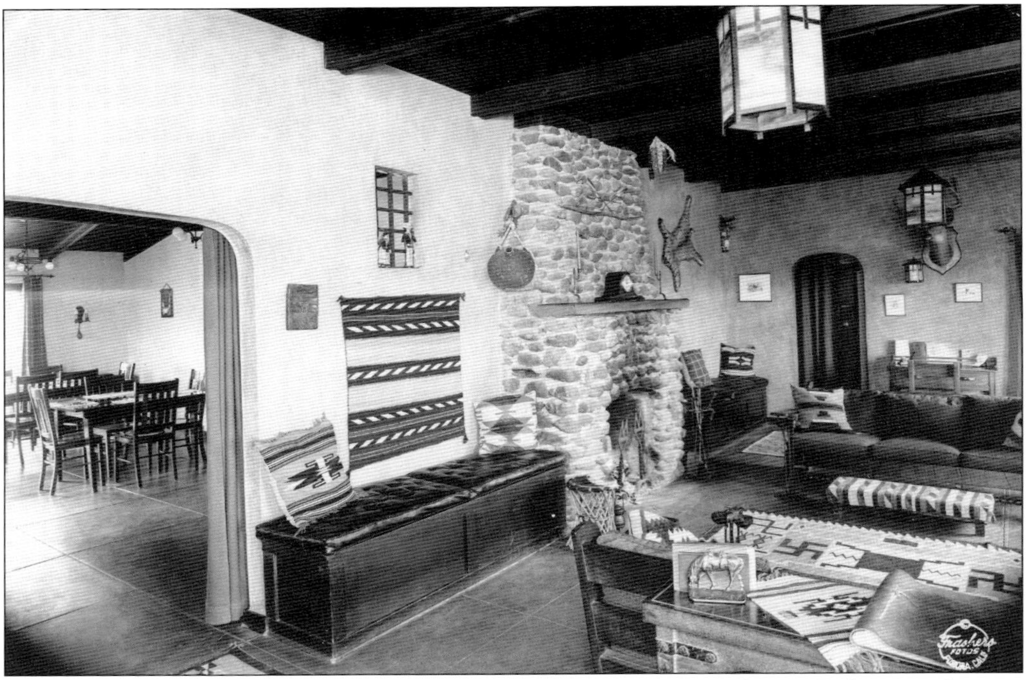

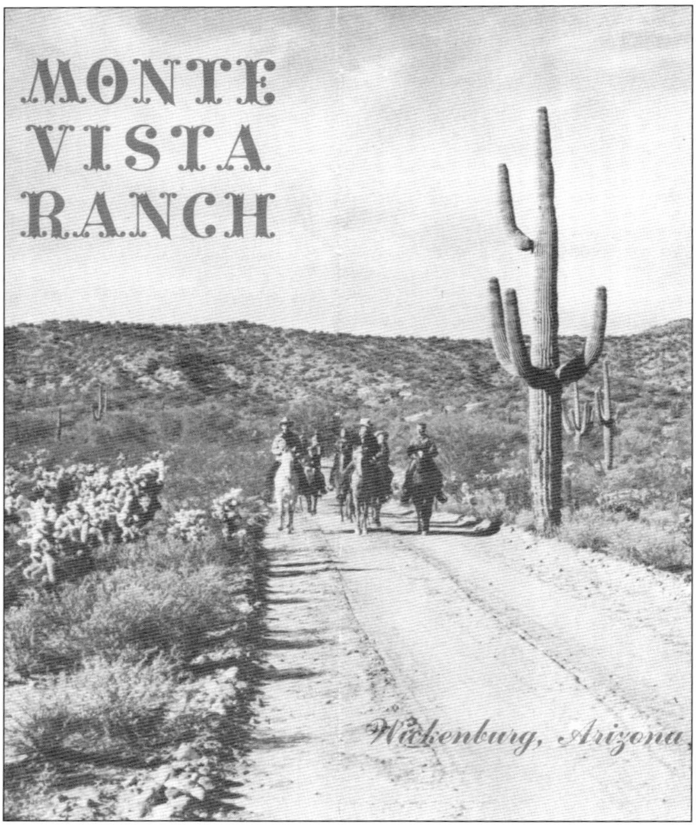

This 1927 photograph of the main lodge at the Monte Vista shows how local crafts and Southwest decor were considered part of the dude ranch experience. In the summer, when the ranch was closed because of the oppressive heat, the windows were covered with paper to eliminate glare and the Native American rugs were taken out for cleaning.

In 1949, the Monte Vista was sold to Carl and Verna Beilen. By the 1950s, guests could participate in ranch routines, including working and branding cattle. Each guest was assigned a horse and saddle to his or her liking for the duration of their stay. In 1963, Cook and Warren Pleister bought the Monte Vista, but it closed in 1965.

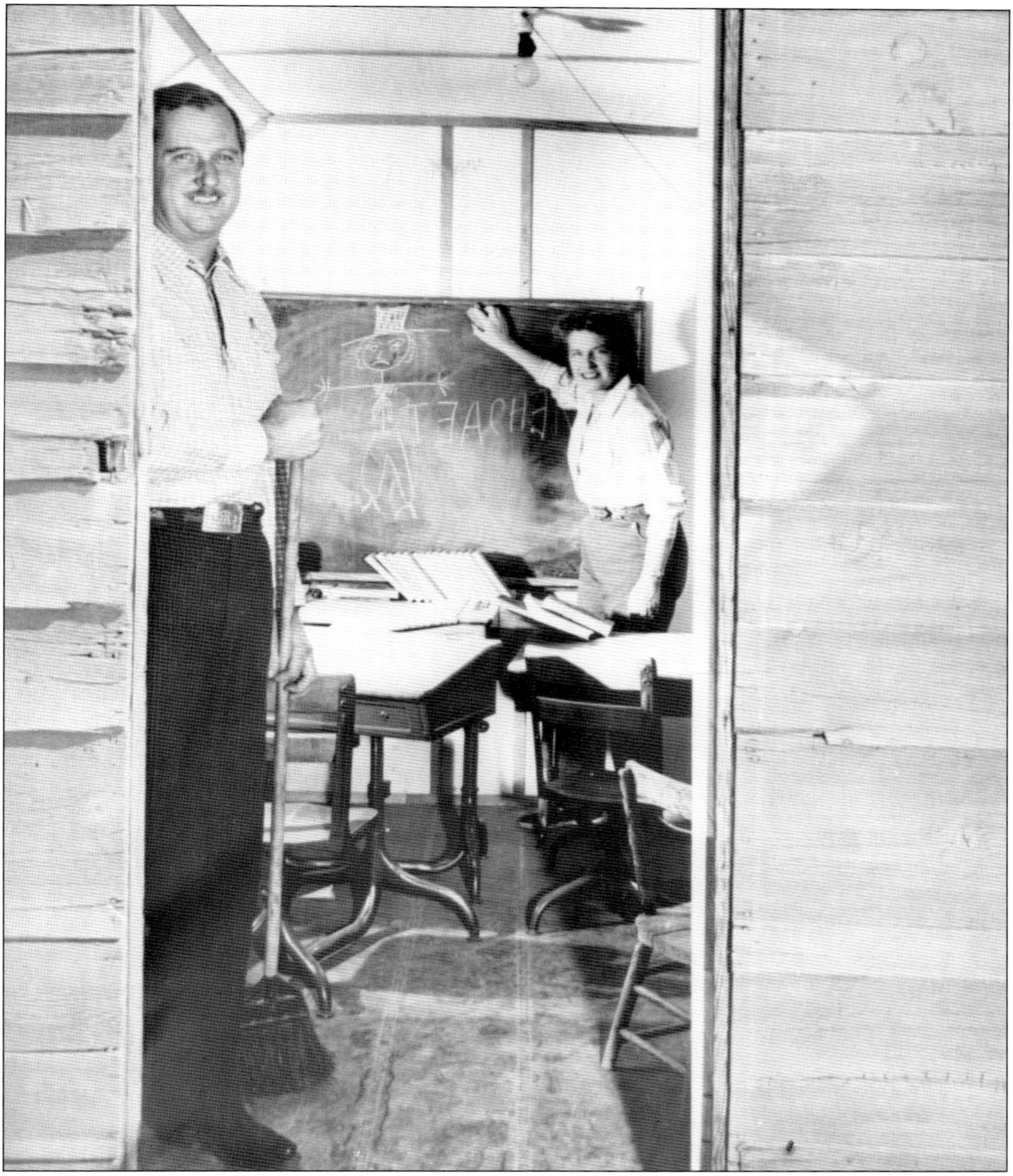

Jack Burden came to Arizona in 1925 for his health, as he was suffering from rheumatic fever. While in Wickenburg he met Bob White, and the two men decided to open a small guest ranch. They rented part of the Bar FX Ranch and named their enterprise Remuda, which is Spanish for a string of saddle horses. While visiting the Wickenburg Chamber of Commerce in Phoenix, Burden met the Fletcher family, including a young woman named Sophie. The two were married the following year and bought out White's share of Remuda (White went on to open the Monte Vista Ranch). Two years later, F.X. O'Brien's widow reclaimed the property, and the Burdens opened the Remuda Ranch at a new location near the Hassayampa in December 1928. Here, Here, Pete and Billie Fletcher – the brother and sister-in-law of Sophie Burden – pose in the ranch's schoolroom, originally built in 1932 for the Burden children, and the children of visitors who stayed at the ranch for an entire season. Jack Burden died in 1943. Sophie Burden ran the ranch until it was sold in 1968; she passed away in 1996.

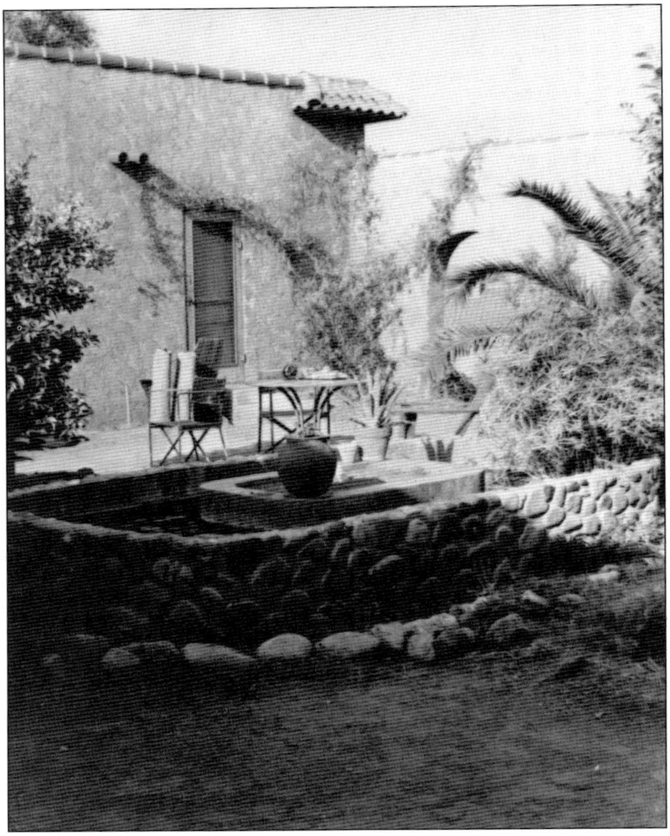

The Burdens gave the new Remuda Ranch all of the appeal that the Southwest could offer, and this extended to the architecture and grounds. Jack Burden incorporated the Remuda Ranch Rodeo Association to stage the popular "Out Wickenburg Way" annual rodeo, which drew people from all over the United States between 1930 and World War II. Celebrities such as actors Robert Mitchum and Joel McCrea and author Erle Stanley Gardner enjoyed the ranch's authentic ambience.

In this 1931 photograph, Jack Burden (second from right) poses with the ranch's Ford station wagon—the first one seen in Arizona. It was first used to explore the area and eventually hauled supplies for the ranch.

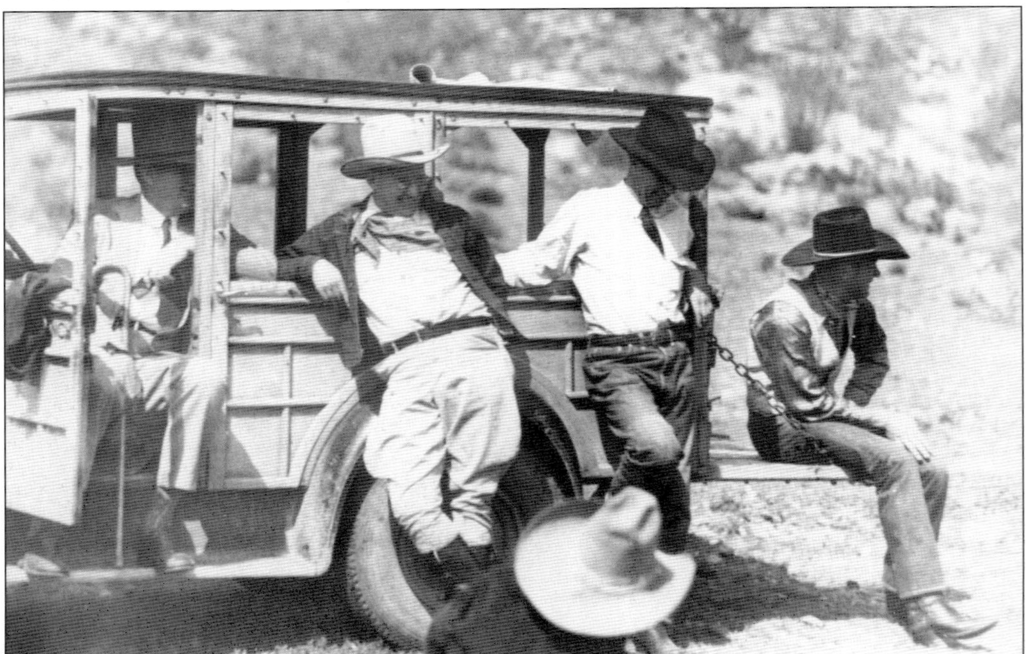

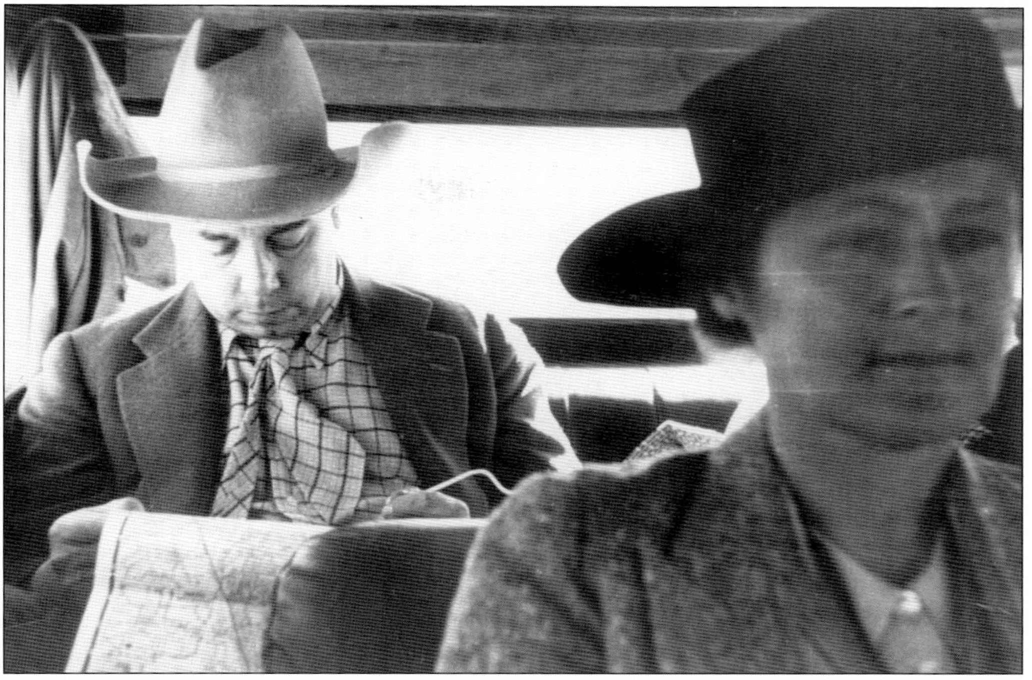

British author J.B. Priestley and his family spent the winter of 1935–1936 at the Remuda Ranch, where the Burdens built him a one-room writing studio outfitted with a wood stove. Dubbed the "Priestley Palace," the author used the studio to write novels and a memoir of his Western experience called *Midnight on the Desert*. Priestley also dedicated the expanded children's schoolroom. He is pictured here with his wife, Jane.

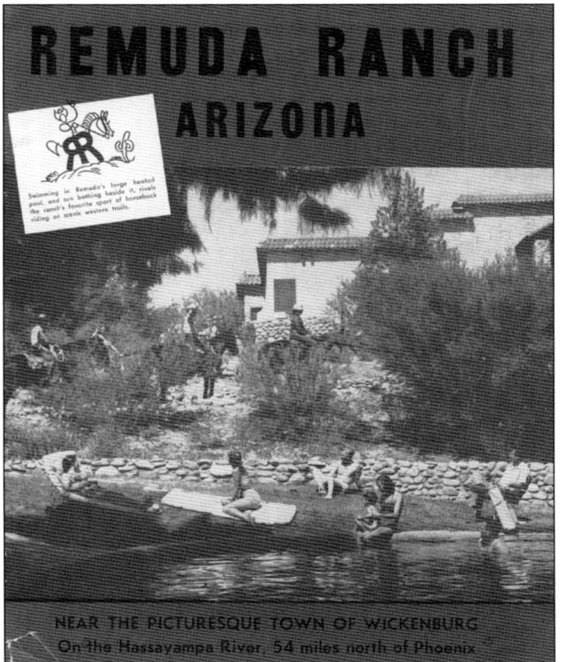

In the 1950s and 1960s, Remuda guests could enjoy a variety of activities, and when they left for home, a cannon was fired as they headed down to the highway. Other members of the Burden family helped run the ranch, and in 1964, the governor of Arizona honored Sophie Burden as the "Dean of Arizona Guest Ranch Women." Sophie was also honored by the Arizona Hotel and Motel Association (cofounded by Jack Burden) as the "First Lady of Arizona Innkeepers," and November 7, 1964, was declared "Sophie Burden Day" in Wickenburg. The ranch was sold in 1969 and went through a number of owners. In 1990, the Remuda Ranch reopened as a treatment center for eating disorders.

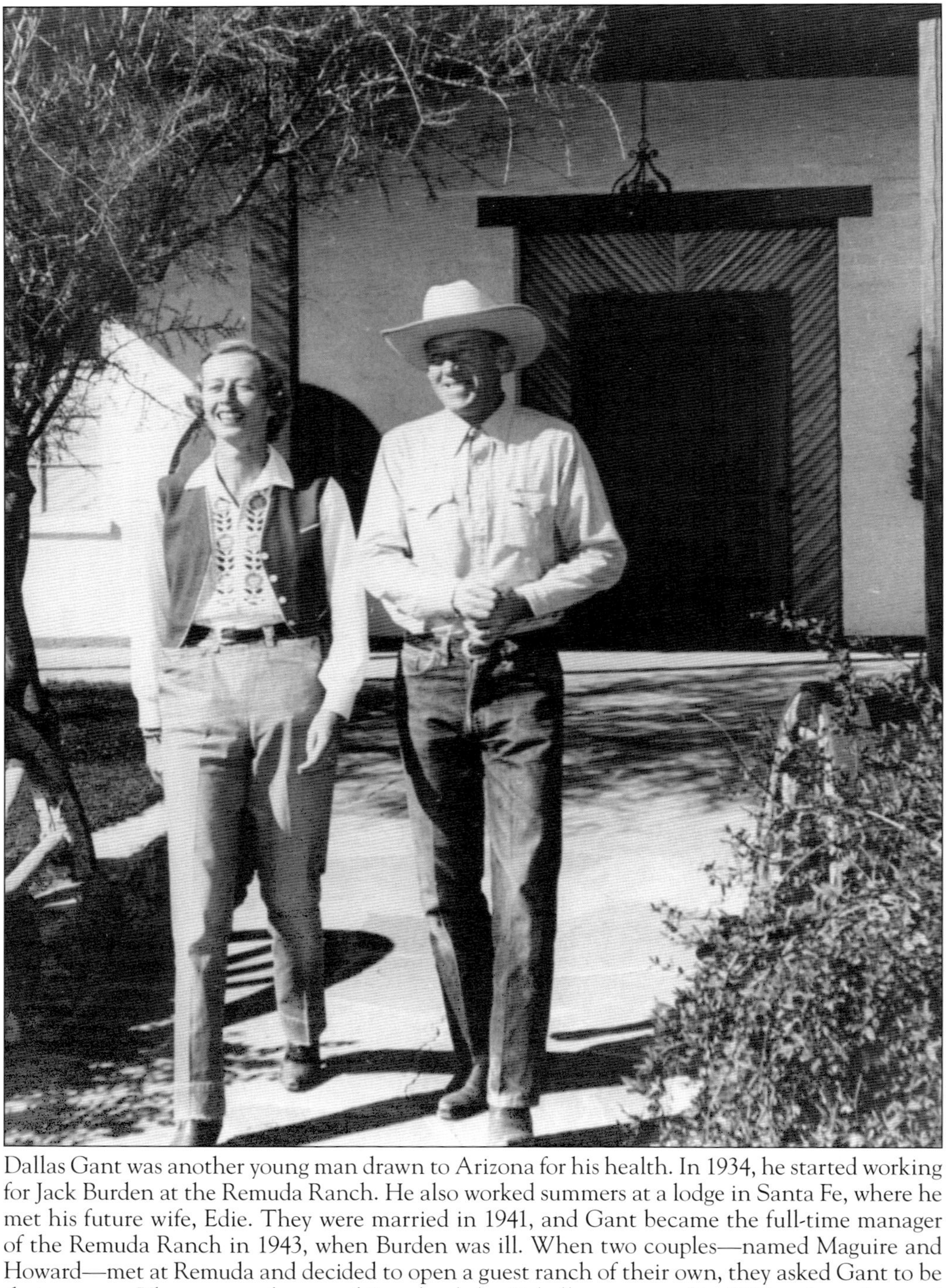

Dallas Gant was another young man drawn to Arizona for his health. In 1934, he started working for Jack Burden at the Remuda Ranch. He also worked summers at a lodge in Santa Fe, where he met his future wife, Edie. They were married in 1941, and Gant became the full-time manager of the Remuda Ranch in 1943, when Burden was ill. When two couples—named Maguire and Howard—met at Remuda and decided to open a guest ranch of their own, they asked Gant to be their partner. The new ranch, named Rancho de los Caballeros, opened in 1948 and was designed to offer resort-like amenities to its visitors. A few years later, "Los Cab" began a cattle business and registered the Sun C brand. Dallas Gant died suddenly in 1967, and Edie passed away in 2005. Los Cab still welcomes guests today.

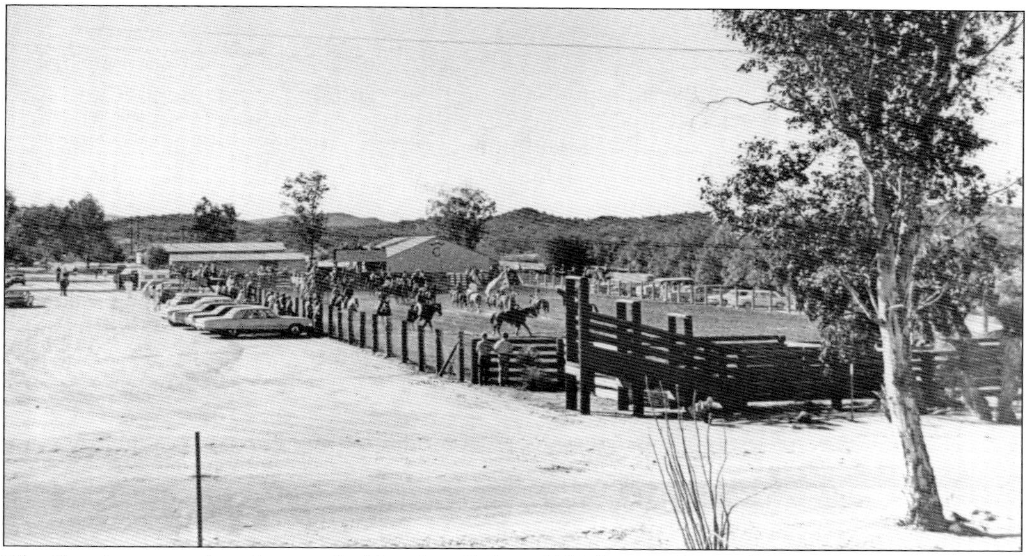

The first inter-ranch rodeo was held at Los Cab in 1951 for members of the Desert Sun Ranchers Association. A trick rider from Gene Autry's rodeo show performed for the crowd, and members of the Wickenburg Saddle Club sold "wickenburgers" and cowboy coffee from their chuck wagon.

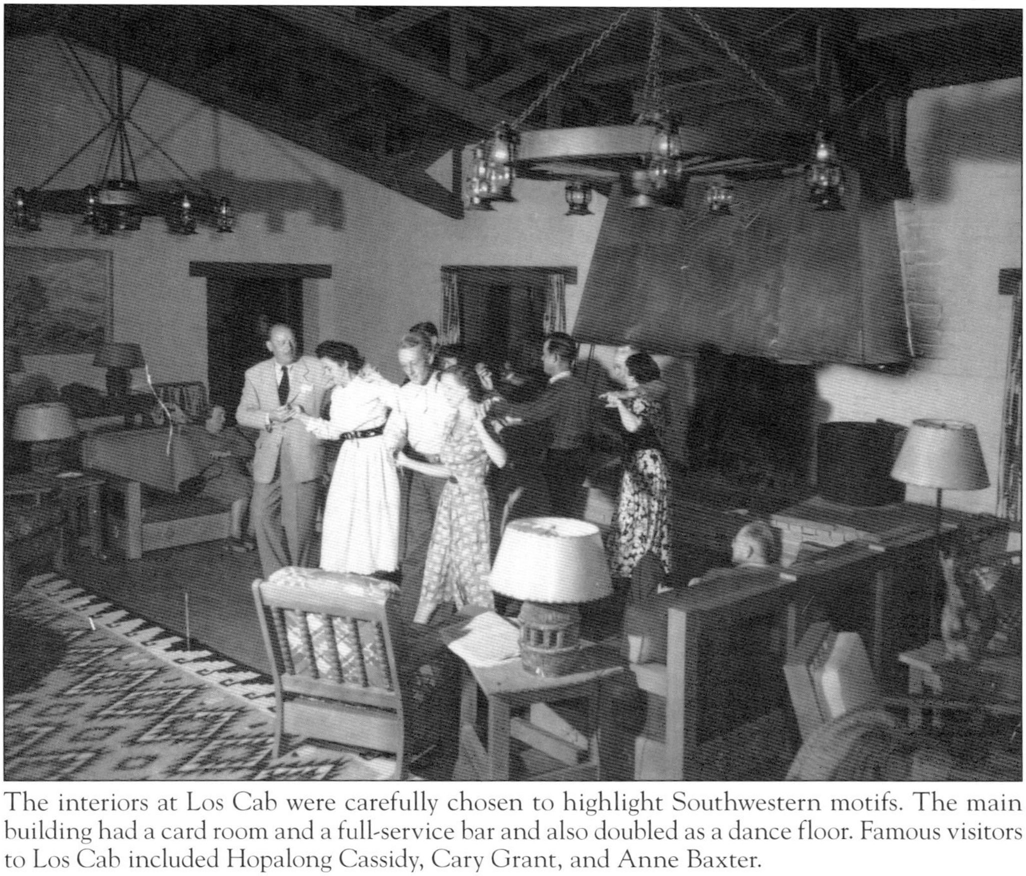

The interiors at Los Cab were carefully chosen to highlight Southwestern motifs. The main building had a card room and a full-service bar and also doubled as a dance floor. Famous visitors to Los Cab included Hopalong Cassidy, Cary Grant, and Anne Baxter.

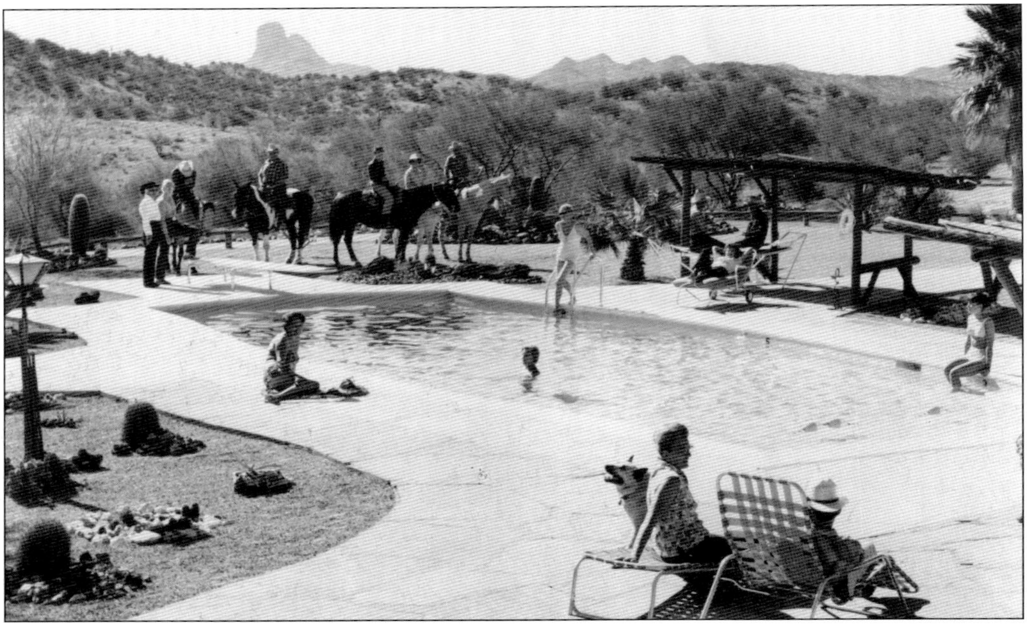

With Vulture Peak as a backdrop, guests at Los Cab could enjoy activities ranging from swimming to horseback riding, often in the same place. Members of the Desert Sun Ranchers often came for dances. During one memorable year, visitors wore silly hats and competed for prizes. After dinner and a visit to the bar, a Los Cab guest led participants in a conga line that took people straight into the pool.

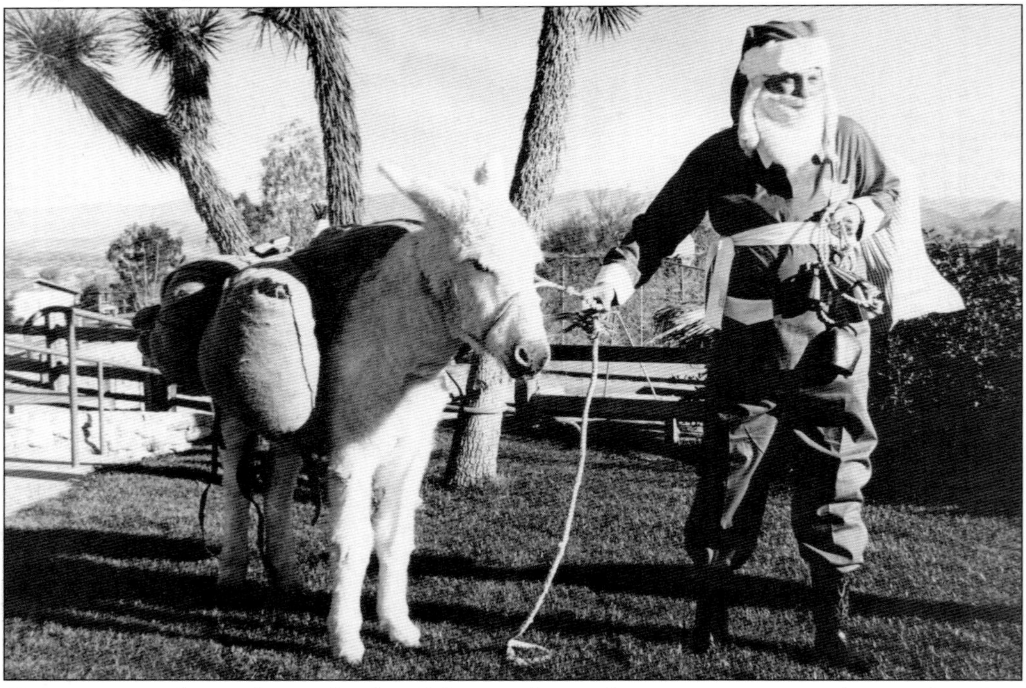

Christmas was always observed at Los Cab, complete with tree trimming, caroling, and cowboy boot stockings hung on the living room's copper fireplace.

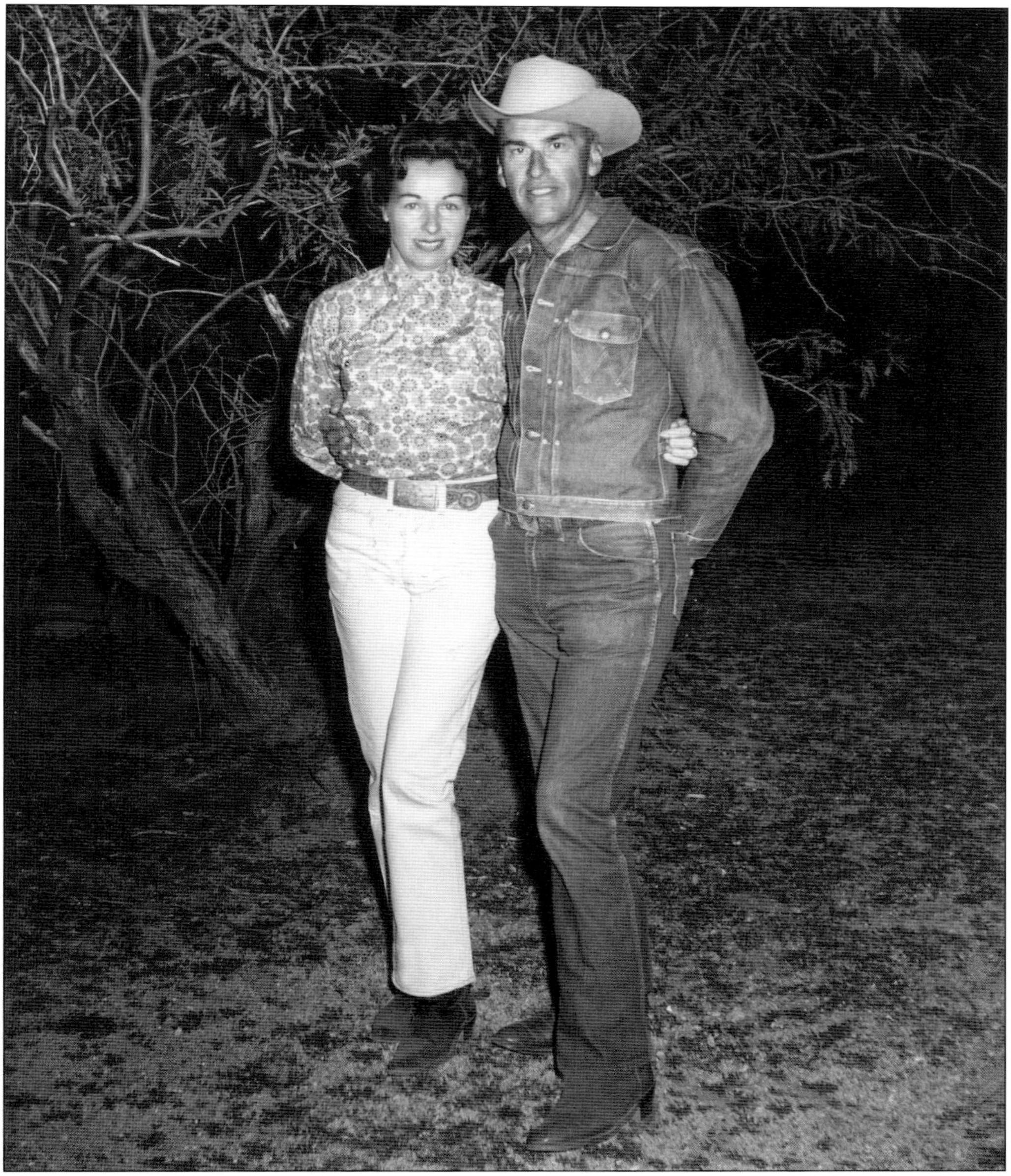

Bellflower, California, residents George and Vi Wellik first saw the Flying E Ranch from the air in April 1949 while on their way to a Texas guest ranch. After flipping a coin, they decided to try the Flying E instead. Lee Eyerly established the Flying E in 1946 as a cattle ranch and opened the ranch to guests in 1947. The Welliks came back frequently, investing money to build a pool and new guest quarters. By 1960, they owned the Flying E. One of the most popular traditions started by Vi Wellik was the process of "britches branding," which involved painting the Flying E brand on the backside of a guest's jeans or other "britches." In 1969, George gave 100 acres of private land to Wickenburg for a municipal airport and Vi gave 40 acres to create a town park. George Wellik died in 1983, and Vi continued to be a generous local philanthropist until her death in 2004. Today, the Flying E continues to thrive as "The Riding Ranch," in addition to being a working cattle ranch. (Courtesy Steve and Andrea Taylor, Flying E Ranch.)

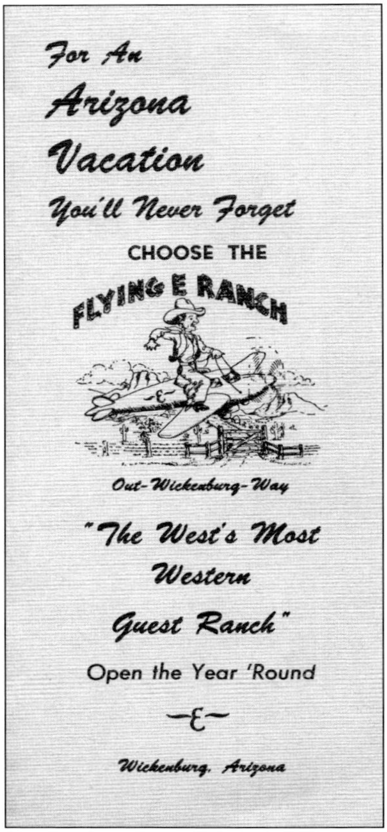

This early brochure shows the Flying E's original logo reflecting George Wellik's interest in aviation and skills as a pilot. Later, more Western themes were incorporated into promotional materials, reflecting both the traditional and innovative activities held at the Flying E. One of these was the "dudeo," created by famous rodeo star and ranch wrangler Everett Bowman. Guests played games on horseback, and cowboys exhibited their rodeo skills; Bowman came up with "dudeo" to distinguish the event from a real rodeo. (Courtesy Steve and Andrea Taylor, Flying E Ranch.)

The Flying E acquired an original 1870s stagecoach in the late 1940s, and by the early 1960s, it brought guests into town to go shopping. One of the coach's drivers was Everett Bowman, the Flying E's famous rodeo champion and popular wrangler. For a time, the coach was used as a school bus. Today, the stagecoach is on display at the Desert Caballeros Western Museum in downtown Wickenburg. (Courtesy Steve and Andrea Taylor, Flying E Ranch.)

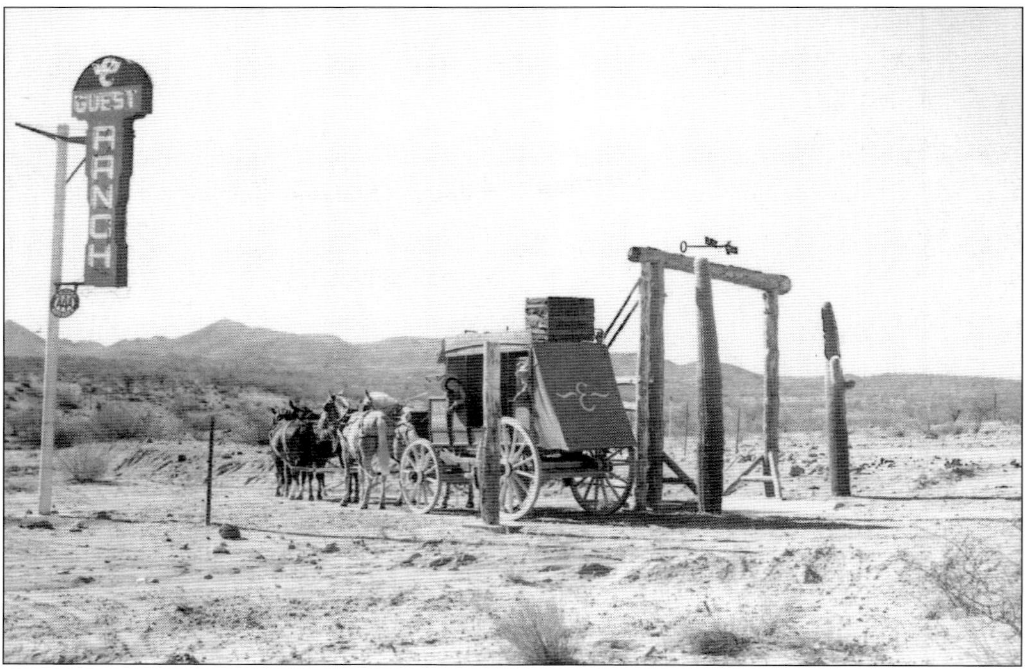

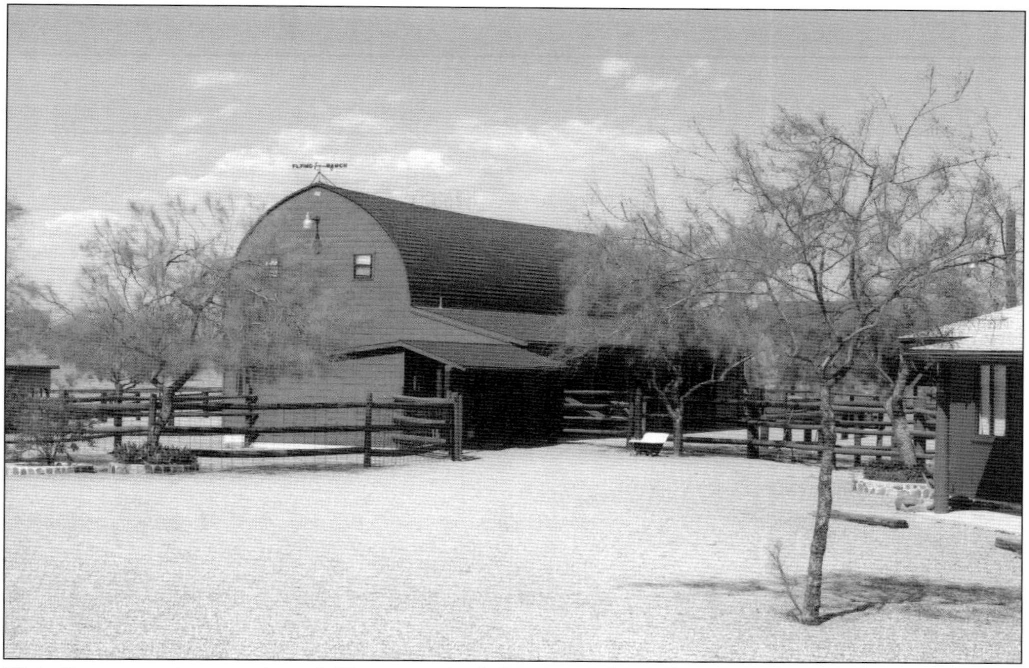

This Oregon-style, round-roofed barn was built by original ranch owner Lee Eyerly, who was from Salem. It is one of the iconic images of the Flying E. The interior of the roof is vaulted polished wood, and the hayloft, outfitted as a dance floor, was a venue for popular public dances for many years. The barn was refurbished in 1985 and is still used today for square dancing, line dancing, and group activities. (Courtesy Steve and Andrea Taylor, Flying E Ranch.)

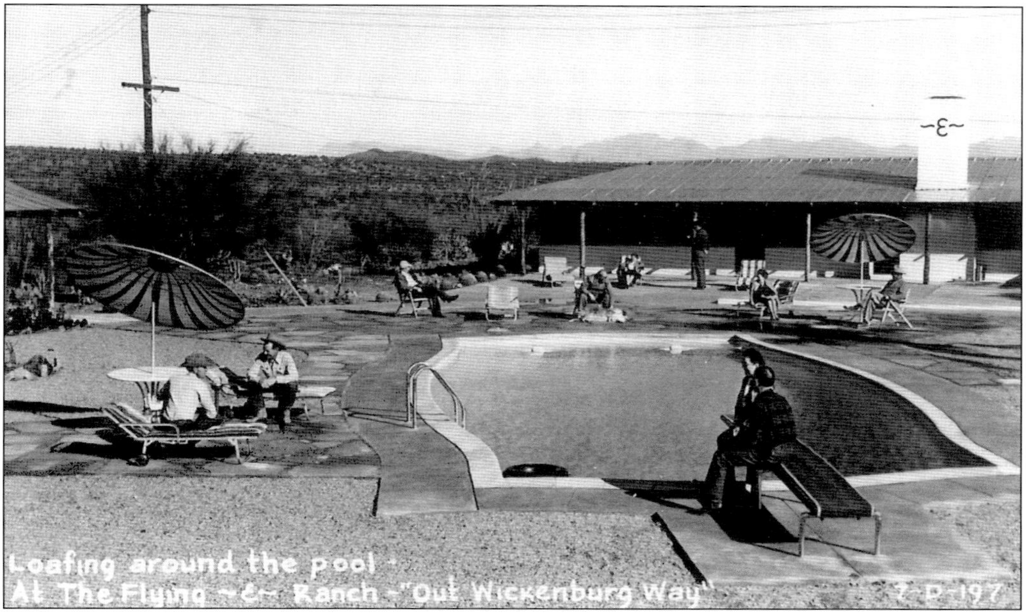

The pool, shown here in a postcard from the 1960s, is still a focal point at the Flying E. Both the pool area and the winding drive from the highway to the ranch offer spectacular views of Vulture Peak.

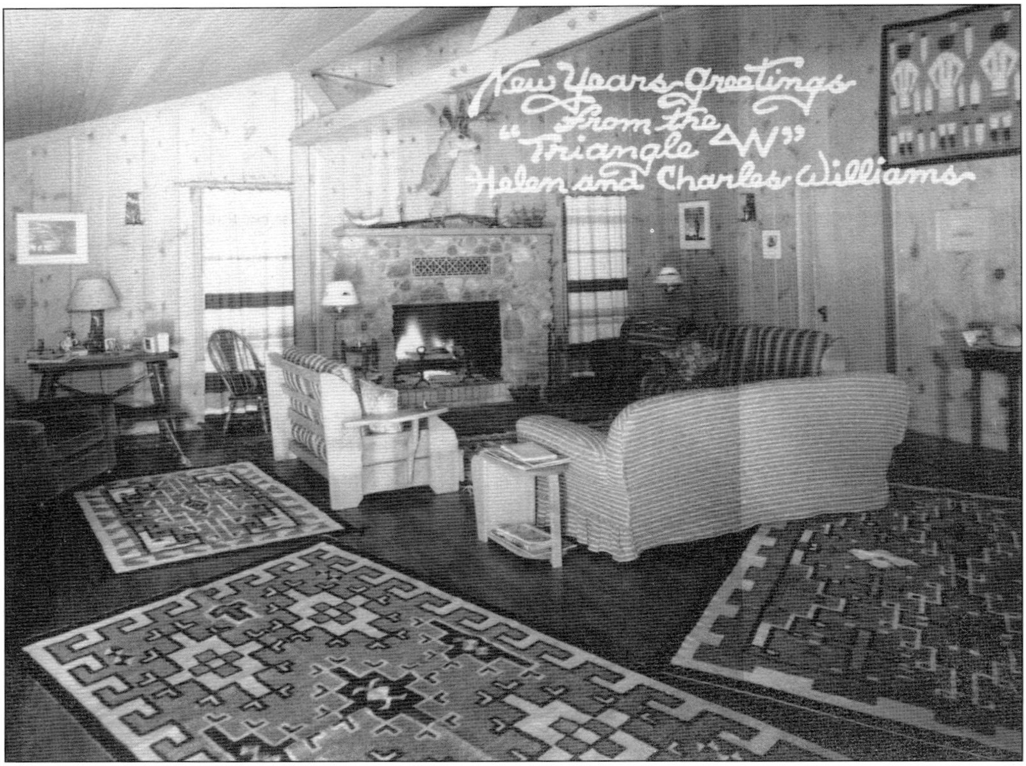

The property that became the Triangle W was a working cattle and guest ranch that went through a variety of names and owners in the 1920s and 1930s. Charles D. Williams purchased the property in 1939 and renamed it the Triangle W. It remained a cattle ranch even as it continued to take in guests, and many visitors came for their health as well as for the western activities. Famous visitors included baseball agent Christy Walsh and actress Irene Dunne. It was sold a few more times between the 1940s and 1950s and is now an outpatient facility for the Remuda Ranch.

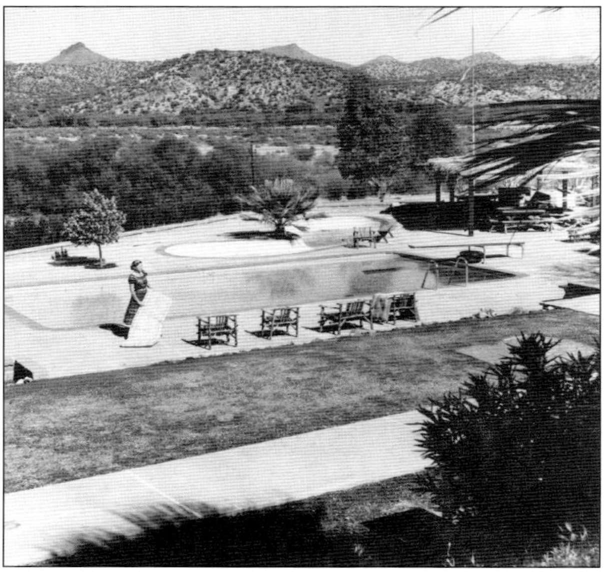

The Slash Bar K brand was registered in 1946 by Don and Margie Kerr of Chicago when they purchased the property from previous owners Vernon and Lena Knight. The Kerrs started a guest ranch, expanding the existing building and later adding a pool, a herd of horses and other livestock, and facilities for activities like shuffleboard and target shooting. William Bendix and Alan Ladd were some celebrity guests of the Slash Bar K. The property changed hands a number of times into the 1960s and 1970s, and part of the old ranch is now a rehabilitation center called The Meadows.

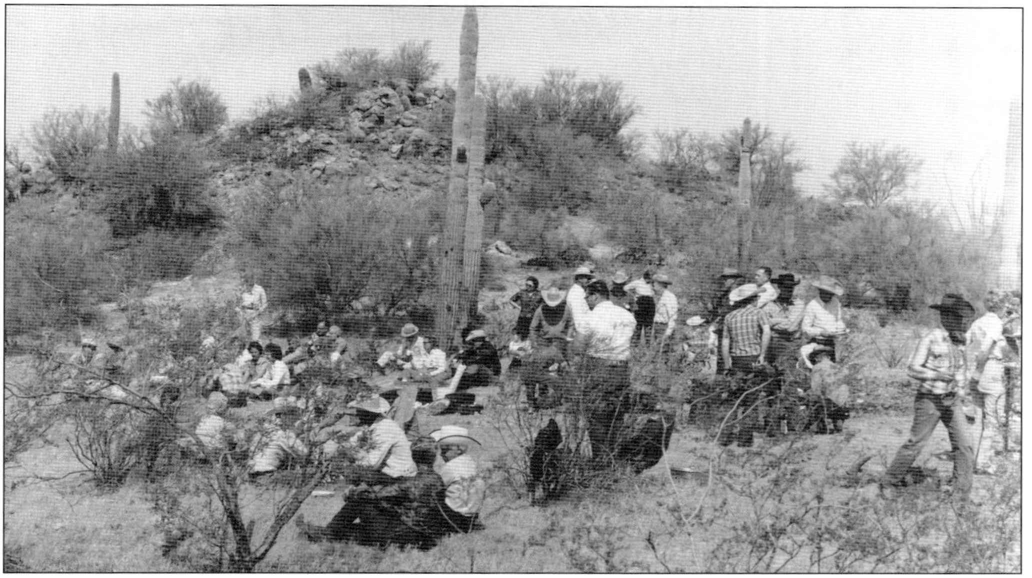

Food has always been a big part of the dude ranch experience. The outdoor cookout and breakfast ride—still featured at some ranches—introduced many visitors to authentic Western cuisine. Guests who had only seen a chuck wagon on television or in the movies were charmed by its appearance on these outdoor excursions. The Flying E published its own cookbook in 1998 and compilations of dude ranch recipes can be found on bookstore and museum gift shop shelves throughout Wickenburg.

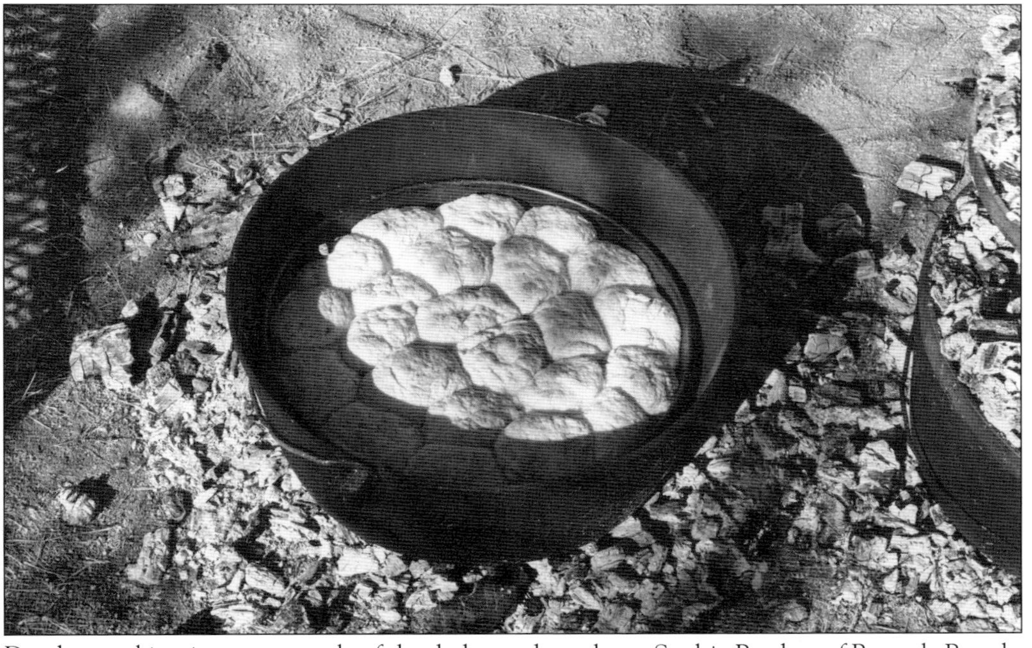

Dutch oven biscuits were a staple of the dude ranch cookout. Sophie Burden, of Remuda Ranch, was especially renowned for her biscuits, which she started making with beer when a guest drank all the milk she had planned to use in the recipe. One year, she won first prize for her biscuits at the Arizona State Fair.

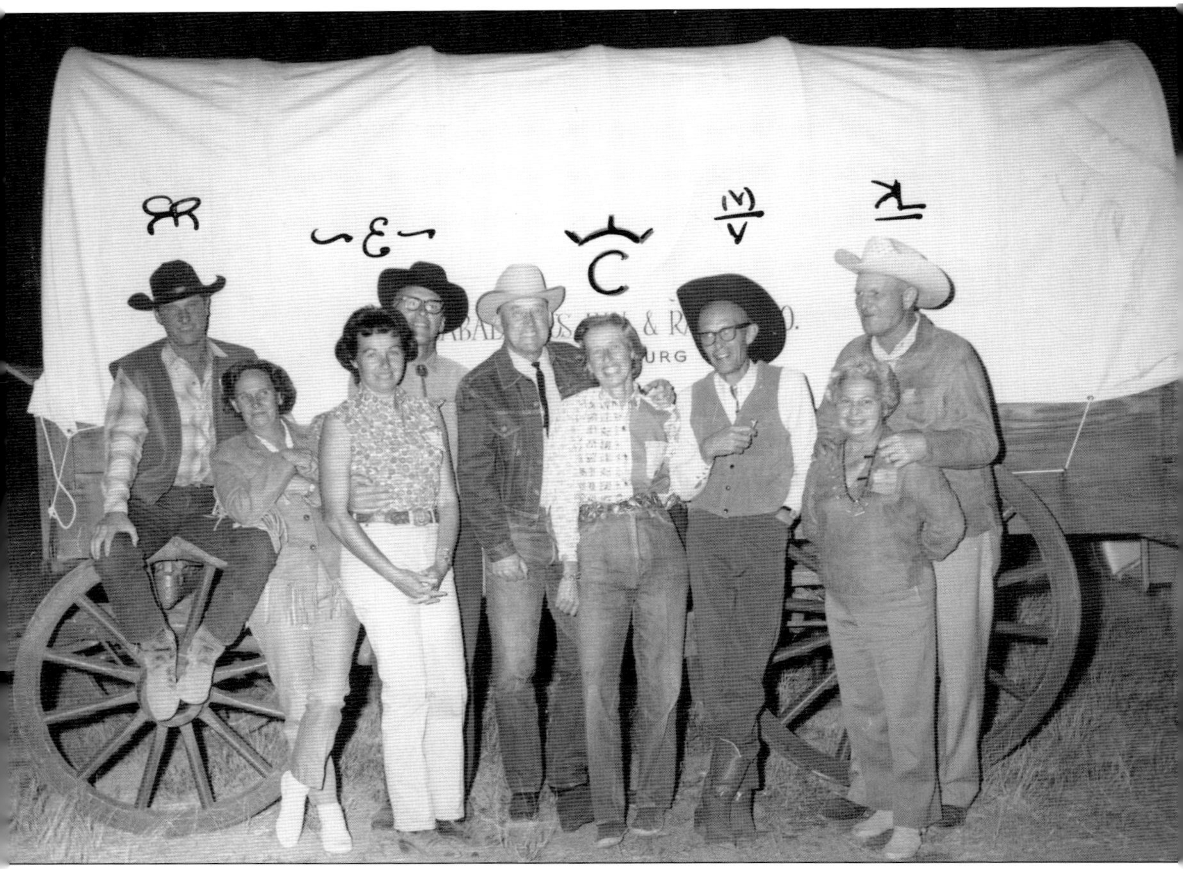

In the early 1960s, a few members of Wickenburg's "dude ranch royalty" posed for this group photograph. Pictured here are, left to right, Pete Fletcher and Sophie Burden (Remuda), George and Vi Wellik (Flying E), Dallas and Edie Gant (Rancho de los Caballeros), Warren Pleister (Monte Vista), and a Mr. and Mrs. Rogers. (Courtesy Steve and Andrea Taylor, Flying E Ranch.)

Eight

Riding into the Sunset

As the United States entered World War II, guest ranches and mining continued to provide income for the people of Wickenburg. However, the closure of western mines that were not contributing to the war effort removed some jobs, and many workers left town (though some remained to work the area on their own). The void left by the demise of organized mining changed the city's character, but the postwar years brought a new kind of prosperity.

Americans were hitting the road, taking advantage of highway improvements and affordable cars. More people passing through town on US 89 and US 60 meant a need for more restaurants, stores, gas stations, and Western clothing stores. Within a few years, Wickenburg had a new town hall, library building, and a bank. Newly opened dude ranches shared the tourism business with motels and auto courts.

The Wickenburg Chamber of Commerce worked diligently to make Wickenburg appealing to a variety of tourists. The Desert Caballeros ride, inaugurated as a point-to-point five-day trek across 100 miles of desert and mountains, is still going strong. "Gold Rush Days" continues to bring people to town.

The name "Wickenburg" became code for "classic Western town" and was often used as a plot point in television shows. In 1958, the series *Have Gun–Will Travel* aired an episode entitled "The Road to Wickenburg," written by future *Star Trek* creator Gene Roddenberry, and *Alias Smith and Jones* featured an "Exit From Wickenburg" episode in 1971.

In the early 1950s, a group of history-minded citizens—many of whom participated in the creation of the Desert Caballeros Ride—began to lobby for the creation of a town museum. The result was the Desert Caballeros Western Museum, which opened its doors in 1969.

But prosperity could not last forever. Interest in the old West dwindled as the world moved past the 1960s and into the "Me Decade" of the 1970s. Dude ranches closed, people moved away, and it seemed that the past was no longer able to fuel interest in the town on the Hassayampa.

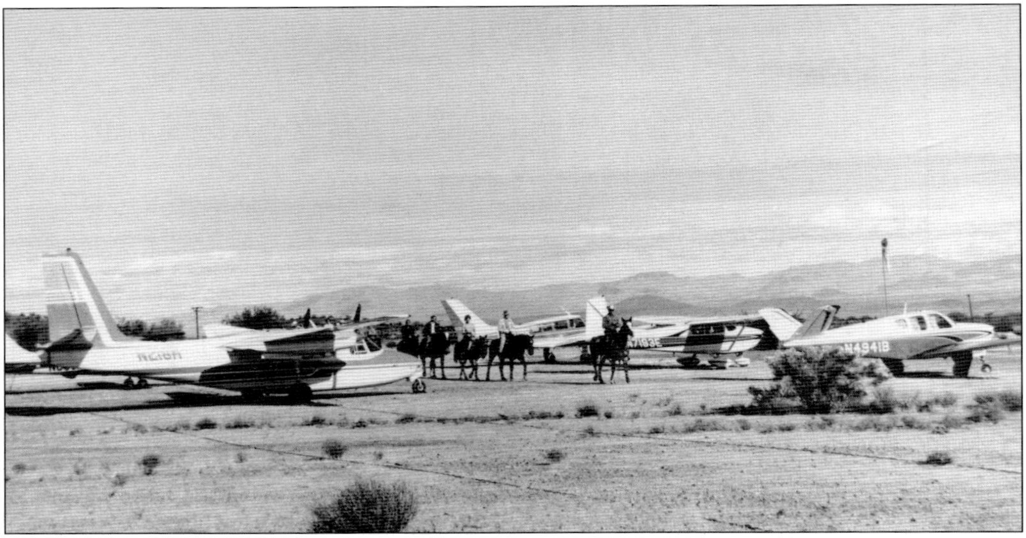

Wickenburg has had an airfield since the 1940s. In the early years of World War II, the Army Air Forces selected Wickenburg as the site of a glider pilot training school. Rancher Miguel Echeverria donated part of his property for the runway and trainees boarded at the Remuda Ranch. When the war was over, the field was turned over to the city and served as a municipal airport until the late 1960s, when George Wellik donated land to Wickenburg for a new airport (now called Wellik Field).

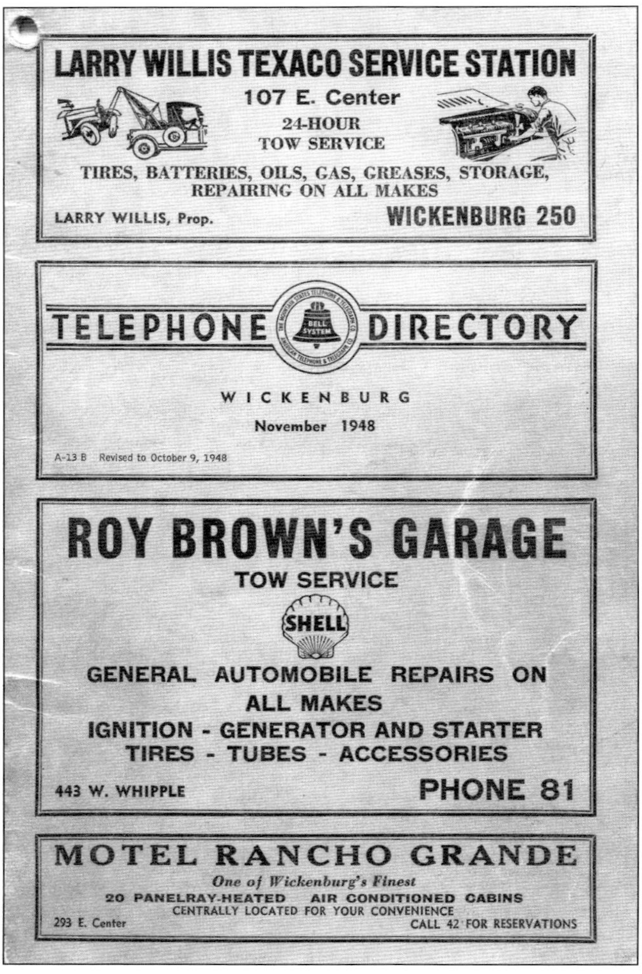

LARRY WILLIS TEXACO SERVICE STATION
107 E. Center
24-HOUR
TOW SERVICE
TIRES, BATTERIES, OILS, GAS, GREASES, STORAGE,
REPAIRING ON ALL MAKES
LARRY WILLIS, Prop.
WICKENBURG 250

TELEPHONE DIRECTORY
WICKENBURG
November 1948
A-13 B Revised to October 9, 1948

ROY BROWN'S GARAGE
TOW SERVICE
SHELL
GENERAL AUTOMOBILE REPAIRS ON
ALL MAKES
IGNITION - GENERATOR AND STARTER
TIRES - TUBES - ACCESSORIES
443 W. WHIPPLE
PHONE 81

MOTEL RANCHO GRANDE
One of Wickenburg's Finest
20 PANELRAY-HEATED AIR CONDITIONED CABINS
CENTRALLY LOCATED FOR YOUR CONVENIENCE
293 E. Center
CALL 42 FOR RESERVATIONS

The cover of this 1948 telephone directory reflects the sort of businesses that thrived in Wickenburg at the time thanks to Western tourism.

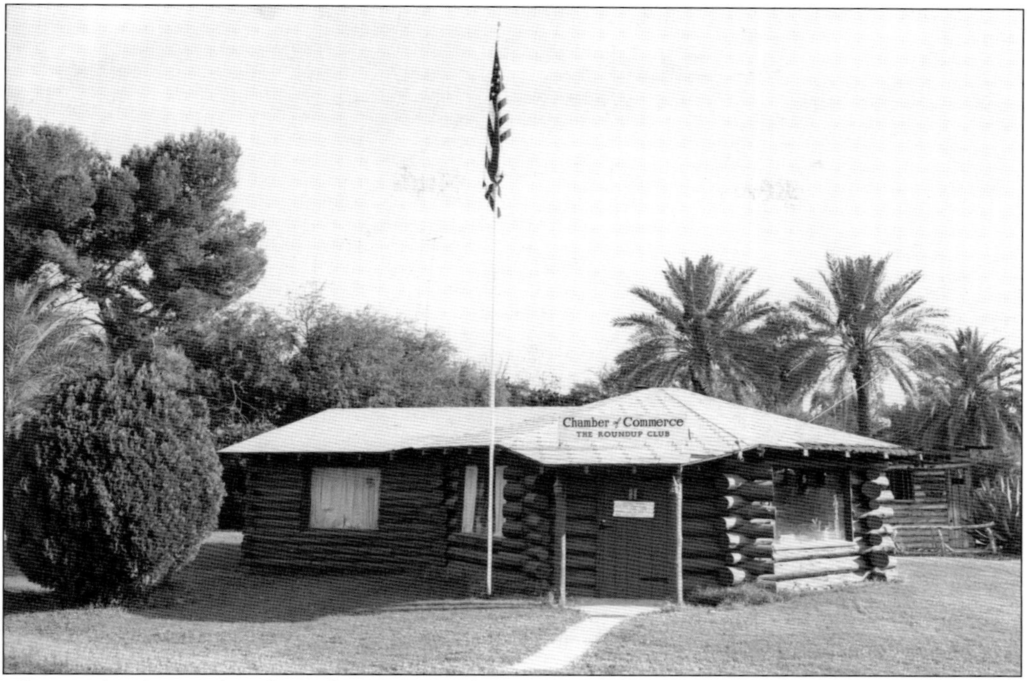

The Wickenburg Chamber of Commerce became a powerful partner in bringing visitors to Wickenburg, though for many years it was called by its original, Western-themed name: the Round-Up Club. This photograph dates to the 1940s. In 1987, the Santa Fe Railroad depot on present-day Frontier Street was restored and dedicated as the chamber's headquarters and Wickenburg's official visitors' center.

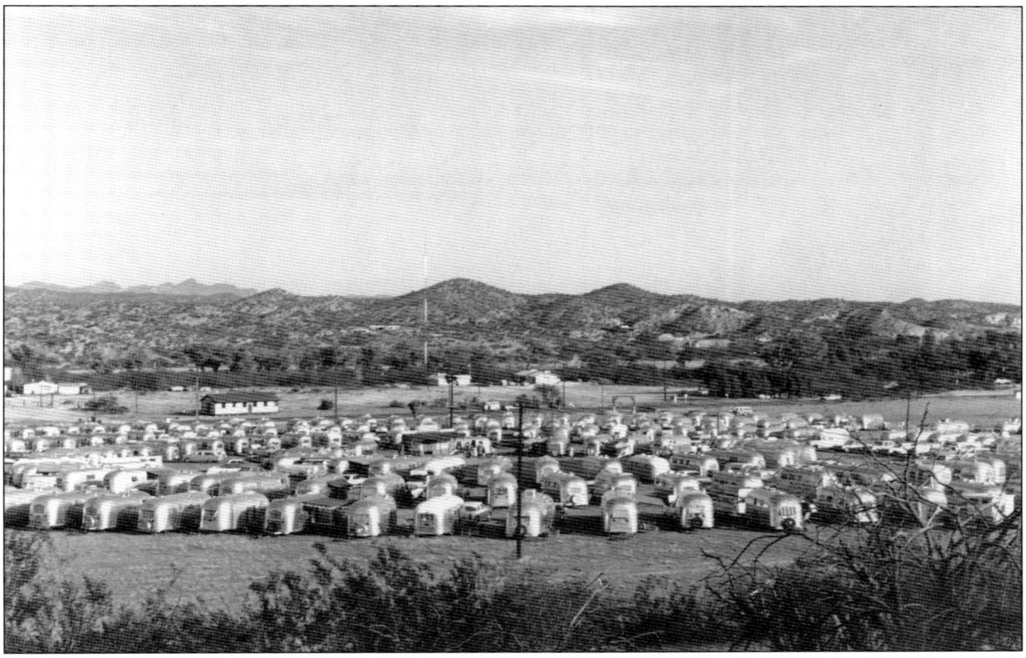

Airstream enthusiasts held a convention in Wickenburg in 1964.

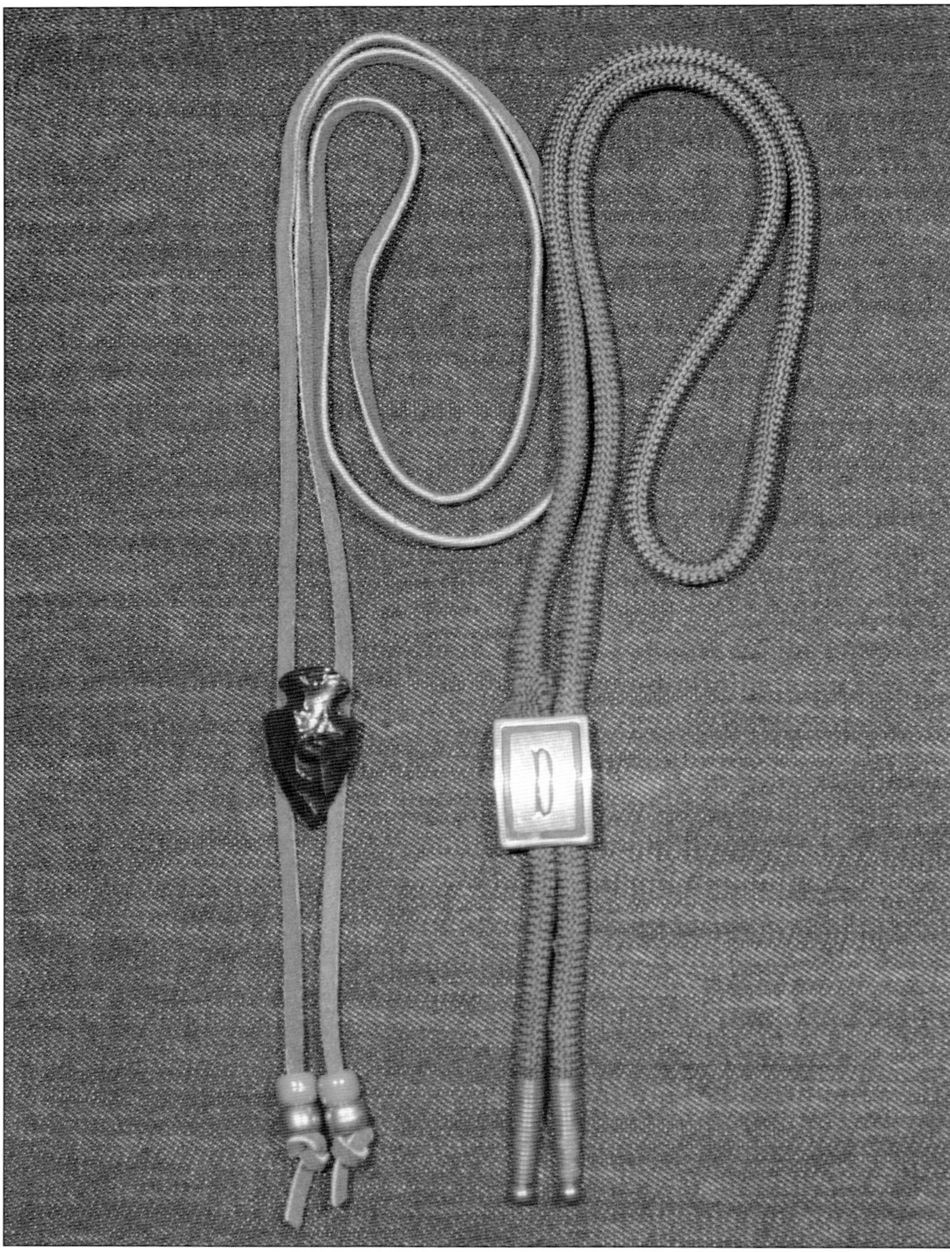

One of the quintessential pieces of Western apparel is the bola (or bolo) tie, a version of which was invented by Wickenburg resident Victor Cedarstaff in 1949. While riding in the Bradshaw Mountains, Cedarstaff's hat fell off and the hatband separated from the brim—he put the band around his neck and a fellow rider teased him about his "new tie." Cedarstaff was a silversmith and decided he could make a tie by using a leather strap and a metal clasp, giving birth to the bola. The name comes from "boleadora," a lariat used by the gauchos of Argentina. Its fame spread when Phoenix anchorman Bill Close wore bola ties on camera. The bola was named the official Arizona state neckwear in 1971, and the Desert Caballeros Western Museum has a stunning collection of ties on display. (Collection of the author. Photograph by Hangauer/Kissinger.)

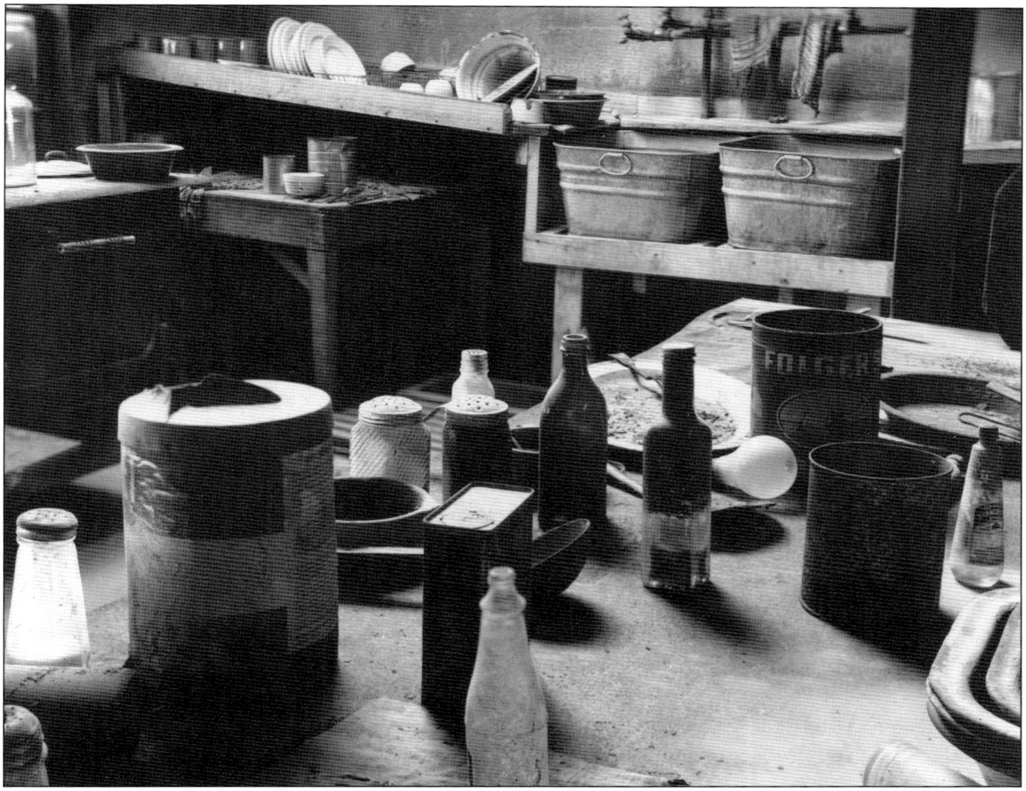

In 1942 the US government shut down all mines whose metals were not essential to the war effort, in order to concentrate resources on extracting coal, copper, iron, and others. The gold mines that ringed Wickenburg were shuttered and, in some cases, their machinery sold as scrap. At the Vulture Mine, bottles, coffee cans, tubs, dishes, and other artifacts of daily life were left behind, as seen in this 1950s photograph of the mine's galley.

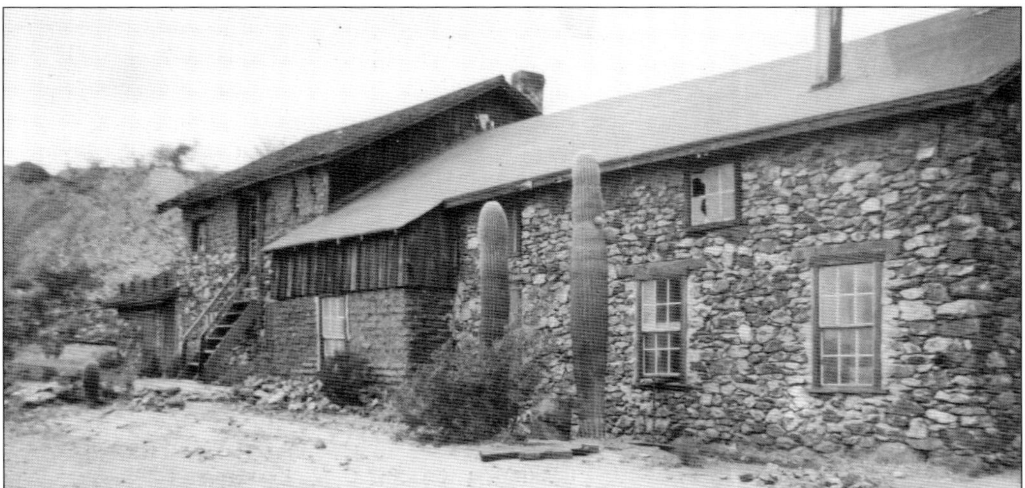

Although the Vulture Mine was officially closed, that did not stop people from working the old tailings and exploring abandoned buildings, such as the old assay office.

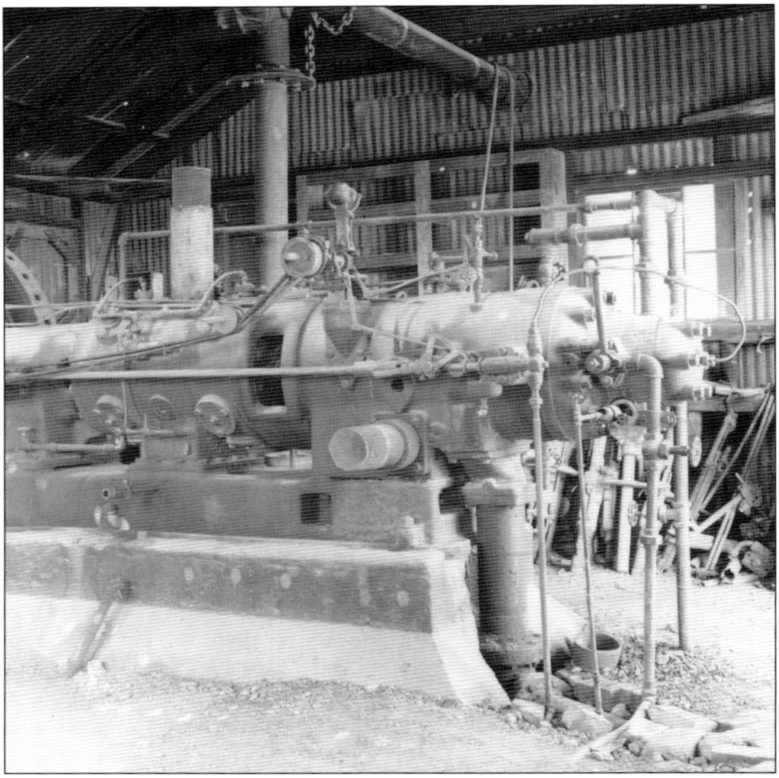

The Vulture Mine's machinery, including this compressor, was left on the property when it was closed. Now that the area is silent, it is hard to imagine the effect the sound of the massive power generator had on the people of Vulture City, though the heat that it generated must have made working in the building easier during the winter.

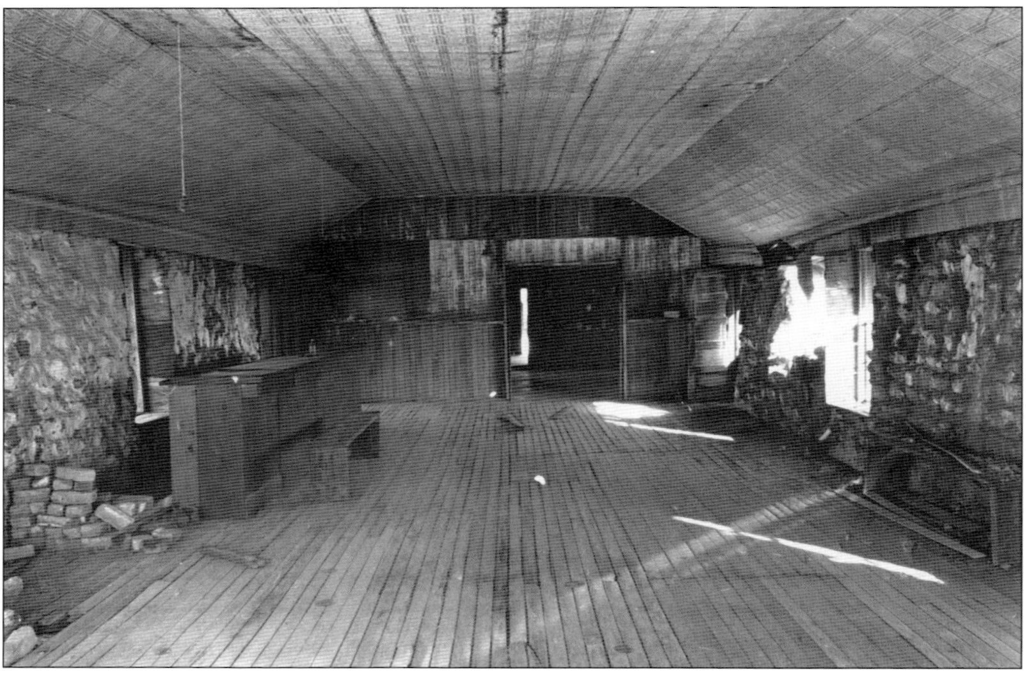

This 1970s photograph of the Vulture Mine mess hall is a reminder of the vast population of miners who took meals in shifts in the mine's heyday. (Photograph by Paul Hughes.)

By the late 1930s, the rodeo sponsored by Wickenburg's businesses became part of a new tourist attraction created by the Wickenburg Chamber of Commerce: Gold Rush Days. The multiday event, still held each February, celebrates Wickenburg's historic past as a mining and ranching center with parades, a rodeo, gold panning, and other western activities. (Collection of the author.)

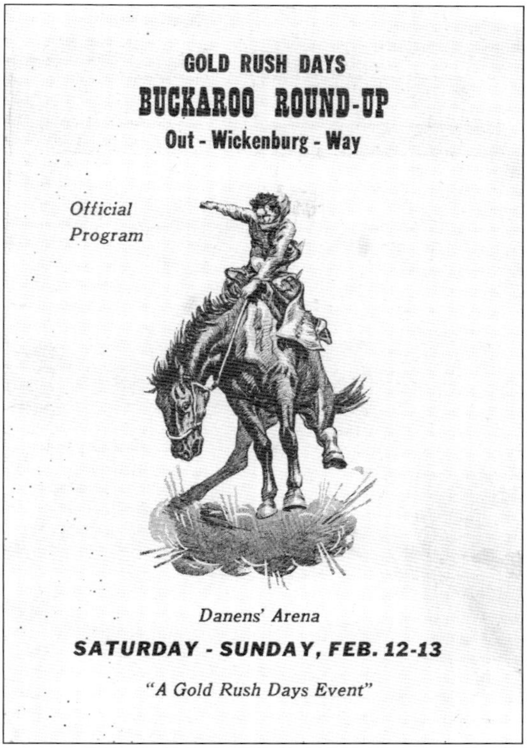

On April 27, 1946, Wickenburg residents arrived in cars, wagons, and on horseback to celebrate the opening of the Valley National Bank. On May 8 of that year, Railroad Street was officially renamed Frontier Street, though some residents had referred to the thoroughfare as Santa Fe Street for a number of years.

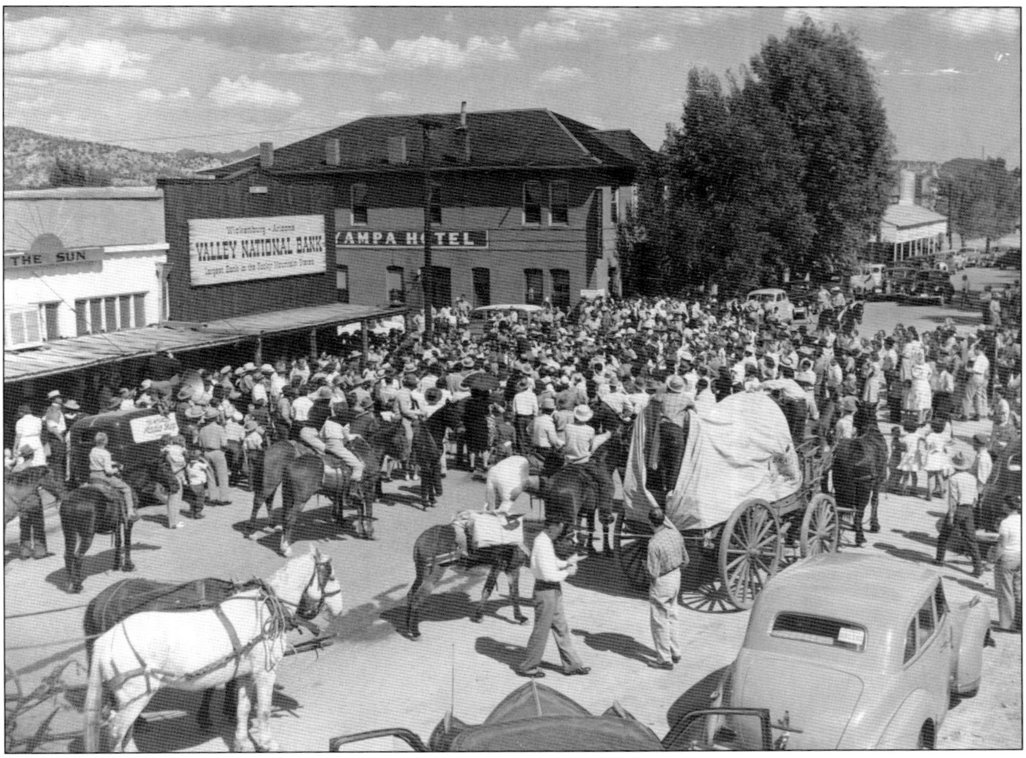

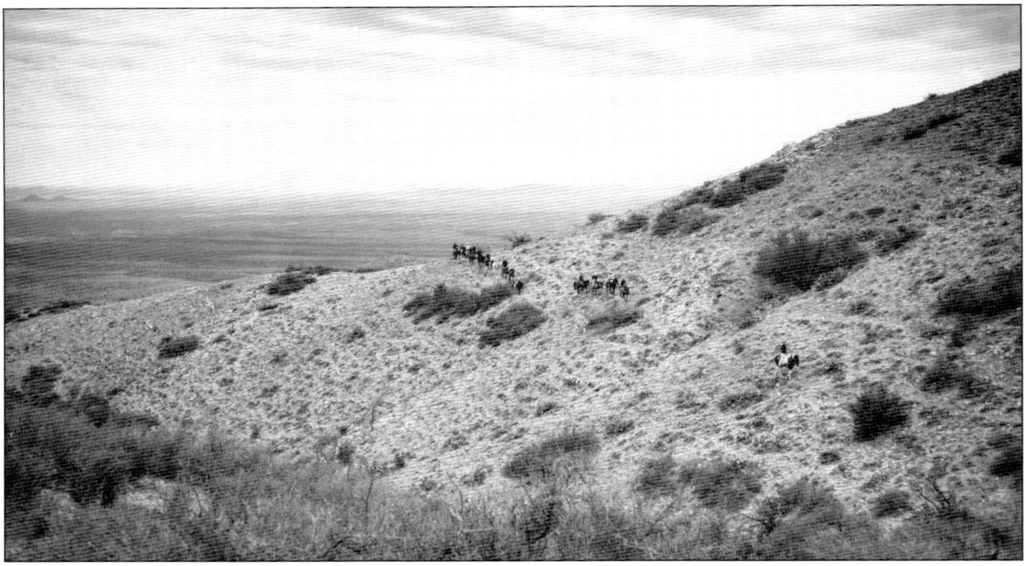

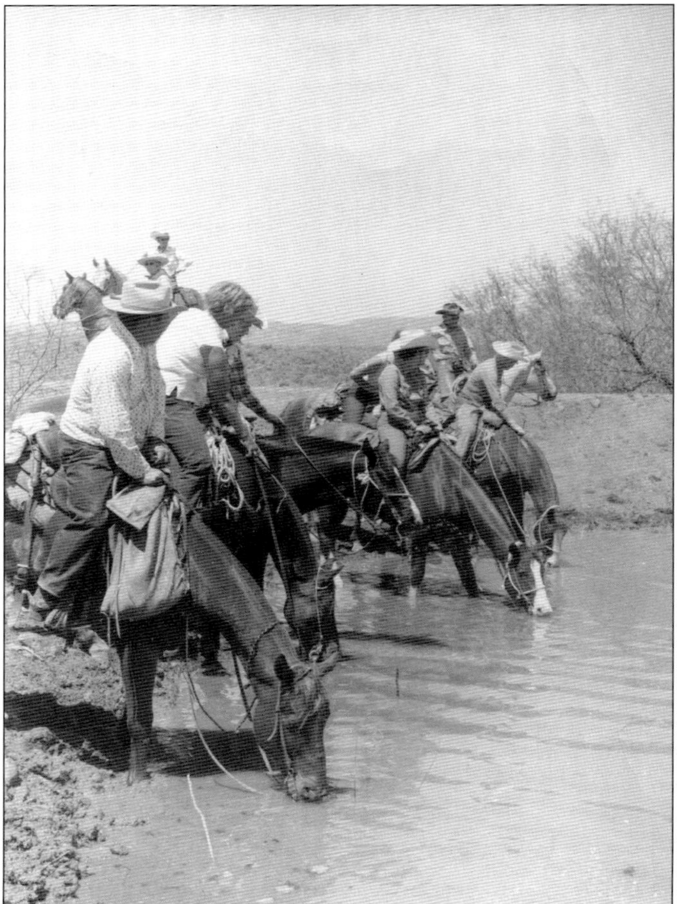

After World War II, the Remuda Ranch, along with other local ranches, stopped sponsoring the rodeo that had been held every spring. Instead, a group of business and ranch owners got together to create a new event. Calling themselves the Desert Caballeros, the men took off on a multiday horseback ride in the spring of 1947. Today, the Desert Caballeros Ride—or "DC Ride"—is as popular as ever, with approximately 200 riders converging on Wickenburg from all over the country each year to participate. (© McLaughlin & Company, Phoenix.)

One year after the Desert Caballeros took their first trail ride, a group of female residents, business owners, and seasonal visitors created their own group—Las Damas. They took their first ride in 1948 and the all-female rides continue today.

During the 1941 Gold Rush Days celebration, the city of Wickenburg dedicated this monument to its founder and namesake, Henry Wickenburg. (© Frasher's.)

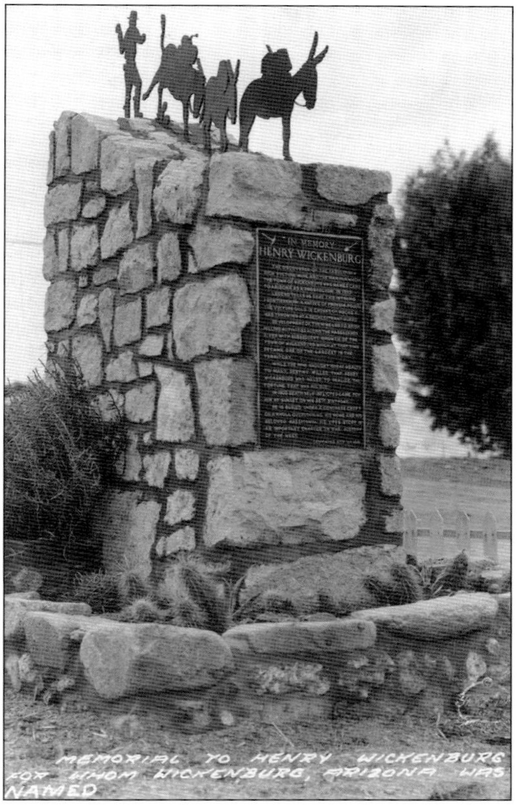

In 1965, a contingent of volunteers relocated the old Santa Fe train to Stone Park, and it was relocated to its current location on Frontier Street in 2003.

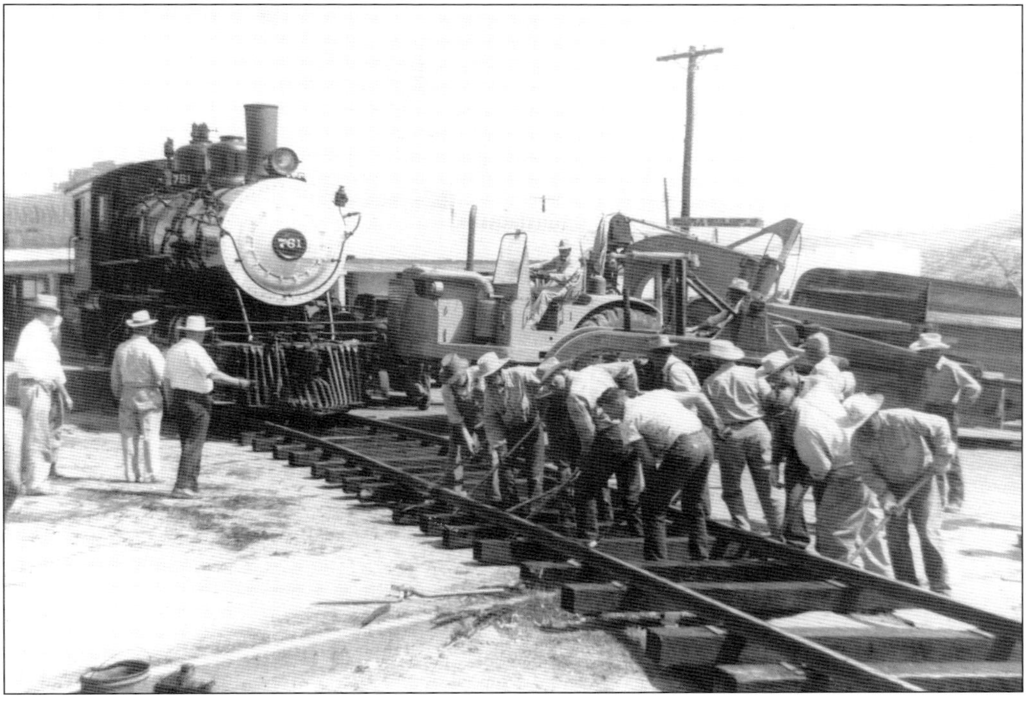

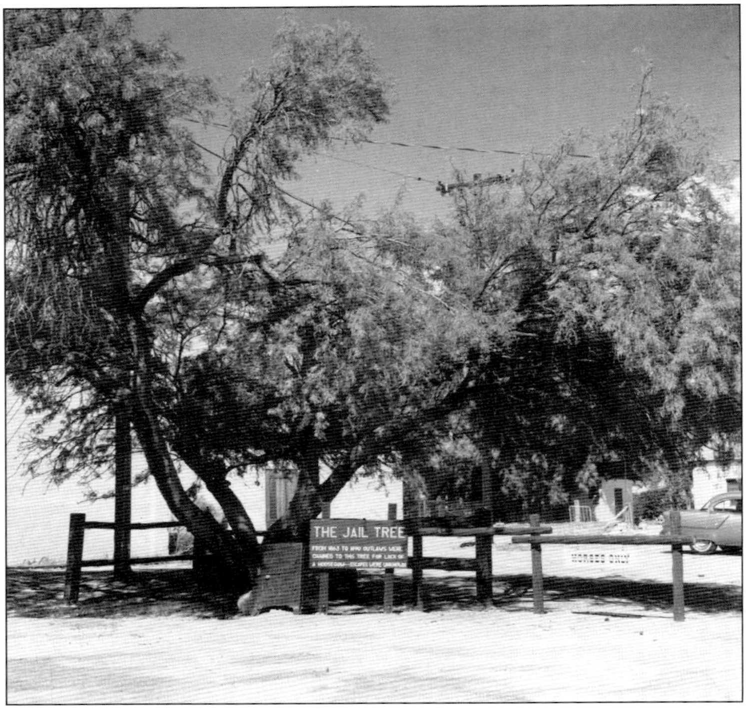

The Jail Tree is a 100-year-old mesquite that, according to legend, served as a town jail from the 1860s until 1890. In many western towns, offenders were chained to such a tree, and there were no recorded escapes. The Wishing Well is another downtown fixture. Next to the rock-walled well is a signboard featuring the Andrew Downing poem "The Hassayampa Legend." The "legend" says that "those who drink its waters bright" will never tell the truth again.

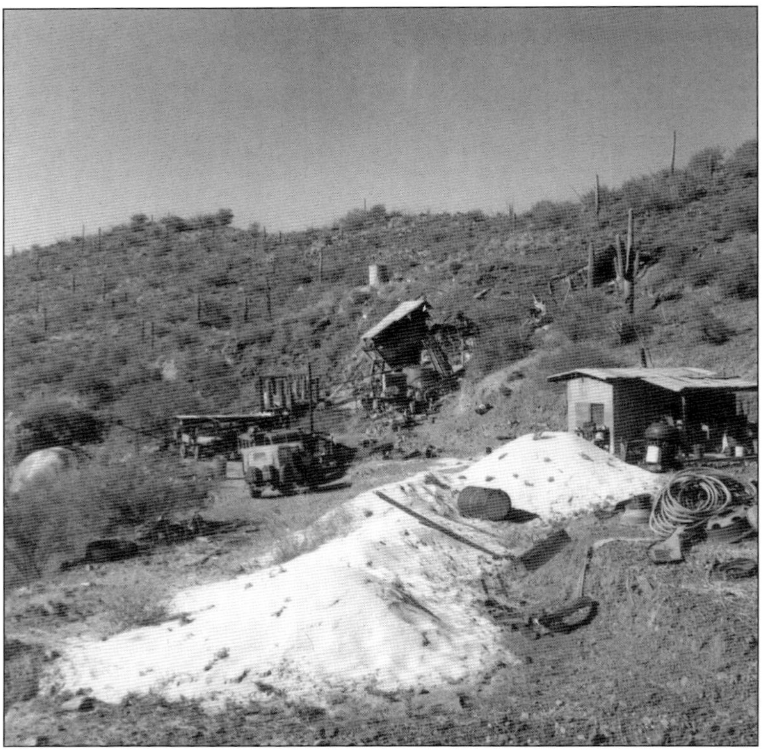

Large-scale mines may have closed forever, but individuals continued to find plenty of places to look for the metals still rumored to be in the mountains around Wickenburg. This photograph is captioned, "Anderson's Camp in San Domingo Wash."

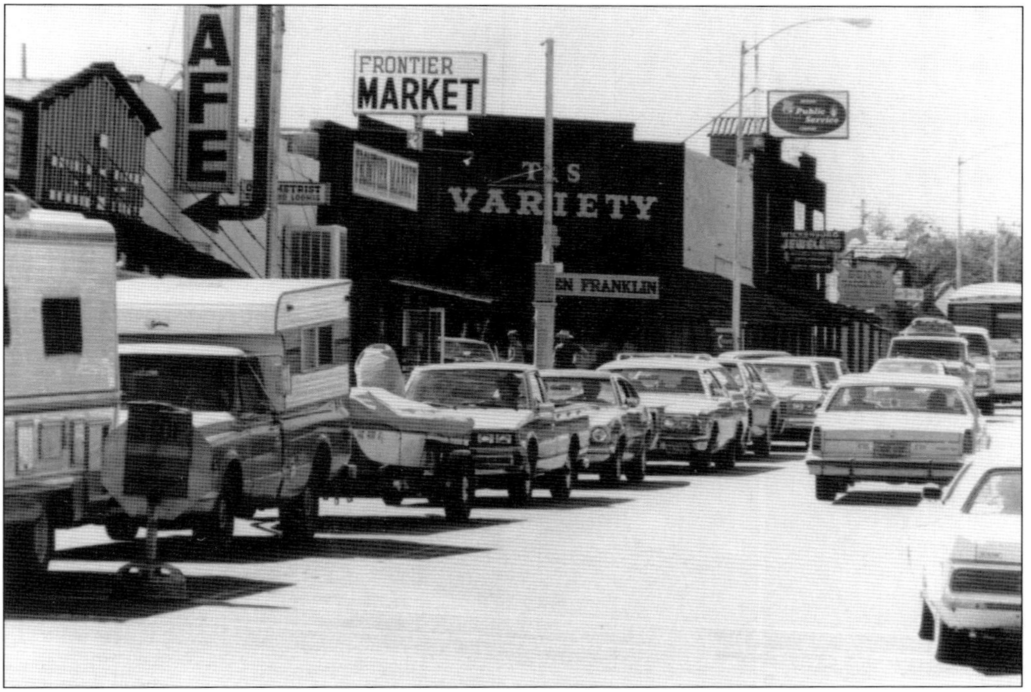

At the height of the tourist season, traffic jams like the one shown in this 1970s image reflect Wickenburg's continuing popularity with campers, fishermen, and other outdoor enthusiasts.

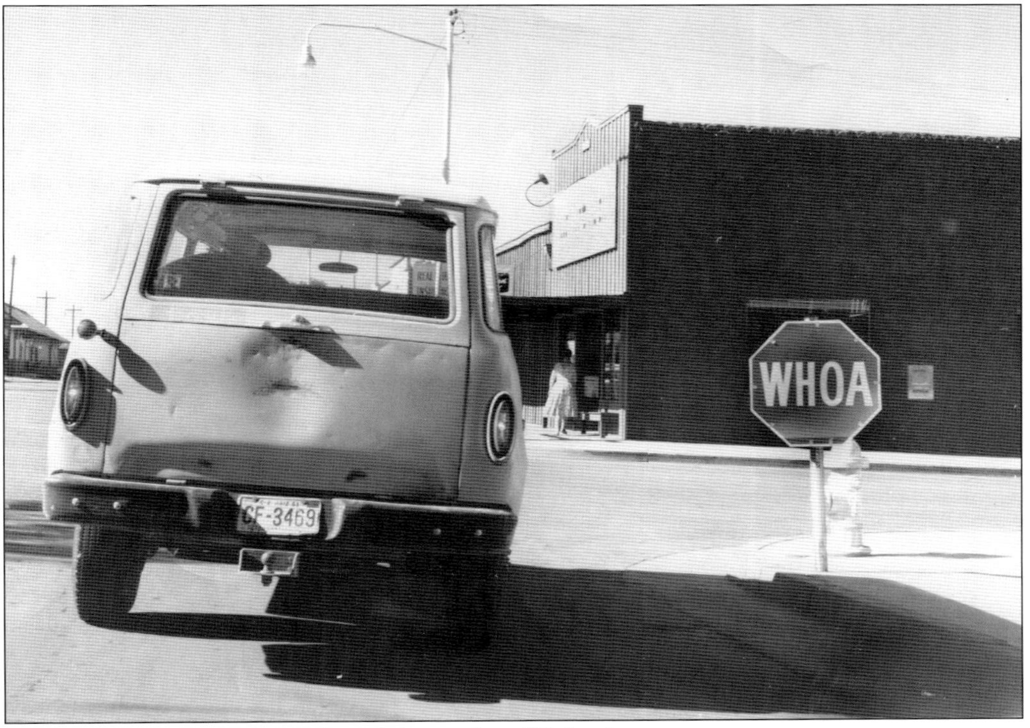

Cars and horses have always shared the roads in Wickenburg.

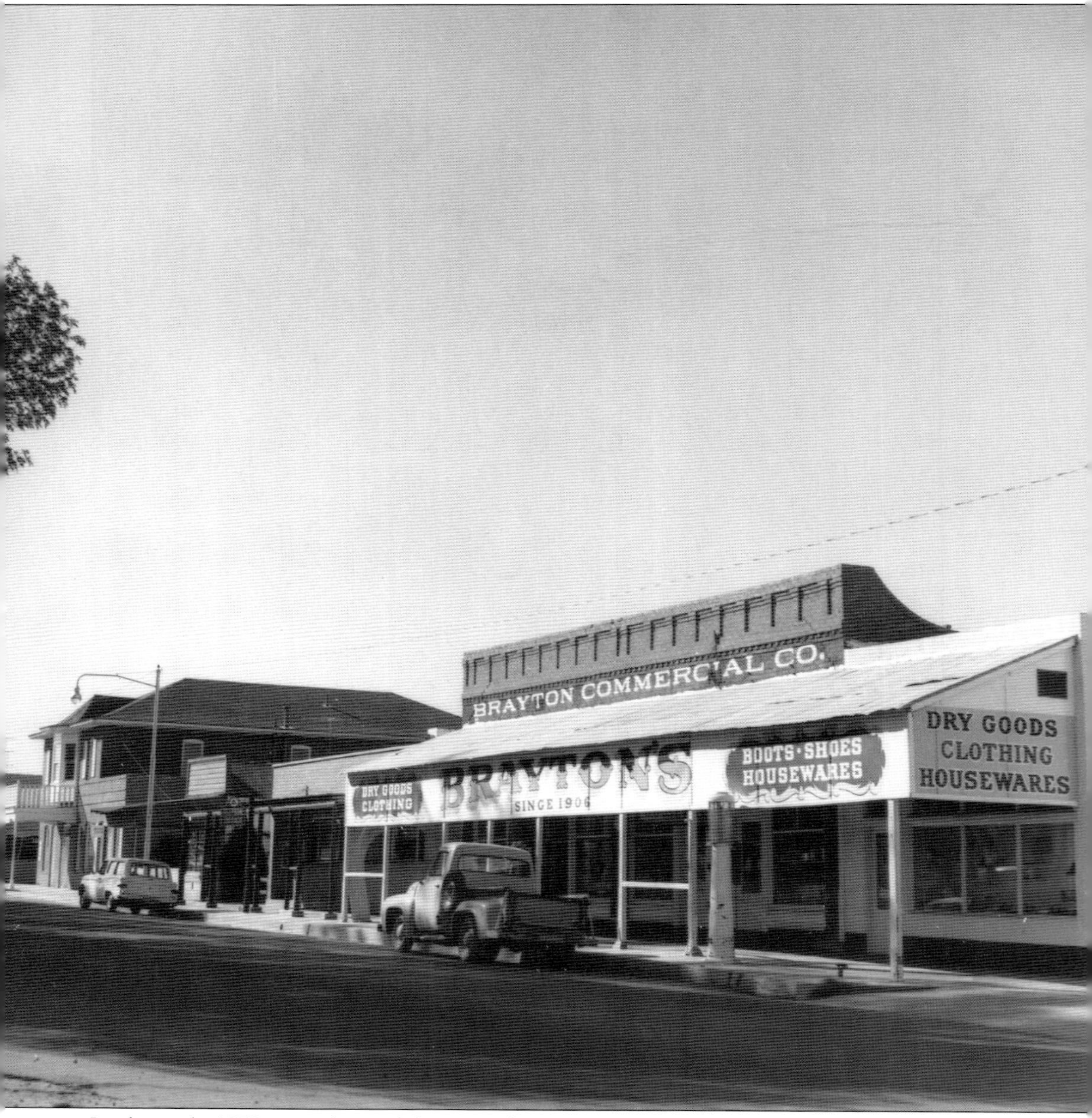

In the early 1950s, members of the Round-Up Club formed a local history committee chaired by public school superintendent and Arizona history enthusiast H.K. "Mac" MacLennan. The committee drummed up support for a town museum throughout the decade and incorporated the Desert Caballeros Western Museum in 1960. Thanks to generous donors and committee members, the group purchased the former Brayton Commercial Co. property on Railroad (now Frontier) Street in 1966, after the store closed that same year. For the next three years, committee members and volunteers turned the former general store into a museum with spaces for exhibits and office. The Desert Caballeros Western Museum officially opened its doors on May 8, 1969, displaying local historic artifacts donated by longtime families and other items collected by museum officials.

Nine

A Modern City

The demise of television westerns, the closing of some dude ranches, and a devastating fire, which destroyed the Desert Caballeros Western Museum, could not keep Wickenburg down.

One reason that Wickenburg continues to thrive is the multigenerational nature of its residents. As they do everywhere, young people left town to go to college or see the world, but many of them return to find jobs and/or raise families. Drawn to the tranquility of the area, retirees continue to relocate here, building new homes and supporting local institutions.

International visitors fascinated by the West and new generations of people discovering the beauties of the Sonoran Desert also started coming through town. They were greeted with new museum exhibits, still-operating dude ranches, hair-raising tours of abandoned mining districts, and the Hassayampa River Preserve. The Del E. Webb Center for the Performing Arts brings world-class talent to town. Wickenburg is also a stop on the rodeo circuit, with events held at the Everett Bowman Rodeo Grounds.

The arts thrive in Wickenburg. Thanks to a public art program, statues of historic characters and wildlife—such as a Gila monster and a rattlesnake—now stand throughout downtown Wickenburg, with an audio system providing tales of local lore narrated by state historian Marshall Trimble. Visitors can smile back at the statue of Elizabeth Smith in front of the building that housed her Vernetta Hotel.

If a city's character is judged by its people, then Wickenburg has the sturdy heart of its namesake. The residents care deeply about their home, and this is evident in everything from the Wickenburg Clean and Beautiful program to local pride in the new bridge across the Hassayampa.

Wickenburg is the kind of town in which rich history is evident everywhere and prized by all, but that does not mean it lives in the past. Wickenburg stands solidly in the history of the American West but always looks ahead to its role as an important 21st-century city.

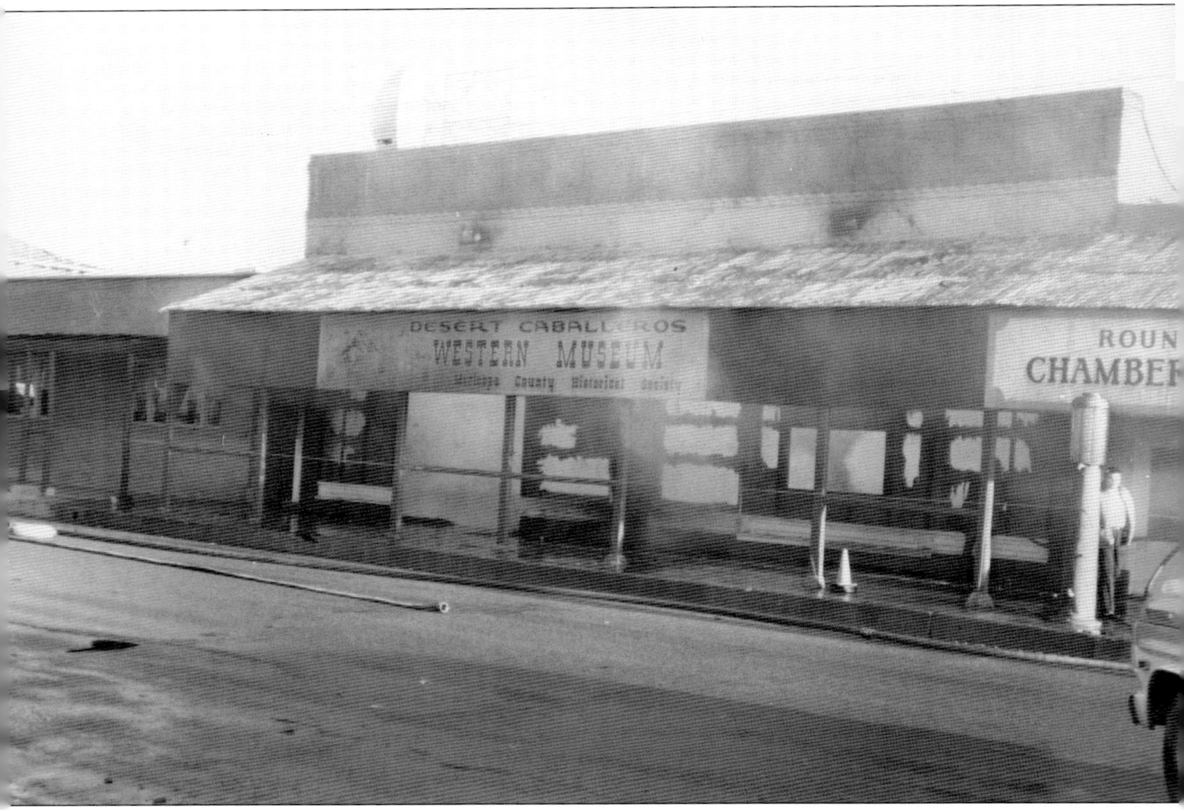

On a December night in 1972, just a few days before Christmas, a fire began inside the Desert Caballeros Western Museum, and by the time it was extinguished, it had destroyed the building and nearly all of its exhibits. The only surviving items were two bronzes by renowned artist Frederic Remington, which fell through the ground floor into the basement, unharmed. A rebuilding campaign began within weeks, garnering donations of materials, money, and labor. The following year, a women's auxiliary was formed and dubbed Las Senoras de Socorro—The Ladies of Help—and they pitched in with volunteers and other services. As work continued, the museum's mission was transformed to celebrate Western art as well as Wickenburg history.

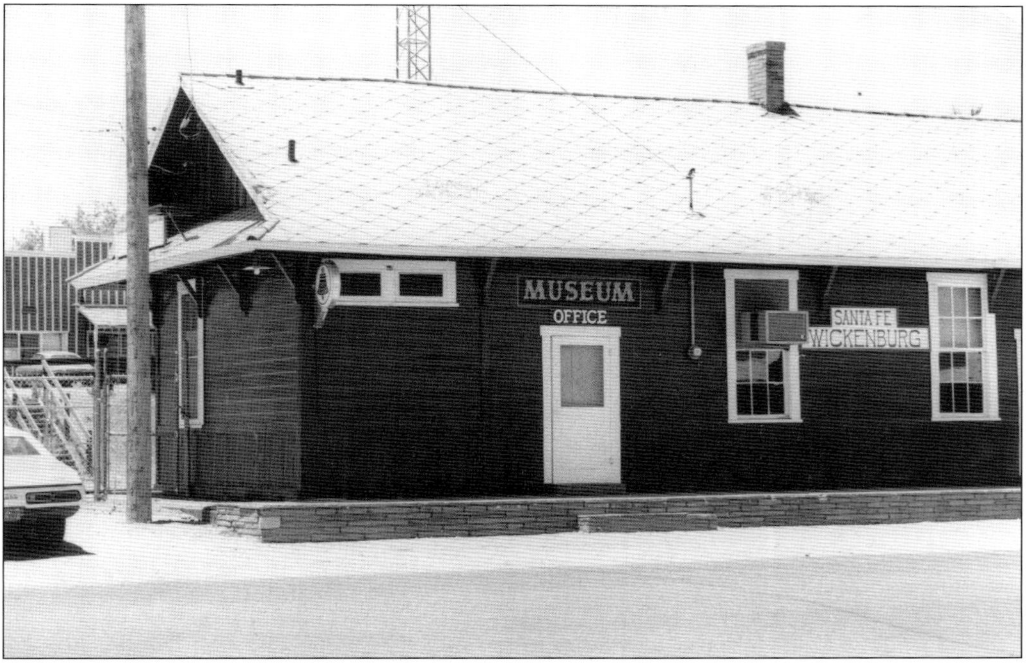

The rebuilding efforts for the museum were coordinated in temporary headquarters at the Santa Fe depot. Exhibits about local history and Wickenburg life were re-created and historic and contemporary Western art was collected, reflecting the new mission of the museum. The Desert Caballeros Western Museum reopened on December 21, 1975, barely three years after burning to the ground—a testament to the power of community.

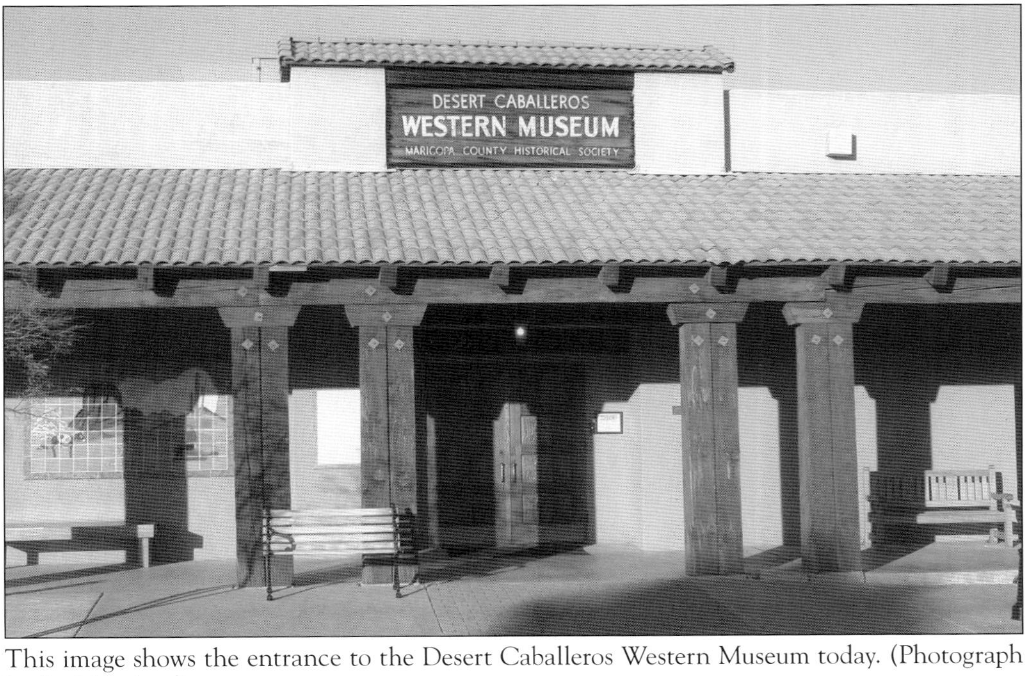

This image shows the entrance to the Desert Caballeros Western Museum today. (Photograph by Paul Hughes.)

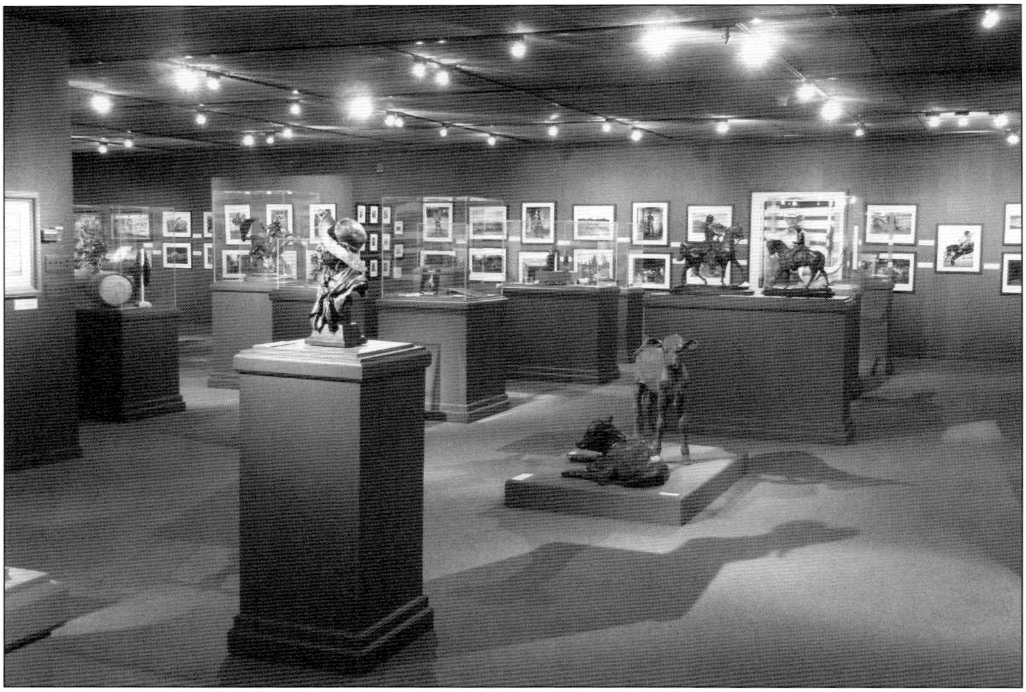

The Desert Caballeros Western Museum contains a stunning collection of classic Western artwork. (Photograph by Paul Hughes.)

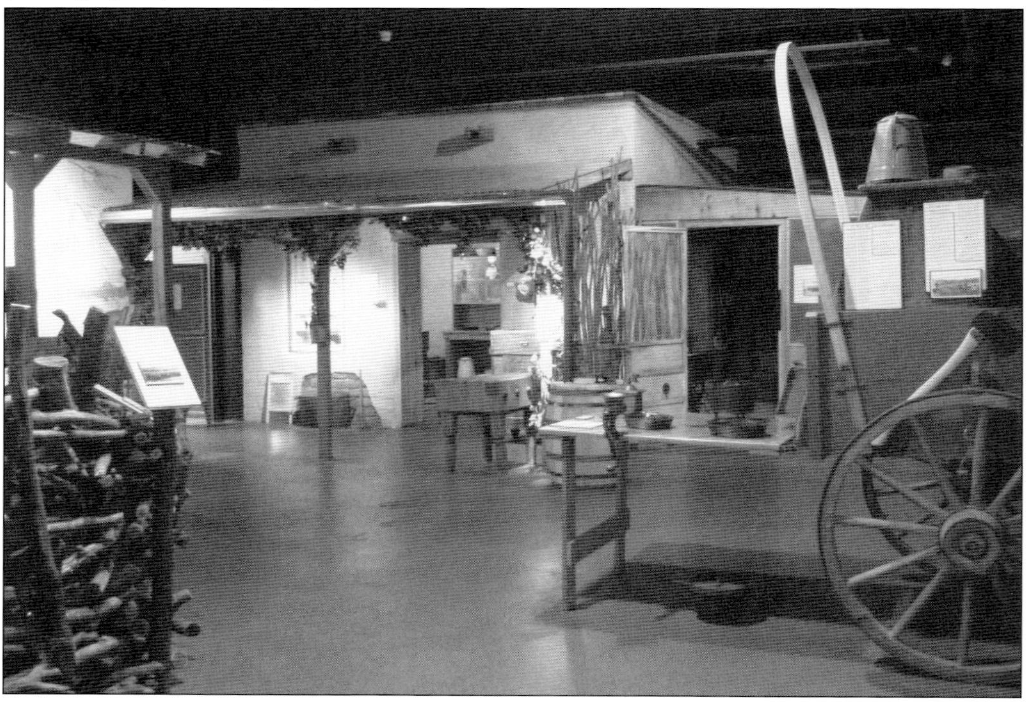

Historical exhibits at the Desert Caballeros Western Museum tell the full story of Wickenburg's past. (Photograph by Paul Hughes.)

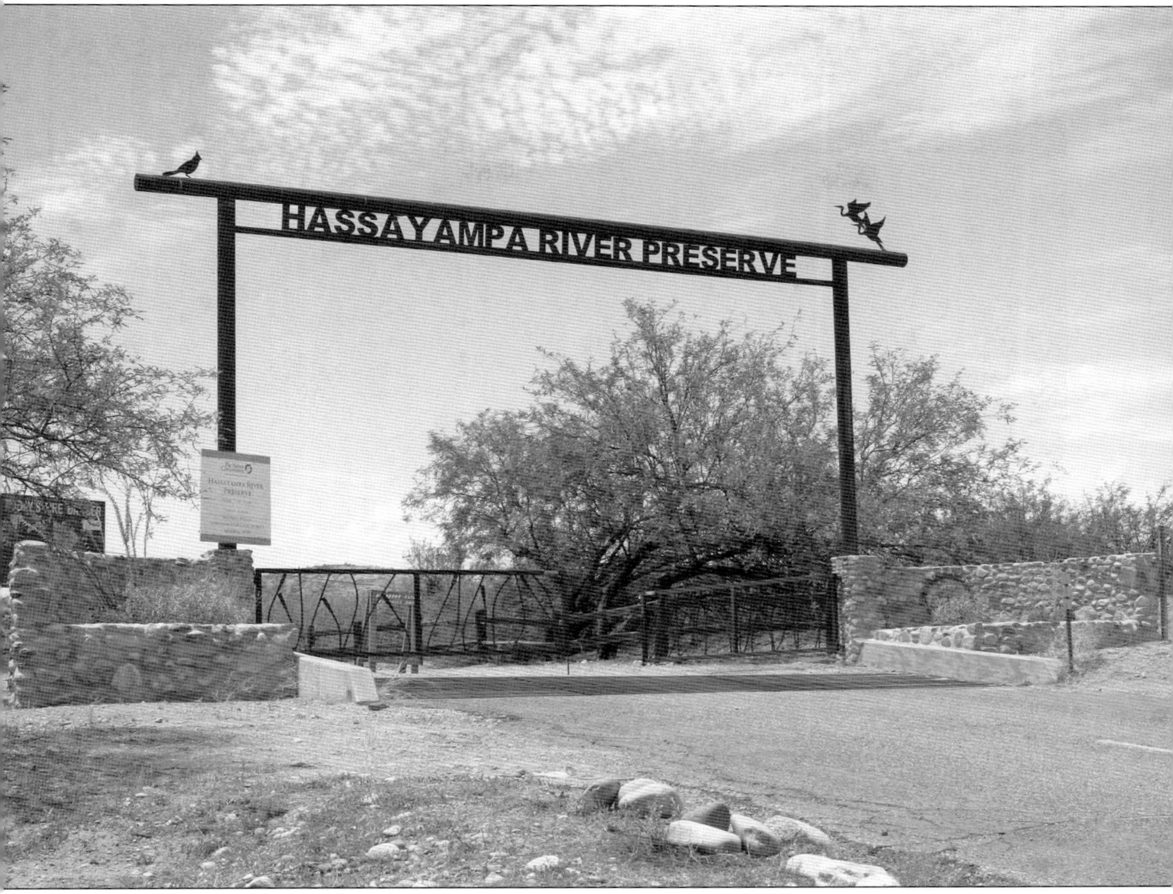

The former locations of the Garden of Allah, Circle Flying W, and Lazy RC guest ranches are now part of the Hassayampa River Preserve. The Nature Conservancy purchased the property from the private owners in 1986 and has doubled its size through the acquisition and donation of over 300 acres of desert foothills. The Arthur L. Johnson Visitor Center has interactive displays featuring local wildlife and ecology, and the Hassayampa River Preserve maintains miles of self-guided hiking trails. (Photograph by Melissa Oehler.)

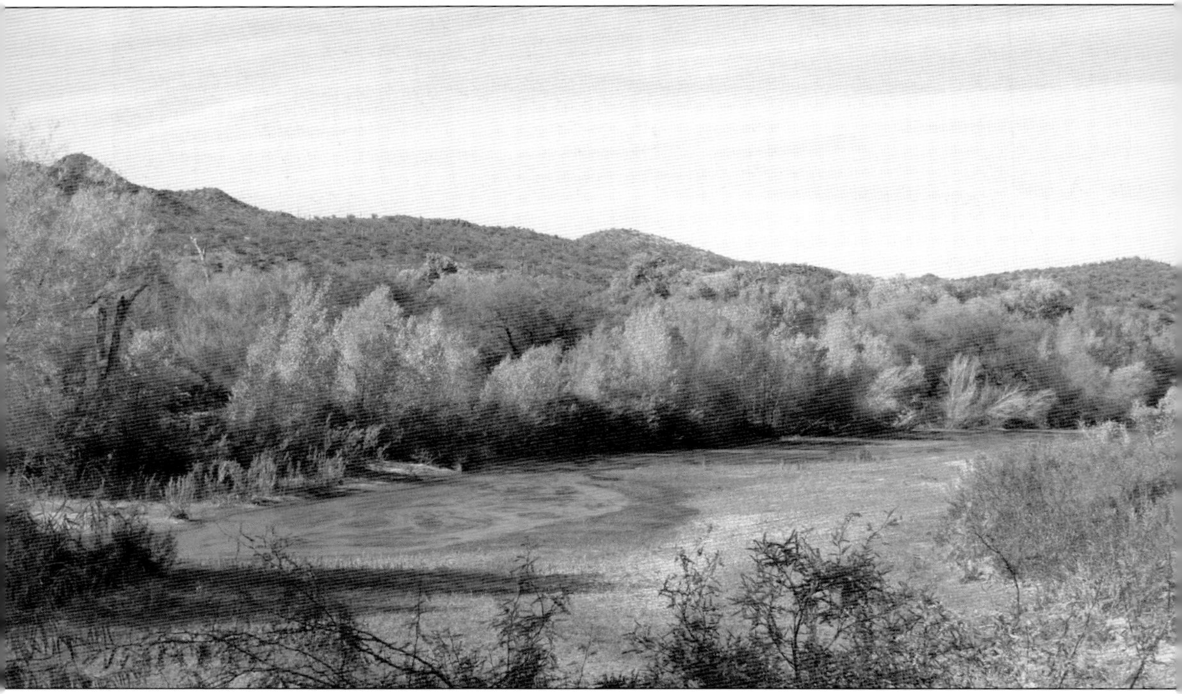

The Hassayampa River continues to provide sustenance and shelter for the wildlife of the Sonoran Desert as well as peace and recreation for Wickenburg's residents and visitors. (Photograph by Melissa Oehler.)

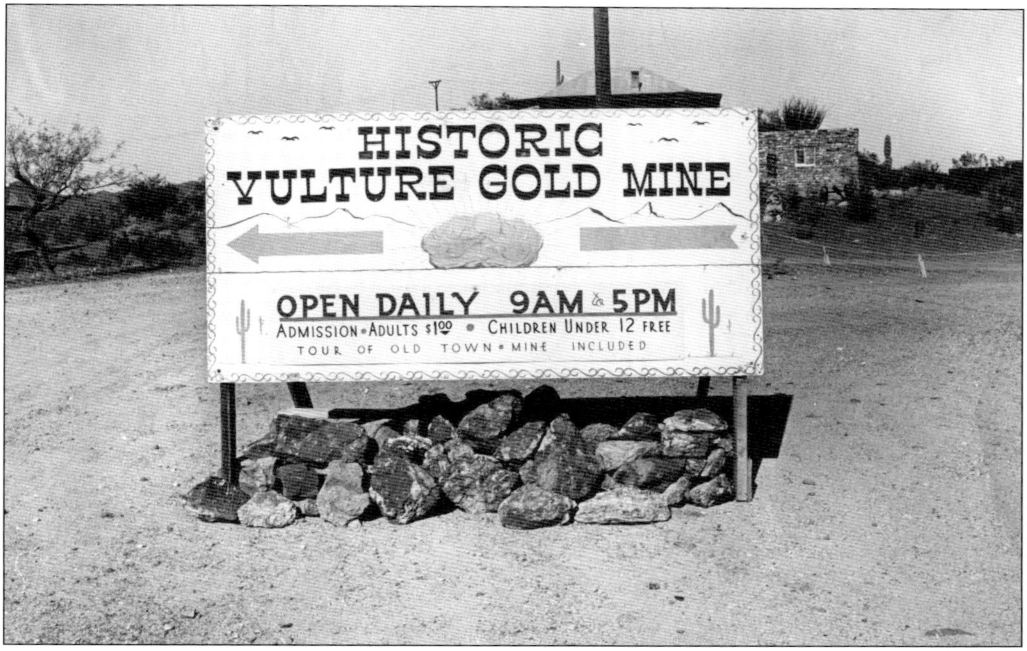

The Vulture Mine passed into private hands in the 1960s, and by the following decade, visitors were welcome to take self-guided tours of the remaining Vulture City buildings.

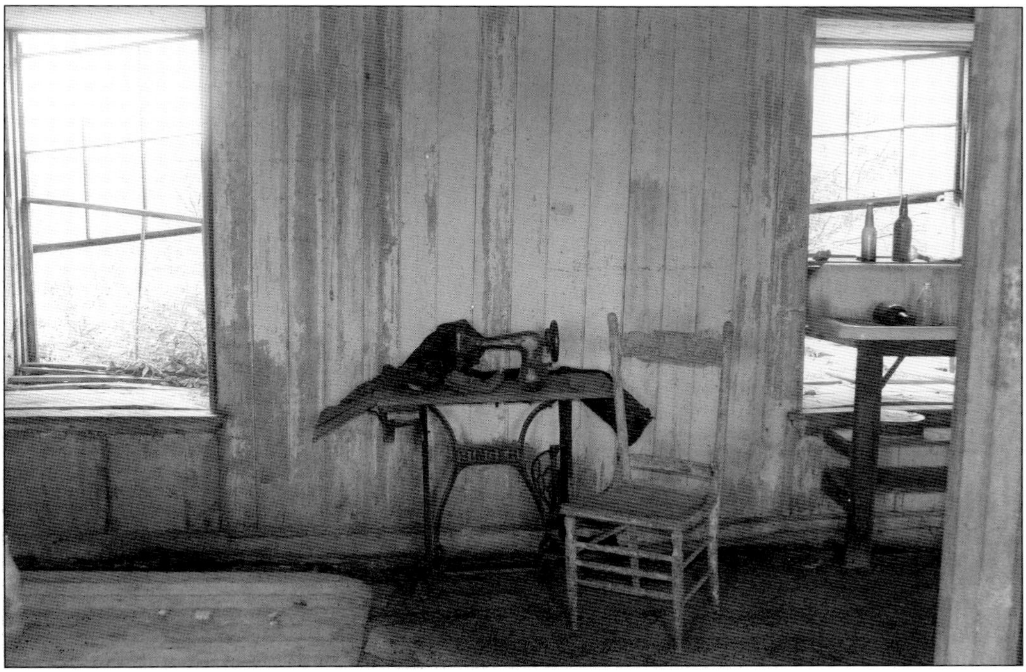

Time, the elements, and vandalism transformed Vulture City and its mining structures into a ghost town. (Photograph by Melissa Oehler.)

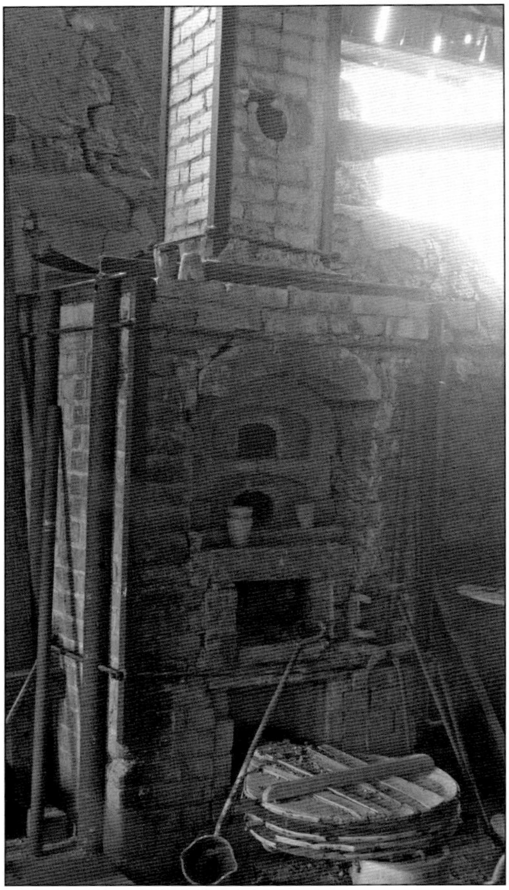

Furnaces like this relic at the Vulture Mine were once used for assaying. (Photograph by Melissa Oehler.)

The 1881 schoolhouse is one of two school buildings that still stand at the Vulture Mine. Both were used by generations of teachers and children. (Photograph by Melissa Oehler.)

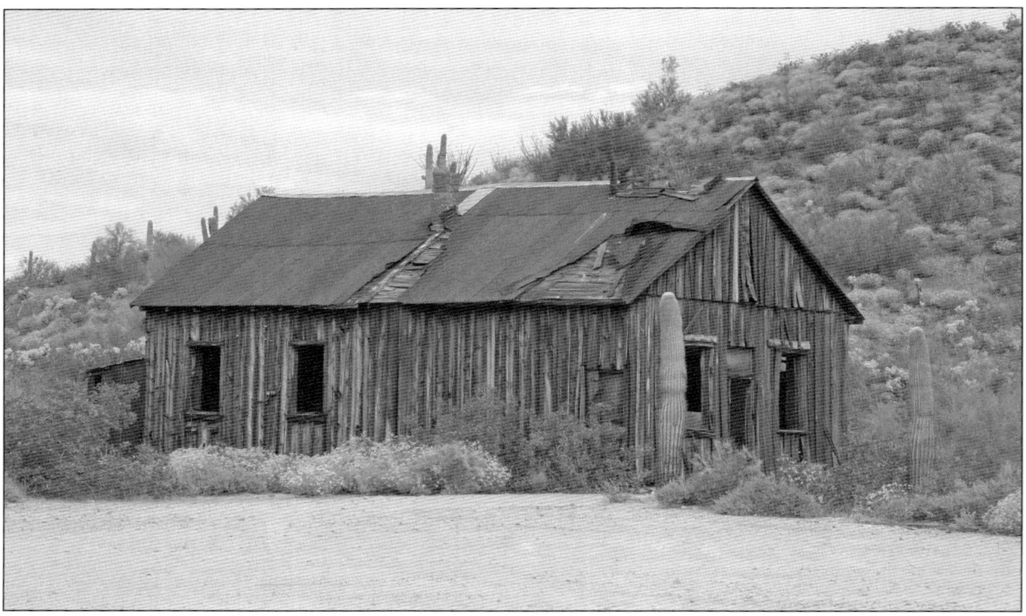

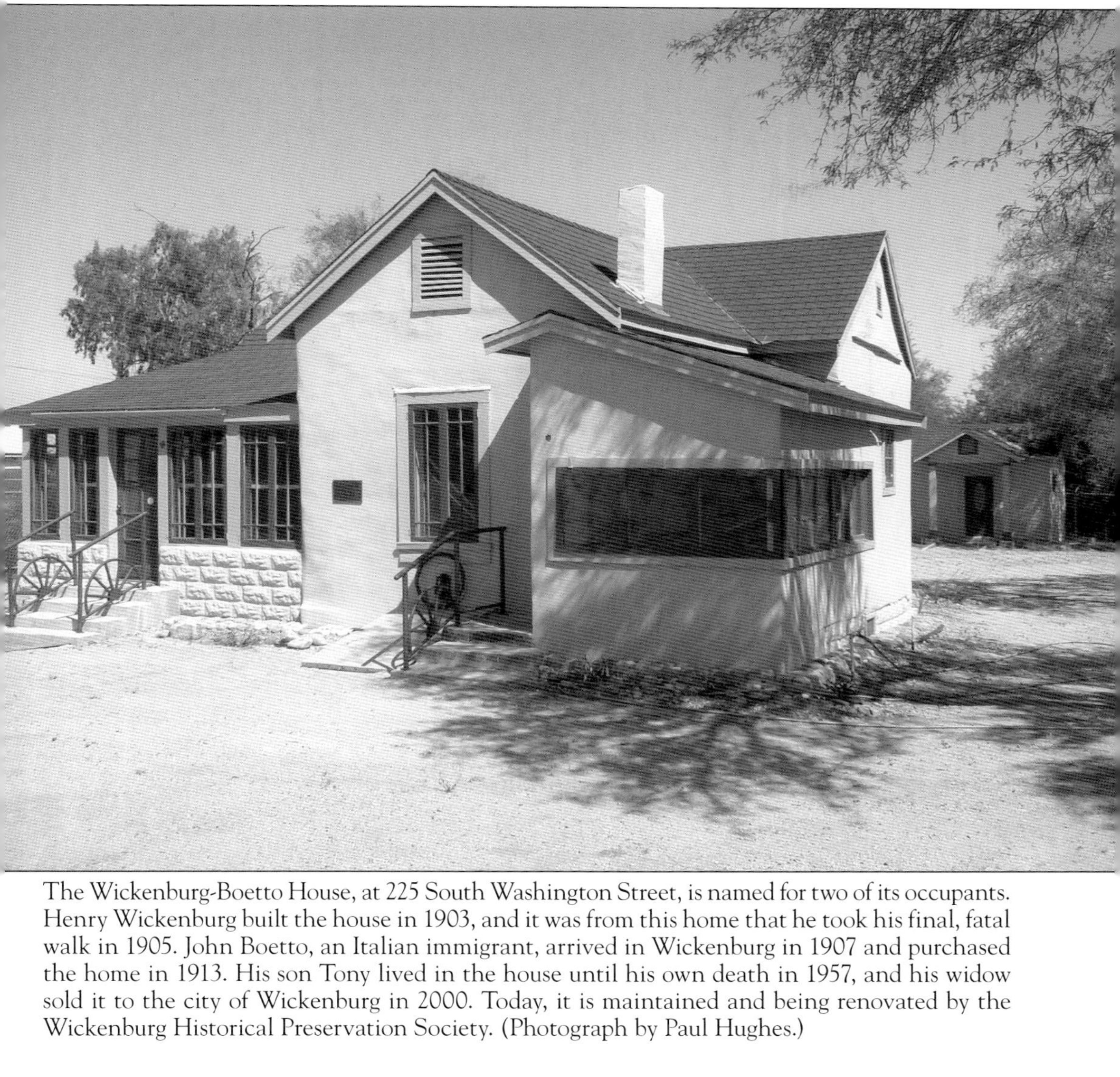

The Wickenburg-Boetto House, at 225 South Washington Street, is named for two of its occupants. Henry Wickenburg built the house in 1903, and it was from this home that he took his final, fatal walk in 1905. John Boetto, an Italian immigrant, arrived in Wickenburg in 1907 and purchased the home in 1913. His son Tony lived in the house until his own death in 1957, and his widow sold it to the city of Wickenburg in 2000. Today, it is maintained and being renovated by the Wickenburg Historical Preservation Society. (Photograph by Paul Hughes.)

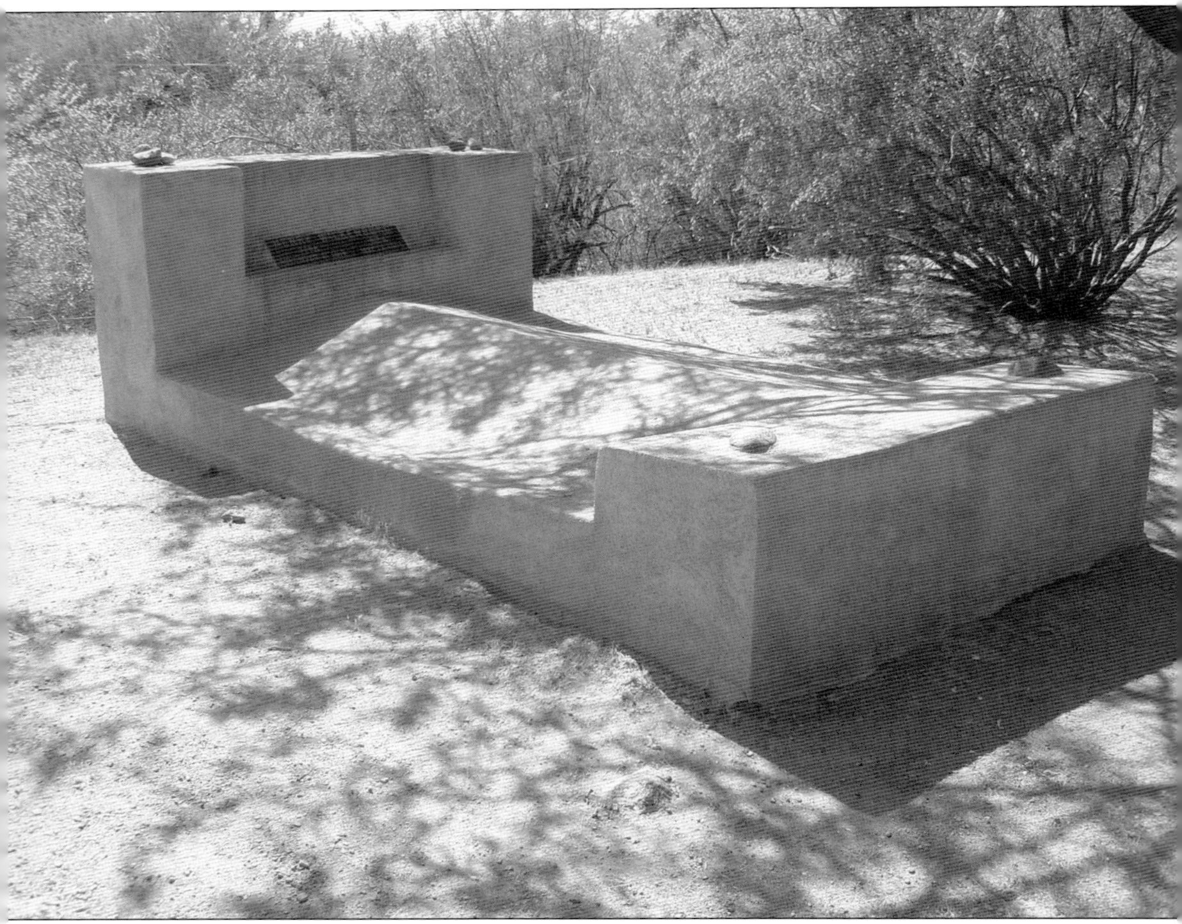

Henry Wickenburg is buried in the Pioneer Cemetery located at the intersection of Adams Street and Howard Court. The cemetery was listed in the National Register of Historic Places in April 2011. Other town notables interred in Pioneer Cemetery include Wickenburg's first mayor, Henry Cowell, his wife, and her brother; James Chase, a member of the Walker Party; and William Weise, a friend of Wickenburg's. (Photograph by Paul Hughes.)

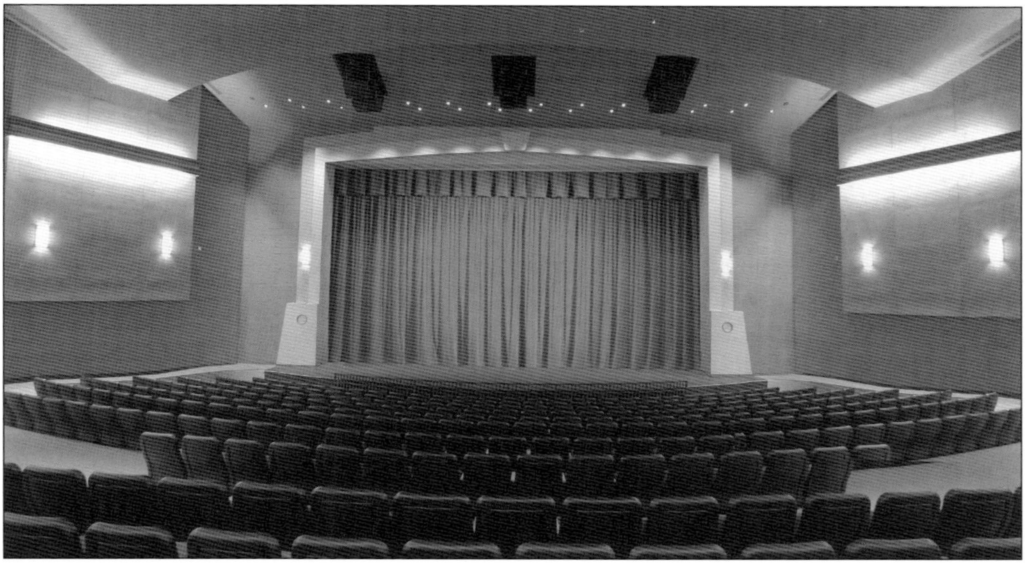

The Del E. Webb Center for the Performing Arts, a state-of-the-art 600-seat theater on the Wickenburg High School campus, opened in the fall of 2001. It hosts everything from performances by internationally known entertainers to after-school classes and arts residencies. (Courtesy Del E. Webb Center for the Performing Arts, © David James.)

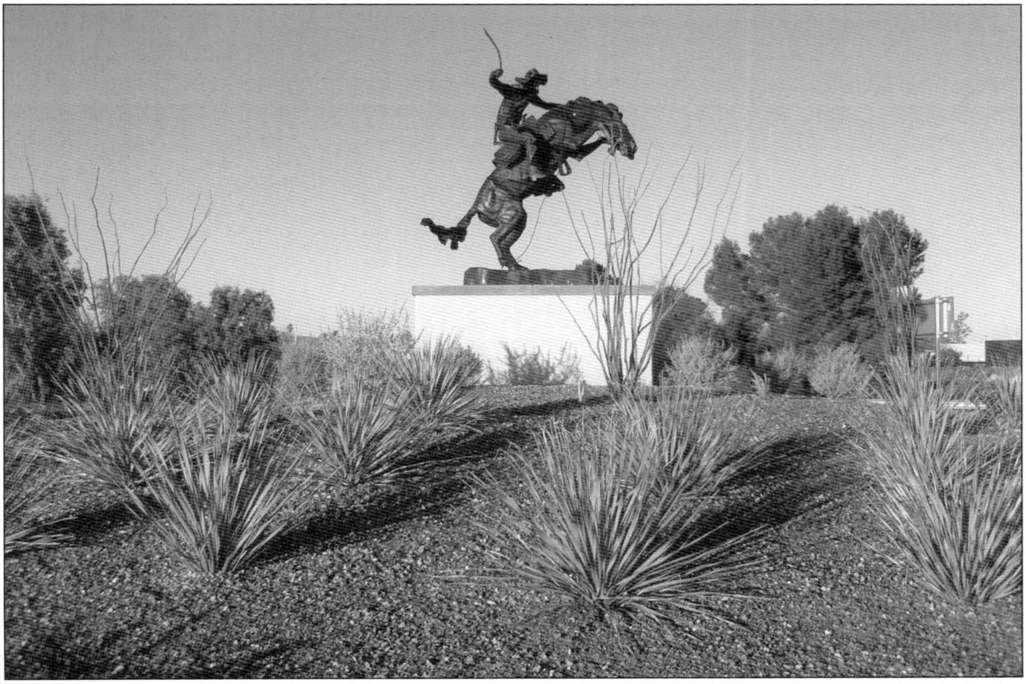

The roundabout at the intersection of Highways 60 and 93 opened in September of 2009. In the center is a life-size replica of a famous Frederic Remington bronze called "Broncho Buster." The modern roadway, coupled with this classic representation of Wickenburg's past, is the perfect symbol for present-day Wickenburg—a thoroughly up-to-date city with a heart as big as the West. (Photograph by Paul Hughes.)

Additional Information

Desert Caballeros Western Museum
21 North Frontier Street
Wickenburg AZ 85390
(928) 684-2272
www.westernmuseum.org

Wickenburg Historical Preservation Society
(928) 684-5129
www.wickenburghistory.org

Wickenburg Chamber of Commerce
216 North Frontier Street
Wickenburg AZ 85390
(800) 942-5242
www.wickenburgchamber.com

Hassayampa River Preserve
49614 N. U.S. Hwy 60
Wickenburg AZ 85390
(928) 684-2772
http://www.nature.org/wherewework/northamerica/states/arizona/preserves/art1970.html

BIBLIOGRAPHY

Borne, Lawrence R. *Dude Ranching: A Complete History*. Albuquerque, NM: University of New Mexico Press, 1983.

Botts, Gene. *The Vulture: Gold Mine of the Century*. Phoenix, AZ: Quest Publishing Group, 1995.

Brooks, Julia Macias. *Wickenburg Hispanic Pioneer Families: Nuestras Memorias*. Wickenburg, AZ: Wickenburg Chamber of Commerce, 2011.

Burden, Dana W. and Joe Stevens. *Where The Past Lives: Constellation Road*. Wickenburg, AZ: Pathfinder Publishing, 2006.

Crampton, Frank. *Deep Enough: A Working Stiff in the Western Mine Camps*. Norman, OK: University of Oklahoma Press, 1982.

Dippie, Brian W., Terrence Moore, and Gregory McNamee. *Crossroads: The Desert Caballeros Western Museum at Fifty*. Wickenburg, AZ: Maricopa County Historical Society, 2010.

Echeverria, Sophie Burden. *When in Doubt, Step on the Gas: A Ragged Memoir*. Wickenburg, AZ, and Jackson Hole, WY: Self-published, 2010.

Hawkins, Helen. *A History of Wickenburg to 1875*. Wickenburg, AZ: Maricopa County Historical Society, 1971.

Joy, Betty E. Hammer. *Angela Hutchinson Hammer: Arizona's Pioneer Newswoman*. Tucson, AZ: University of Arizona Press, 2005.

Liggett, Jim. *Arizona's Worst Disaster: The Hassayampa Story, 1886–2009*. Wickenburg, AZ: Pathfinder Publishing, 2009.

Melchiorre, Erik. *Octave Gold Mine: The Golden Queen of Rich Hill, Arizona*. Rock Doc Publications, 2008.

Priestley, J.B. *Midnight on the Desert: Being An Excursion Into Autobiography During a Winter in America, 1935–1936*. New York, NY: Harper & Brothers, 1937.

Pry, Mark E. *The Town on the Hassayampa: A History of Wickenburg, Arizona*. Wickenburg, AZ: Desert Caballeros Western Museum, 1997.

Rowe, Jeremy. *Early Maricopa County: 1871–1920*. Charleston, SC: Arcadia Publishing, 2011.

Works Progress Administration. *The WPA Guide to 1930s Arizona*. Tucson, AZ: University of Arizona Press, 1989.